To: Sharon
May God richly bless
you —
Bishop Gurley
03-02-08

Light
Not
White

Racism and the Church

By

Dr. G. Randolph Gurley

Previous book by author:

My Brother's Keeper

...a book which addresses the missions outreach of the
Church. A historical perspective of missions is
presented, as well as current Missiology, world
evangelism, and urban evangelism methodologies.

ISBN: 1-879854-51-1

Printed in the United States of America

Published by GMI Publishing
P.O. Box 2690
Laurel, MD 20709

This book is dedicated to my best friend, companion and partner, and above all my loving wife, Pastor Manon Esther Gurley. Without her encouragement and research this book may never have been written.

Secondly, I want to thank all of our dear friends of Hispanic, African, and Asian origin, who have taken me into their homes and their hearts over the years and demonstrated the true meaning of "the Unity of the brethren." Bishop Roderick Caesar, Luciano Padilla, Marilu and Carlos Reyes, Luis Capdevila, Dr. A. V. Thomas, Bishop Ezra Williams, and so many other brothers and sisters, may God richly bless you and your families for your love and your friendship and the impartation into my life.

And to my long time friend and travelling companion with whom I have wept and laughed with over the years and who thought that this book would never materialize, Dr. Stan DeKoven, President of Vision International University and Bible College; Thanks Brother!

Acknowledgements:

A special word of gratitude to Sister Bonnie Ramsey, whose labor of love and passion for the subject matter of this book has been a great asset to its completion.

A special word of thanks and gratitude to Brother Brian Fairchild, who lovingly took the cover of this book through the many design changes needed to bring it into its final form.

Table of Contents

Section 4: Racism, Past and Present

Preface

The Church and Racism is such a controversial subject, yet it is one that needs to be addressed properly if there is going to be healing and unity in the body of Christ.

We have now entered into the 21st century, and this great nation of America is probably more racially divided today than at any other time since the Civil Rights movement of the 60s. Many news commentators, ministers, political figures, and even former President Bill Clinton himself have spoken about this alarming trend. In a news broadcast near the close of 1999, former President Clinton said, *"There is more racial division in America today than at any time since Jimmy Carter was in office."* I believe that assessment became evident in the midst of the 2000 presidential election between Al Gore and President George Bush. Inflammatory statements such as *"Bush will put us back into slavery"* and *"We will lose a century of civil rights progress"*; remarks concerning a disenfranchised people, and so on certainly did little to ease racial tension and helped to polarize racial factions. What an indictment against this country!

Many will ask, "Do you mean to say that, even with all of the debates, education, affirmative action programs and the push for racial equality, we are digressing instead of progressing?" That certainly appears to be the case when all of the facts are reviewed.

The 90s opened the door to a new decade of continuing racial strife. What appeared to be a time of reconciliation has proven to be a time of greater separation. The Rodney King Riot, the O.J. Simpson trial, and a new generation of radical activists have heightened the division among the races. These activists are ready, willing, and able to champion their cause. They are motivated by concepts similar to those that stirred the hearts of the freedom fighters of yesterday. Each has an ideal of justice and equality; each represents their own race and what they believe are the needs of their own people.

Some talk of race wars. Both White and Black separatists are calling for an *American Renaissance*, which would include partitioning America into two or three ethnically-based nations—one All White, one All Black, and one that would be mixed for those who would prefer an integrated state. Advocates of this radical solution to racial tensions are few in number, thankfully.

Paradoxically, there is also a new racial and cultural awareness in America. The walls of ignorance—lack of knowledge and understanding—are coming down, ushering in a host of new sentiments. Unfortunately, many old sentiments have been rekindled as well.

The Internet has facilitated the growth of hate groups. As we entered the new millennium, over 400 of these groups had web sites, devoted to propagating their brand of hatred on the Internet.

Open declarations of hate are not limited to the "Information Superhighway." White Neo-Nazi skinheads stand on one corner, shouting racist slurs at all ethnic people and denying the Jewish Holocaust ever happened. On the opposite corner their Black skinhead counterparts—void of swastikas and tattoos, but complete with shaved heads and Kente cloth bow ties—disperse their own brand of racism. They speak of a reversal of discrimination, of Black domination instead of White, saying it is the Cushite's—the Black man's—time to run.

One faction after another, complete with bodyguards and radical followers, dispenses its doctrines of hatred and violence, prejudices, murder and genocide. Squared off like gladiators of old, often insulated with ignorance against the truth and armed with falsehood and lies, they continue their vigilance. From the street corners of the cities to the talk shows and tabloids, they spread their venom. Nazis and Jews, Muslims and Christians, Cushites and Aryans—each making inflammatory statements about the other. They grow in number as the unlearned and misinformed are drawn into their ranks by their rhetoric. Meanwhile the racial chasm that divides this great nation continues to widen.

Unfortunately much of the Clergy and the Christian Community seem to have been drawn into this arena of conflict. The result is that racial discrimination and prejudices continues to raise its ugly head in the Church. Many have said, ***"The most segregated time of the week in America is about 11:00 am on Sunday morning!"*** What kind of a message does this send to the world? How can we effectively work to bring healing and unity in our nation when we have not achieved an adequate level of unity within our local churches or within the Church at large?

Jesus himself posted a warning to us concerning the destructive nature of division. He said, *"A house divided can not stand."* (Luke 11:17) A church divided cannot stand. Neither can a nation.

Whether we are struggling for cultural identity, self-worth or seeking to elevate our social or racial status, we must be cautious that we do not violate God's principles. Even when we want to secure a place of racial identity in Biblical history, we must be sure that we are speaking and understanding the truth. The Christian Community can not, under any circumstances, allow itself to be divided for any reason. We must remember that God's truth will bring healing, not division in His body.

Racial discrimination has been a major source of division in the Christian community. There has been a great deal of discussion about this, and many have attempted to bring about **racial reconciliation** within the Church. Some leaders of major denominations have made public apologies to Black Christians on behalf of White Christians. All of these attempts have been admirable and have certainly helped to some degree. However, the truth of the matter is—and this must be made plain—the simple fact is that there has never been conciliation between the races in these United States. Of course, it is impossible to **re-concile** something where there has never been **conciliation** in the first place.

Brothers and Sisters—Red, Yellow, Black and White—we must join not only our hands, but also our minds and our hearts, to help free each other and this great land called America from the continuing presence of racism. We must become one and begin to show the world that we are truly His disciples because we <u>Love one another</u>!

Political, Scientific, nor even Ecclesiastical debates have not eased the racial tension nor brought about a solution. However, a praying, believing, and loving church can and will make the difference.

If there has ever been a time for the church to stand together as one, it certainly is the hour in which we live. There is political unrest, moral decay, AIDS, drug addiction. Murders are of epidemic proportions. Sin abounds on every hand. There are laws being presented on every level of government that, if passed, could virtually put an end to the church organization as we know it today. We must, in light of all of this, and the needs of a dying world, learn to put away our deep-rooted jealousies and prejudices and present a unified front to the world.

We can argue over anthropology, archeology, and dissect our heritage point by point. We can adhere to the Word of God for a moment and then point to science and the theory of evolution the next. We can run to the Koran or to humanism, but it will all be to no avail. The answer to the peace and fulfillment for which all mankind seeks does not lie in racial pride, Darwinism, or Islam, but in Jesus Christ, who is The Lord of all!

Whether Jew or Gentile, bond or free, Black or White, Protestant or Catholic, the battle lines are drawn. The arguments will continue....

But where does Jesus stand in all of this? I believe He has assumed the same posture that He had on Calvary. He stands with arms outstretched between believer and scorner alike...

....loving both equally as He loves all races, nations, and people,

...reiterating to His disciples again and again, *"They will know that you are my disciples, because you "love" one another."*

...praying as He did in His final petition on earth before His ascension, *"Father, make them "one" as we are one."*

...and finally instructing us on true prosperity and victory in our Christian life by saying once again, *"The most important of all the commandments is that you love God with all your heart and love each other as well."*

On these commandments, we can hang all of our genealogies, culture, ethnic and racial differences.

We must remember that, when we receive Jesus as Lord and Savior, we become part of a new supernatural race upon the earth—a race that supersedes all other factors or race or creeds—and we simply become "Christians." In this kind of atmosphere, we can not only accept one another; but we can treasure the differences that once divided us.

We must present Jesus to all peoples the way He truly is:

...in respect to spiritual matters, forever occupying the center position for all things;

...in natural matters, as a Light Shemite, not a Black Cushite nor a White Japhetite.

Jesus was light, not White.

Finally, if indeed it is Cush's time to run, I pray that he runs away from the Koran, Darwinism, and all humanistic attempts to explain his origin; and I pray that he finds his "roots" in the book of Genesis instead. We can then effectively continue the mandate Jesus has left us to invite the world to come and hear the "Real Gospel" and that is the Christ-Centric Gospel.

It is my sincere prayer that this book be received by all of my Brothers and Sisters in Christ with the same spirit of love and concern in which it is written and with an unbiased concern for the Family of God.

Section 1: An Overview of Racism in America

Chapter 1: The Mulberry Tree

I was raised in Central Florida. From the late 1940's until the late 1960's I had a firsthand look at the ugliness of racism. My father was a law enforcement officer for over thirty years in the county where we lived. At one time he was over the county jail system. It was there that I observed the *Good Ole Boy* philosophy that fueled a great deal of the racism and racial bigotry of that era, not to mention the atrocities and physical violence.

We were totally segregated in those days. Exactly as the terminology suggests, totally segregated meant absolutely no mixing of the races. People of color—Blacks, Hispanics, Asians, and anyone else who was dark-skinned—were excluded from all white privileges. They could not eat in the same restaurants, drink from the same drinking fountains, or even use the same restrooms in the gas stations where they filled up their automobiles. At some stations there were bathrooms labeled "Colored."

People of color were only allowed to reside in all-ethnic neighborhoods. These neighborhoods were usually referred to as the *Nigger Quarters* or just simply, *The Quarters*.

I never played with Black children or played sports against a team with Black players. I did not eat with them, or even know one of them on a personal basis until I entered the military at eighteen years of age. That was indeed a learning experience! After a number of confrontations that left me with black eyes, cut lips, and even a concussion, I began to realize that indeed Uncle Sam wanted us integrated.

During that time, I came to realize that I had been deceived for eighteen years concerning the races. I realized that much of what has been propagated in the South concerning the Black man was more than old wives' tales; it was down right lies.

Some of my closest and dearest friends in those days were Black and Hispanic. I praise God that many of my most cherished friends today are the same. What a contrast with those early years of my life when I observed first hand the hatred and bigotry that remains as a dark shadow on the South's History to this day.

There was no such thing as equal rights in those days. The Black man had virtually <u>no</u> rights at all. Unfair treatment of minorities by police officers was common. Blacks were arrested without "just cause" and without proper warrants. The police often intimidated them into confessing to crimes they had not committed. Often false evidence and witnesses were presented against the innocent in order to convict them.

Sometimes the false evidence was deliberately planted. Police officers actually carried weapons such as _throw-down guns or knives_ to plant at crime scenes. When an innocent or unarmed suspect was shot, the officers threw one of these weapons down beside the suspect and claimed self-defense. Of course, fellow officers always substantiated their report. No one spoke of police brutality in those days, yet many Black people were brutalized without any recourse whatsoever.

THE MULBERRY TREE:

In the small town where I graduated from high school there was a famous landmark—a mulberry tree. This tree was both the focal point of town and its namesake. The old tree stood in the front of the train depot in the center of the town. It was here, as history records, that the town was founded. The mail train left the mail at the mulberry tree; thus the town became known as Mulberry.

We had a gold mulberry tree on our class rings, and our yearbook was titled, _The Mulberry Tree._ We even had a school anthem that spoke of _Ole Mulberry Tree, Ole Mulberry Tree, how proud you stand,_ or something to that effect.

In addition to the historical sentiment surrounding the tree, it held a far greater significance to the local residents, for it was also known as a "hanging tree." For a period of half a century or more, the Mulberry tree served as an instrument of fear in the community, especially to the ethnic community. It was a constant reminder of white supremacy and justice or injustice, depending on the situation.

More than once when a Black person supposedly committed a crime, I would hear someone say, *"Let a few of them dance on the Mulberry tree, and that would put a stop to these things!"*

In reviewing the tree's past, I found out that there had been some people hanged on it, both Black and White. Just how many I did not find out.

I have seen the Klan marching and crosses burning. I have heard the racial slurs, the name-calling, the disrespect, and the deep-rooted hatred that was passed from generation to generation. The ignorance continued from father to son to grandson.

SEPARATE BUT EQUAL:

One key manifestation of racism was an educational principle called *Separate but Equal*. This principle was, in theory, based on the supposition that although the schools were segregated, the Black students would be housed in and have access to the same quality of facilities and academics that the White students had. The working out of this principle fell far short of this goal. It was evident to all that, even though the races were separate, they were never equal.

Employment opportunities for Blacks were restricted to menial service jobs or manual labor. The trade unions and skilled labor jobs were closed to them, as were any administrative or professional positions. College graduates had to migrate to the North to practice their professions or be restricted to serving their own race only.

Often the Black educators were products of substandard educational institutions and unfortunately were ill equipped themselves. Thus their students would be ill equipped and would find it difficult to pass state exams.

Until the mid-sixties, this trend continued. Under the leadership of Dr. Martin Luther King, Jr., the Civil Rights Movement brought about dramatic changes in the South. Integration was instituted, and finally the schools, restaurants, and public facilities were racially mixed.

Unfortunately a change in peoples' hearts cannot be legislated by Federal laws. I do know however from personal experience that God can change a heart from one filled with hatred to one filled with brotherly love for all men and all races *IF* the individual is willing to have his heart changed.

Something Got a Hold on Me!

When I was a teenager, some of my friends would drive through the black neighborhood and throw stones or oranges at homes and pedestrians. One night I accompanied them on such a rock-throwing trip. One of the favorite targets of these wayward youths was a small Black church down on the highway that ran through the town.

The night I went with them, we arrived at this church after dark. The service was in full swing, and the congregation was having what is often referred to as "A Jericho March." They were marching around the building singing, *"When the Saints Go March'n In"* and playing a big bass drum. They were blowing a slide trombone and playing their tambourines.

I don't even think that they noticed the pounding the little building was taking from the rocks and the oranges we were throwing. It was evident that they had *"the joy of the Lord"*—a term that I would not be familiar with until fifteen years later.

I stood there with this orange in my hand, observing the people and listening to the music. For some reason, I could not bring myself to throw the orange at the building. Now understand that I was no more principled against it than my peers, but like the old song declares, *"Somethin' gotta hold on me!"*

Later I said to my best friend, *"You know, if I ever get religion, that is the kind that I want!"* Of course his response to my statement was, *"What would you ever want out of a N____ church?"* Little did I know that God had started something in my life that night that would eventually bring me to where I am today. Until this day my favorite style of music is, you guessed it, Black Gospel.

We can all change if we are willing to do so. If we will allow God's love to purge us of our carnal ideas and let His love permeate our hearts, change will come. Then and only then can we love each other without fear.

By the way, I still enjoy a good old fashioned, Jericho march once in a while.

Chapter 2: A Nation Divided

America is a nation divided, a nation fragmented and shattered by various groups of people, philosophies and ideals. Once referred to as the great melting pot, with Lady Liberty standing tall in New York harbor, She beckoned to the world and all nations to send their outcast to these shores. Some were in despair and depression when they arrived here. Others were fleeing tyranny and torture. Some were chasing the proverbial pot of gold at the end of the rainbow or just the opportunity to pursue the American dream. Whatever the reason, they came, boatload after boatload, all seeking freedom.

Come they did, by the millions, from all nations. First the Spanish, then the English and the Dutch, the French and other Europeans, each group of settlers seeking religious and political liberty and justice for all. They came of their own freewill, following their dreams and adventures.

There was, however, one particular group of people who did not come to this new land with smiles on their faces or joy in their hearts. Neither did they come following their dreams or personal desires of prosperity. They came as chattel—not passengers aboard the schooners that transported them to the New World, but as cargo, mere trade goods to be bartered and sold like so many beasts of burden, to work this fertile land called The New World.

These people did not choose to come here. They were uprooted and enslaved by their own tribesmen or by those from neighboring tribes. They were subsequently sold into slavery to foreign traders, who grew rich marketing fellow human beings.

Africa's enslaved came by the millions, with many of them dying on the grueling and inhumane portage aboard the sailing vessels. They were stacked like wood below deck with limited space and only stale air to breathe. They were given very little to eat and were forced to endure being covered with the defecation and vomit of those stacked above them. Racked with pain and filled with fear, beaten and bloody, terrorized and near death, they arrived.

A Poor Welcome:

Those who came by choice were greeted by friends and family standing on the docks and cheering their arrival. But there was no one there to embrace these beleaguered, bewildered Africans. Their only embrace would be the chains hammered on their limbs and the scars indelibly printed on their hearts. With freedom still in their spirits and a hope for returning to their own homeland—to the land of their forefathers, the continent of Africa—someday still in their hearts, they submitted to their captors. Thus a new epic had begun—an epic of shame that would last more than 200 years.

The blood of many who arrived aboard the slave ships and of those who were born and died under the lash of the slaver's whip flows through many African-American's veins today. There is still a "Cry for Freedom." You can almost hear the sound of the chains in some parts of this country. But they are not alone in their quest for equality. Joining them in the struggle are Asians, Orientals, Hispanics and Native Americans—people of color from every nation, kindred and tongue, all seeking the same freedom and equality.

Prejudice Comes in Many Forms:

We live in a world that is filled with hatred, bigotry, prejudicial attitudes and violence. Discrimination comes in all shapes, sizes and colors. It is present on every stratum of society, in every human dimension. Racism is only one of the many types of prejudices that we face daily.

Bigotry is another factor that divides our nation. Bigotry goes beyond race and skin color. It starts at the very top level of our society and trickles down to the lowest stratum—everyone with their own agenda, their own ideals and philosophies, all vying for their piece of the American dream. White supremacists, clad with swastikas and rebel flags, are hurling their racial insults and displaying their obvious ignorance on television talk shows. Their black supremacist counterparts with their own racist propaganda do the same.

Unfortunately, bigotry doesn't end with a few radicals trying to impose their version of truth on society. Its influence touches the poor and the rich, the illiterate and the educated alike—from the Korean shop keepers to the homeless or those who have AIDS, to the obese or to the immigrants who come to quote, "Take our jobs!" Whether poor Black Haitians or Vietnamese boat people or those who swim the Rio Grande River, the list of victims and victimizers is endless. Not even the Church is immune to bigotry's influence.

Not surprisingly, there is a great deal of controversy today surrounding the subject of the races and their rightful place and heritage in the Kingdom of God. People, who are seeking to raise the cultural awareness of their race or nationality, are attempting to establish justice for the past wrongs perpetrated upon their people. They should be commended and encouraged to do so.

While the fact remains that you do not have to give up your cultural heritage to become a Christian, it is also true that we cannot allow our culture to take precedence over the Word of God. Therefore, it is necessary to impose a warning: In our attempts to make corrections, we dare not overcorrect. It is so easy for the momentum of any crusade that is bent on finding and purporting the truth, to become so hyper in its pursuit that it pushes the pendulum beyond balance into the opposite extreme. There is indeed an apropos adage that states, *"Two wrongs do not make a right."*

It would be absurd to deny the inequities and fallacies concerning the teachings about race and color in the past, and the neglect of proper Biblical exegesis, which often provided a so-called scriptural basis for them. Denying the absence of proper historical and cultural teaching based on scriptural truths in Bible Colleges and Seminaries over the centuries would be equally absurd. Certainly we cannot turn a blind eye or deaf ear to the racism that has existed for centuries within the Christian community

itself. Racism has not only been tolerated; it has often been reinforced from the pulpit and through the educational forums of the
"church."

A SEARCH FOR THE FACTS:

There is no doubt that it is time to properly define the Biblical
and Historical facts concerning people of color as seen in the
Word of God, as well as those whose origin and cultural genealogy is not of color. It is vital that the correct vehicle and methodology, which is used to establish the truth, has a firm foundation in Biblical truths. The Christian scholar, the expositor of
truth, the Preacher of righteousness must, at all costs, endeavor
to find the truth, understand the truth, revere the truth, protect
the truth, and expound only the truth.

So many times when the word "racism" is used people immediately seem to migrate to the "Black-White" issue. But, unfortunately, it is not limited to those two racial factions. Indeed, it
can be found in all walks of life and social structures.

I have traveled to many nations and observed racism in many
forms and practices. It is as diversified as the many peoples
who populate the nations themselves. It is just as ugly, as cruel,
and as unpleasing to God as "Black-White" racism. It is a stench
not only in His nostrils, but also to all who affirm God's principles of love and equality as Holy.

In Africa, there are tribal differences so strong that they have
cost the lives of millions of people. Many of the Black extremists today speak of the Holocaust that took place in
America during the slave era when so many of their ancestors
died; but very few of these people speak of the horror that is
taking place in places like Liberia and Rwanda today.

A former government official in exile from Liberia told me that
young Liberian students came to the United States to study and
learn about finding their "roots" and establishing their tribal
identity. As a result, they came back to Liberia and created
social and tribal unrest that resulted in the deaths of over 250,000
of their fellow countrymen.

Newsweek magazine carried the photos of a massacre of 1200 people, including many Priests, in Rwanda. These people were killed in a church. Their bodies were left to decay where they fell. Their only crime was being born into the "wrong" tribe.

Africa is certainly not the only place where racial prejudices and bigotry are present. All over the world, man is still abusing, enslaving and often killing his fellow man because he is racially or socially different or just simply because he refuses to submit to a totalitarian rule that strips him of all dignity and individualism.

The term "ethnic cleansing" became a reality as the world watched the news reports from Kosovo. Bosnians and Croatians, Arabs and Jews, Vietnamese and Cambodians, Iraqis and Iranians, North Koreans and South Koreans, Irish and English—the death toll climbs higher and higher. So often the only reason for the slaughter of innocents is simply *"they are not like us."*

OTHER GROUPS PERSECUTED:

Some of my family background consists of Jewish and Native Americans. The Jewish part of the family lost all that they owned in Europe because they were Jews. The Native American part of the family lost all they had in this country simply because they were American Indians. When "Good-OLE-Boys" like Andrew Jackson passed a law that no Indian could own land, my family became very personally acquainted with racial prejudice.

The Gurley family has fought against oppression and racial inequities for generations. Dr. Phineas Gurley was Abraham Lincoln's pastor. He often prayed with him from the going down of the sun until it would rise again the next day during those agonizing years of the Emancipation and the Civil War. Before that, Reverend Randolph Gurley, Secretary of the American Colonization Society, traveled to Liberia and established a colony there of freed slaves and other ex-slaves who had run away to the North. He named this new country Liberia and its capital, Monrovia, after his friend James Monroe. Liberia was the first Democratic State in Africa.

During that time, the settlers had to fight the local tribesmen along the Ivory Coast border, killing 200 in one battle. The local tribesmen said that the Colony interfered with the slave trade. As one tribal chief said, *"I have dealt in slaves like my father before me and his father before him. If indeed it is profitable, why then should I not continue?"* This is quoted from the book, *Liberia Old and New*, by James L. Sibley, 1928. Sibley also tells of a slave revolt during that time—not Black slaves verses White slave owners, but Black slaves against their Black slave owners.

ESTABLISHING RESPONSIBILITY:

When the responsibility- is truly fixed for the inhuman treatment of any people by another it should be evident that everyone who took part in that dark portion of human history should accept their rightful share of blame.

It has been said that, *"History is often written in favor of those who are writing it."* I pray that this is not the case in "Light Not White."

Where does the church stand in all of this and what is the Christian's role and responsibility? Good question. Read on, and I think we will find the answer as we seek the truth together.

Chapter 3: Racism Defined

The term Race is defined as, *"Any of the different varieties of mankind, mainly the Caucasoid, Mongoloid, or Negroid groups, distinguished by kind of hair, color of skin, etc. Any geographical, national, or tribal ethnic grouping, or any group having the same ancestry or the same habits, ideas, etc. Same as the term breed."*[1] From the word Race comes the word, Racism or Racialism, which properly defined is *"...a doctrine, without scientific proof, that claims the superiority of some one race."*[2] The word Racism is the same as Racialism but extends the idea of *"...the practice of racial discrimination or segregation."*[3]

Discrimination and prejudices can be found in every segment of our society. The various forms of these prejudices are as diversified and sundry as the people who are involved. There are so many forms of discrimination that it would be impossible to list them all. Around the world, discrimination exists in every culture, nation, people, and tongue. The wealthy often discriminate against the poor, employer against employee, the businessman against the laborer, white-collar worker against blue-collar worker, and farmer against field hand. Often the educated are prejudiced against the uneducated, the cultured against the uncultured, and so on. The list is endless.

Discrimination works its way down the sociological strata until they reach the very bottom rung of the social scale. From there a reversal takes place. Prejudicial attitudes become inverted and start working their way back up the ladder.

At the bottom of the scale or the top, depending on the individual's perspective or vantage point, you will find the worst form of discrimination that exists—the most painful, the most emotionally debilitating, and the most subjugating form known to man, and for sure the most displeasing to God. There you will find racism.

There can be no greater destructive interaction in the human race either past, present, or future than racism. Racism has fostered wars, slaughtered families, produced widows and orphans, enslaved nations, and has cost millions of people their lives throughout the ages. It is the most dehumanizing and dangerous form of discrimination on earth. Left unchecked, it can turn law-abiding, Sunday-go-to-meeting church folk into a murderous hate-filled lynch mob.

NOT ONLY A BLACK-WHITE ISSUE:

Most often when the words racism or racial prejudice are used in the United States, peoples' minds immediately turn to a Black and White issue. This happens simply because the most prominent form of racial prejudice in America has been between the Whites and Blacks. But no nationality that has been part of the settlement and building of this nation has been exempt from their own share of discrimination at one time or another.

For example, during the building of the railroads and settlement of the Western Pacific States, the Chinese experienced their own brand of slavery. They were called "Coolies" and were treated as less than human. They were worked in the rain and cold, whether they were sick or healthy. They died where they fell, without medical care or attention being offered. Without rights or legal defense, they died by the thousands at the hands of their persecutors. If a White man killed a Chinese, he was not even charged with a crime, because it was not against the law to kill a "Coolie." Finally they did impose a $50.00 dollar fine for the murder of a Chinaman.

When the Italians came to settle in America, they, too, faced persecution—a persecution not unique to them alone, but the same as so many other immigrants before them had faced. No one wanted the Italians to take their job or part of their business away from them. As a result, Italians found it difficult to find employment or to open their own businesses. Many of them even changed their names to non-Italian sounding names, like Bellino to Bell or Bassiglio to Bass, etc., simply to hide the fact that they were of Italian descent.

The term "Wop" is believed to have originated at Ellis Island, the immigrant induction center in New York's harbor. "Wop" was an abbreviation for "Without Papers." Many immigrants did not have proper documentation when they arrived from Italy, so they were quarantined for a while. They had to wear a sign that identified them as needing to have papers to enter the country. Hence they were called "Wops". This designation soon became a derogatory term.

It is the same as the term, "Spic," an abbreviation that stands for Spanish Person in Custody. This would also become a slanderous term, as would the term "Wetback," which describes the Mexican people who swim the Rio Grand River to gain illegal entry into the United States.

The Italians found work on the shipping docks and became strike breakers for the unions. Their struggle for equality gave rise to the importation of the Mafia and Cosa Nostra, which translates "Our Thing", from the Old Country as a means of survival. Many other immigrants would also develop their "Own Thing" in order to survive in their new homeland.

It was no different when the Irish came to the shores of this great land of the brave and free, fleeing the potato famine of the mid-19th century. Over one million of them died, and another million headed for America. When they got here, they had to fight for jobs, housing, business capital and every other thing simply to exist in this new land. They were called, "Mics," because so many of their names began with "Mc." Like most other abbreviations for the names, "Mics" soon became an insult.

Next would come the Jews. As in all parts of the world, people were highly suspicious of and prejudiced against these foreign "invaders." These newcomers were shrewd businessmen who had the reputation of being unscrupulous in all of their business dealings and practices.

Jews were called "Christ-killers" and "Kikes." As a result of their reputation in business it became common to use the term, "Jewed Down", when bargaining for a better price in a transaction. So vehement was the persecution against the Jewish people that often signs were posted, "No Jews or Niggers Allowed." Civic organizations, Fraternities, and private clubs denied them membership on basis of their race and religion. Unquestionably, we must also include the Jews in this list of the persecuted.

INCREASING PREJUDICE AGAINST THE JEWS:

In 1905 a fictitious document, entitled *The Protocols of the Elders of Zion*, was first printed in Russia. These protocols are supposedly the minutes of an alleged conference of senior leaders of world Jewry. This document outlined a satanic plot for the Jews to conquer and enslave the world. This imaginary conspiracy concerning the Jews helped to produce the Holocaust and untold suffering of the Jewish people by inciting racial bigotry and persecution worldwide, especially in the last century.

The majority of the Jews came from Europe to flee the horror of racial prejudice—the very type of persecution they found themselves experiencing in America. They had fled the discrimination and punishment being inflicted upon them by fellow citizens who were Gentiles. These successful Jewish businessmen, professionals, craftsmen, shopkeepers, and educators, along with farmers and field hands, arrived in America with only the clothing on their backs. They had been forced from their homes, jobs, and businesses by White supremacists and made to live in the ghettos and slums of Europe.

The terror and oppression against the Jews escalated throughout the early to mid-1900s. Their persecutors were armed with Aryan doctrines that were fueled by the Church of Europe and inflammatory remarks made by men like Martin Luther in the past.

A doctrine called Replacement Theology found it's way into the Theological Seminaries of Europe in the 1920s. This theology proclaimed that God was divorced from a literal Israel and that He only recognized a spiritual Israel. Supporters of this theology believed that if God himself had written off the Jews, then man should do the same thing.

This heresy would finally find it's way into the Third Reich and would turn deadly in the hands of the Nazis. It would find its end under the boots of the Nazi S.S. storm troopers as they crushed the life out of Jewish citizens. Ultimately over six million men, women, and children died. Young and old, their bodies would fill the mass graves and furnaces of Europe simply because they were, "Jews"—the victims of Anti-Semitism. Today, over half a century later, young Neo-Nazis display signs saying, "Do six million more!"

WHO ARE THE SEMITES?

The dictionary defines a Semite as: *"1. One of a people of Caucasian stock comprising chiefly Jews and Arabs but in ancient times also including Babylonians, Assyrians, Phoenicians, and others of the eastern Mediterranean area. 2. One of the people descended from Shem."* [4] When it is used as an adjective, the term Semitic is defined as: *"1. Of or relating to the Semites, esp. Jewish or Arabic. 2. Of, relating to, or comprising a subfamily of the Afro-Asiatic language family that includes Arabic, Hebrew, Amharic, and Aramaic."* [5] When used as a noun, Semitic refers to t*he Semitic languages or one of the languages in the Semitic group."* [6]

It is interesting that an anti-Semite is defined as one *"...who is hostile toward or prejudiced against Jews."* The Arabs, although of the same racial origin, are separated from the Jews in terms of prejudice, just as they are in almost all other respects as well.

Can you imagine how the Jewish immigrants felt when they were forced to live in the squalor of the ghettos in the Northeast and forced to work as little more than slave labor in the clothing districts? They worked in the "fabric sweatshops"—as the tailoring business was called in places like New York City—for twelve to fifteen hours a day in the heat and the cold. They were paid mere pennies and were subject not only to their uncaring employers, but were often the victims of brutal crimes. Robbery and rape, beatings and humility were a way of life for the Jews in America. Thus the term, "Anti-Semitic," became a reality to them in the West—the land that they believed was the new Promised Land flowing with milk and honey.

A Crucible of Racism:

Every group of immigrants who came to America suffered from the same racial slurs, the rock throwing, and the name-calling. Broken windows and broken hearts, burned buildings and shattered dreams. Yet they persisted and endured to capture the "American Dream."

Many of the immigrants died before ever realizing their dream. Some of these people were buried in cemeteries in the cities with marble headstones; some in paupers' graves. Others were buried along the roadsides and trails without even a marker designating their place of internment. They were buried on obscure mountain trails and on the open prairies where the wagon trains crossed. Others died without even a friend to send word across the sea or back home to let their loved ones and families know that they were deceased.

Those who were persecuted today would become the persecutors of tomorrow. Those, who had survived and carved out their own niche in America, were now ready to test the determination and tenacity of the next boatload of immigrants who came seeking refuge and fortune in this great country.

The Czechs and Polacks, German and Hungarians, East Indians and Orientals—immigrants from all nations came. In contemporary times, the Hispanics and Haitians, Cubans and Vietnamese Boat people have come along with the Mexicans—all streaming across the border, seeking employment. All have taken or will take their turn in the crucible of racism and the struggle for equality in the United States.

Native Americans, Also Victims of Racism:

All of the nationalities mentioned so far have been immigrants to the Americas. However, there were indigenous people who inhabited this country before any of those named above arrived. They are the Native-Americans—the American Indians. When we speak of racism and racial prejudice we cannot omit these American Aborigines, who have suffered beyond measure at the hands of those who settled the Americas. The term "Holocaust" should come to mind when we discuss their plight.

It is believed that, from the time of Christopher Columbus' historical landing at Santa Domingo in 1492 until the end of the Indian Wars in the late 1800s, over nine million Indians were slaughtered in North, Central and South America and the Caribbean. It would be appropriate to use the word "exterminated" in most cases, due to the mindset of those who were determined to annihilate these Native Americans.

The White settlers' treatment of the Indians is one of the most drastic examples of racism ever recorded. These settlers were driven by greed for land, power, and natural resources, such as gold, silver, oil, and minerals. They had been told that the red-skinned heathens did not believe in God and had no soul, therefore they were not human. Killing an Indian was like killing a wild animal. In fact, they were hunted for bounty. The scalps of women and children, as well as the men, were collected and sold.

These Native Americans were driven from their homelands and hunting grounds. Entire tribes were slaughtered. Finally they began to fight for survival. When they did, they were called the aggressors. In the eyes of the nation, they were seen as a threat to the settlement and civilization process of America. They had to be eliminated. The Army was called in to make war on these indigenous people and rid the plains of their presence and any subsequent threat from them.

The list of atrocities against this once proud people is endless. From the Black Hills of the Dakotas to the Florida Everglades, they were killed and imprisoned. Women and children, young and old, they died. They were starved and driven to the point of extinction. There is a trail of tears and a trail of blood that extends from East to West and North to South, leaving a shadow of shame upon the heritage of this nation. Countless numbers of Native Americans were butchered and massacred. Those who survived were herded like so many cattle onto reservations, where many of their descendants remain to this day.

They were lured into peace treaties with promises of food and freedom—enticing promises to a people who had been disarmed and whose hunting lands had been depleted. Hunger, disease and alcoholism took its toll. Discouraged, they submitted to the White man's terms.

Our nation's treatment of the Native Americans didn't improve even after they were isolated on the reservations. They were cheated and lied to. The government broke every treaty that it ever made with these Native Americans. The term "Indian-Giver" is used today to define one who gives something and then takes it back. Most people think this term describes the Indian, but on the contrary it has the opposite meaning—someone who gave to the Indians and then took it all back.

Racism, in all its dimensions, ravaged our Native Americans, creating a displaced and disoriented people—a people who often live in abject poverty in many states, especially the Southwest and Northern plains states. As a people, they have the highest rate of alcoholism, infant death and teenage suicide rate in the United States. More maladies afflict this group of people than any other group in our nation. Why? It is a result of broken treaties and promises. This is discrimination and racism in its purest form.

THE TRUTH ALONE SETS US FREE:

It must appear to the reader by now that this is an overkill or a beleaguered point in bruising and battering this great nation of ours. But on the contrary, it is but the truth, and the truth will set us free! But, in our pursuit of truth, it is important to understand that the United States does not have a monopoly on racial discrimination. In fact, many of the nationalities already mentioned came to this county, fleeing oppression and racial problems of their homelands.

I have personally witnessed many different forms of racism in my travels around the world. For example, in India there are various tribal differences in addition to the caste system that is very much in place. Even in Christian groups, there is a carry-over from the Hindu caste or social structure, which is based on birth and prohibits the mixing of one caste with another. The lowest of the castes is the Harijans or the "low caste." People of this caste are often referred to as the untouchables and are often subjected to discrimination. They are backward and un-educated. They are on the lowest strata of society. They are the poorest of the poor of the Hindus and Christians, and they have very little hope of improving their station in life. They are discriminated against in every way possible.

It is such a blessing to see how these people are blessed when they become Christians. From that point on, they start an upward mobility in society.

In Africa there are similar situations of racism and tribal differences. West African and Central African nations have experienced a blood bath in the last decade because of tribal differences. From the time that slavery began centuries ago among the African tribes to the present day, there has been senseless slaughter of one tribal people by another. In Liberia, Nigeria, Burundi and Rwanda these ethnic purges have taken the lives of well over a million people. Men, women, and children are slaughtered in the most brutal ways imaginable. Shot, burned, tortured, and hacked to pieces with machetes, not by an invading alien force, but by their own countrymen. We often hear the term "Black on Black Crime" Well, this is one of the worst cases of "Black on Black Crime" in the world to date.

Ill feelings have been harbored for centuries between these different African tribes. Many have not forgotten how the Mother Tribes of Africa dominated and enslaved their ancestors, killing their young warriors and taking their wives and children prisoner.

These ill feelings are not difficult to understand when viewed historically and we learn of the brutality and harsh treatment of one tribe by another conquering tribe, or of the slavery and death that tribal wars brought. People today still carry the bitterness in their hearts that even prohibits fellow Christians from fellowshipping one with another.

A lot of these differences were initiated by European colonists, who sometimes pitted one tribe against another to serve their own selfish interests. Many of these ill feelings are still harbored today and are manifested in senseless slaughter.

Even among Latin Americans and Hispanics and people from Central America there is a great deal of prejudice. In Christian circles, it is often evident that there are divisions among Spanish people according to their nationality.

Much of the discrimination today is not purely racial, but it also stems from differences in political ideologies and dictatorial attitudes of world leaders. A great deal of aggression and social unrest is a result of the ruling class oppressing the poor.

All over the world, even in the time we live—the dawning of a new millennium—man is still abusing, enslaving, and killing his fellow man. Often he kills him because he is racially or socially different or simply refuses to submit to a totalitarian rule that strips him of all dignity and individualism. Whatever the reason, nations are locked in mortal combat.

New Shades of Racism:

Current studies of racism in America reveal that racism is no longer White/Black, White/Yellow, or White/Red phenomenon. Rather division is evident between a multitude of shades of skin tone. In part this is due to the increasing frequency of interracial marriages. Divisions based on shades of skin color are evident in other nations as well. I once read an article in a magazine that in Jamaica there were 33 different distinguishable skin tones—starting with the lightest and going to the darkest. Those with the lightest skin are regarded as being the highest of the social scale.

This trend toward multiculturalism characterizes the history of our nation. The Census of 1860 had only three classifications for race, while the Census of 2000 had thirty with eleven subdivisions for Hispanics. The growing numbers of interracial marriages will continue this trend. [7]

Children of these marriages sometimes feel displaced, like they don't belong in either culture. Others embrace the diversity of their heritage. Certainly, this is one area where healing the divisions between the races will have a great impact.

One example of the new shades of racism is the animosity evident between many Mexicans who have immigrated to the United States in recent years and Chicanos—descendants of Mexicans who immigrated and intermarried with Anglos. A recent article in Newsweek Magazine documented this form of Brown/Light Brown racism. Many Chicanos view the new generation of "Wetbacks" as unprincipled. Chicanos in supervisory positions in the work place often discriminate against the Mexicans. Racial slurs are found painted on walls. Often the Chicanos do not want to be identified with the newcomers even though they share the same ancestral heritage. The Mexican immigrants sometimes resent the Chicanos because they are doing better economically than they are. Then there is the language problem. The Chicanos who do attempt to reach out to the Mexicans find that, after generations of adjusting to the American culture, they no longer speak Spanish properly! [8]

The same kind of Brown/Brown discrimination is sometimes evident in the African-American community. Some who are very fair may abandon any connection with their African-American ancestors. Likewise, some whose racial makeup shows little evidence of mixing of the blood may completely disconnect themselves from their Anglo roots.

In recent years, there has been a growing division between African-Americans and Africans. For all the push to find their roots, African-Americans sometimes look down on their African brothers and sisters because they do not share their heritage of suffering and persecution under slavery. One African professor in a predominately Black Virginia university contends that he was dismissed from his position because he was too African.

One African-American teacher in California reports that the greatest racial conflicts she has to resolve in the classroom are those between the Vietnamese and the Filipino students. She was astonished at the intensity of the division between these two Asian groups. She said the two groups often debate whose people survived the most getting to America, whose people made the quickest transition to the American way of life, and whose people are the most successful. Suffering has not only become a badge of courage to these young people; it has also become a basis for division from one another. [9]

THE RESOLUTION OF RACIAL CONFLICTS:

Matthew recorded Jesus' comments on the seemingly unending conflicts between nations:

"And ye shall hear of wars and rumors of wars: see that ye be not troubled: for all these things must come to pass, but the end is not yet.

For nation shall rise against nation, and kingdom against kingdom: and there shall be famines, and pestilences, and earthquakes, in divers places." (Matthew 24:6-7)

The word that is translated nation here is *ethnos*, meaning race. Again and again, we see race rising against race.

What is the answer to such a senseless slaughter? Can man live in racial harmony and unity? If so, how? These are valid questions, and God gives us the only valid answers.

Paul considered these weighty questions in his letter to the Colossians. Drawing his readers' attention to the oneness, the unity, we all have in Christ, Paul gave them this word of exhortation:

Lie not to one another, seeing that ye have put off the old man with his deeds; And have put on the new man, which is renewed in knowledge after the image of him that created him: Where there is neither Greek nor Jew, circumcision nor uncircumcision, Barbarian, Scythian, bond nor free: but Christ is all, and in all.

Put on therefore, as the elect of God, holy and beloved, bowels of mercies, kindness, humbleness of mind, meekness, longsuffering;

Forbearing one another, and forgiving one another, if any man have a quarrel against any: even as Christ forgave you, so also do ye. (Colossians 3:9-13)

Paul saw the crucial importance of neutralizing the divisive effect that "differences"—racial or otherwise—have within the Body of Christ. Man looks on the external, and divides on the basis of these external factors. God looks upon the heart. The heart that is open to receive Him, is filled with His presence, His power, His glory—each one beloved, each one made holy, each one clothed in Christ; all regarded as the elect of God, all accepted into one family, ruled by one God and Father.

The chains of racism or any other form of elitism are broken in Christ, for He gives each the same gift of grace. There is no room for boasting—for racial superiority or any other worldly basis for classification—in the grace He has given us. If we give His grace full reign in our lives, it will make us one even as He and the Father are one.

Paul also stressed our oneness in Christ in his letter to the Galatians:

For ye are all the children of God by faith in Christ Jesus. For as many of you as have been baptized into Christ have put on Christ.

There is neither male nor female: for ye are all one in Christ Jesus. And if ye be Christ's, then ye are Abraham's seed, and heirs according to the promise. (Galatians 3:26-29)

We are Abraham's seed. Just as natural seed brings forth flowers of many colors and varieties, so Abraham's seed displays God's delight in variety.

We are heirs according to promise, and only one promise is given—that of eternal life with Christ. We are one in Christ—one in His eyes and one in His heart. Because we stand as one before Him, it is imperative that we put off that which keeps us from standing as one with each other.

End Notes:

[1-6] *The American Heritage Dictionary, Second College Edition,* Houghton Mifflin Company, Boston, 1985.

[7] Jon Meacham with Arian Campo-Flores, Vern E. Smith, Karen Breslau, Allison Samuels, and Lynette Clemetson, *The New Face of Race,* Newsweek, September 18, 2000, pp. 58-61.

[8] Arian Campo-Flores, Brown Against Brown, Newsweek, September 18, 2000, pp. 62-63.

[9] Jon Meacham. Ibid. pg. 61.

Chapter 4: Who Are Our Heroes?

There is a song from the past that says, *"Has anybody here seen my old friend, Abraham? Can you tell me where he is gone? He freed a lot of people, but it seems the good die young. I just looked around, and he was gone!"* The song goes on to ask the same question about John, Bobby, and Martin. The writer is, of course, speaking of Abraham Lincoln, John and Bobby Kennedy and Martin Luther King, Jr., all of whom died violently at the hands of assassins. These men were real-life heroes. Not only did they take control of their own destiny, but they also helped to shape the lives of countless millions around them. They were not the products of oral tradition or folklore. Nor were they made bigger than life on the silver screen by Hollywood. They lived and died, and they left a legacy to all of mankind—a legacy that says, *"You can be and do all that your heart desires in this great country of America. The American dream of life, liberty, and the pursuit of happiness is still alive and obtainable to those who dare."* They believed this with such intensity that they were willing to lay down their own lives so that the dream could be realized in the lives of others.

Throughout the ages men have looked to their heroes for inspiration and encouragement in times of adversity and oppression. Whether these heroes are real or fictitious, alive or deceased, we can identify with their character, their feats of daring, and their bold exploits as overcomers.

Unfortunately, many of the superheroes of the past were only the product of some individual storyteller's imagination or someone simply "spinning a yarn" or "weaving a tale" to encourage the discouraged in their time of need. Yet in our minds, we have fought alongside King Arthur's "Knights of the Round Table," Robin Hood, and Rambo. As children we've ridden with Roy Rogers, Gene Autry and John Wayne, to name a few. We've cheered as they struck a blow for freedom and overcame tyranny and injustice.

When we speak of heroes like Abraham Lincoln, John and Bobby Kennedy, and Martin Luther King, Jr., however, we are not speaking of characters in a fable or simply actors in a drama. We are speaking of men and women who were flesh and blood human beings—people who, by example, paid the ultimate price for what they believed.

When we speak of these people, who have gained our admiration and respect for their example or contribution to mankind, we must keep one thing in mind as Christians: We cannot become disciples or followers of anyone who is not totally Christian in thought and deed. This is a simple principle—one that we must neither lose sight of nor set aside for our cultural or racial identification. This principle reminds us that, no matter how popular, revered, or immortalized an individual may become in the eyes and mindset of the world, we cannot become their disciples or followers if their principles do not line up with the Word of God.

I have always personally respected anyone who is willing to lay down their life for what they believe. Even if I don't believe as they do, they still have my respect for their devotion and dedication to whatever cause they herald. Two examples are Malcolm X and Mahatma Gandhi, both of whom died for what they believed. But, as Christians, we cannot make exceptions for the sake of racial identity with anyone living or dead, especially those whose philosophies and religious beliefs are in direct contradiction to the Word of God. Gandhi was a Hindu, and Malcolm X was a Muslim. Both of these men believed and practiced pagan religions.

People such as these can be respected for their social and humane contributions to the plight of their fellowman, but we cannot follow them, regardless of race or culture. The Word of God marks a line that we, as Christians, cannot cross under any circumstances. In fact, there should be a warning posted to all Christians who seek to exalt their culture or ethnicity beyond what the scriptures allow.

Why is such a stance necessary? Our choice of heroes has a tremendous impact on us both individually and corporately. God-directed leaders will encourage us along a path that brings us into a fulfillment of God's vision for our lives. Likewise, God-directed leaders will work to uplift the downtrodden and bring unity and equality among all the races.

OTHER-DIRECTED LEADERS:

Mr. Moon, founder of the World Unification Church, claims to be a Christian but has proclaimed himself as the Christ. There have been many other "Jim Jones" type figures in the last few decades as well. Their agendas have had more to do with building their own kingdoms than God's kingdom.

Nelson Mandela and Louis Farrakhan are living examples of men of vision and perseverance. Yet, Mandela does not present himself as a Christian. The African National Congress, which he led, has encouraged a return to tribal religious practices or Animism, occasionally referring to Christianity as the White man's religion. Mr. Louis Farrakhan, on the other hand, is Neo-Islamic. He propagates his own brand of racial hatred, as well as encouraging the Nation of Islam followers to become activists in the various struggles of the Black community.

Although Mr. Farrakhan fuels the fires of racism from the African-American perspective, he does encourage morality. He also encourages Blacks to be self-sustaining, responsible citizens. In fact, his positive role model concerning the character of an individual professing Godliness is in contrast to the image of many Christian ministers, both Black and White, who have not maintained their own personal reputation as being holy in their life-styles. But neither of these men is a Martin Luther King, Jr. Louis Farrakhan is not leading his people out of bondage, but appears to be leading them deeper into the bondage of racial hatred and bigotry that has gripped this nation for centuries. This is in stark contrast to Dr. King's purpose and methodology. Dr. King worked to lead his people out of political and social bondage into freedom.

THE SIMPSON TRIAL, A RACIAL ISSUE?

One of the most renown news items of the 1990s was the O.J. Simpson trial. As a result, O.J. Simpson has become somewhat of a living hero through his lengthy court battles—even more so than his football career brought to him. There was so much controversy surrounding the O.J. Simpson trial. The debate continues to this day concerning his guilt or innocence. The jury acquitted him during his criminal trial, but their decision has left many unanswered questions. Simpson was later found liable in his civil trial, so the questions are still unanswered.

Was the trial a racial issue? That question has been a major topic on talk shows and panel debates by the experts. Many people believe that the answer is most definitely "Yes". The most likely reason they draw that conclusion is the general reaction of the American public. On the streets, in the work place, auditoriums and even in churches around the nation, people gathered on the day that the verdict was to be announced. When the verdict was read, the reaction of the people was totally opposite between the majority of Whites and the people of Color. The ethnic community shouted and cheered and even cried as they rejoiced in the verdict. Notice, I said in the verdict, not his innocence. It appears that his innocence was never established—just the fact that his guilt was not provable beyond a shadow of doubt in a court of law. On the other hand, there was an obvious disapproval in the White community at the jury's decision.

The mindset of the two factions seemed to differ in one major aspect, and I believe it was somewhat obvious. The White community seemed to be unemotionally attached—they were concerned primarily with "due process"—while the Black community was very emotionally attached. Each group was concerned with the outcome of the trial from opposite perspectives. Why?

O.J. Simpson represents a great athlete to the White community— "The Juice." While to the Black community, O.J. goes far beyond being a Heismann Trophy winner or a great running back. He is a true-to-life hero. He is a living statement to all Black youth in America: *"You can come out of the ghetto or any adverse circumstance in life and become rich and famous. You can be a millionaire movie star and live in Beverly Hills."*

Regardless of his alleged ungodly life-style, drug usage, spouse abuse, or any other flaw in his character, the Black community reveres O.J. He has become an icon, an object of hero-worship to them, even though he was never what you would call a civil rights activist in the past. It was reported that he even took speech lessons to sound Whiter, married a White woman, joined an all-White country club and moved into a White neighborhood. But after his trial, he was elevated for a short period of time in some people's opinion as a spokesperson for the Black community.

Is it wrong for a people to feel this way about one of their own? Absolutely not. Yet again as Christians, Black or White, Yellow, Red or Brown, we must understand that we are bound by a different set of ethics than the public at large. We cannot embrace anyone for any reason that does not exemplify a Godly life-style without posting some type of denouncement for that which is ungodly in his or her life.

It was interesting to listen to Geraldo Rivera and other talk show hosts that had many of the key participants in the Simpson trial as their guests. Both the prosecution and the defense teams were on all of the major networks, along with a myriad of experts. My wife and I made it a point to note those who suggested that O.J. was indeed guilty, based on the large amount of evidence presented, and those who disputed that evidence as being too insignificant to even suggest his guilt. The interesting point here was that, almost invariably, those experts who believed Simpson was guilty—whether they are a part of the trial participants or simply successful lawyers at large—were White. On the other hand, those who represented the opposite view—who disputed the evidence, who spoke of conspiracy and frame-ups, and who held to O.J.'s innocence—were, with the exception of Mr. Dardin, the prosecutor, Black. This almost 100% approval continues, even though he was found liable by a unanimous jury vote in his civil trial.

The civil trial jury's decision was primarily based on all of the evidence, which was not permitted to be used in the criminal trial, and on Mr. Simpson's denial of incidents that were testified to the contrary by many eye witnesses. This obviously reduced his credibility in the minds of the jurors. Yet after the civil trial, the polarization and racial divide once again was evident. Why? Heroes do not "fall from grace" easily.

A MATTER OF JUSTICE FOR ALL:

Am I saying that the Black community is not at all interested in justice? On the contrary, I believe if there are any citizens in the United States who are most interested in justice, it is those who are in the ethnic community. After all, who has seen more injustice in the American Court system than the citizens of the Black community? It is possible, when in search of someone to identify with racially and possess as our own hero, we can even subconsciously lay aside reason and even Christian doctrine to achieve that end.

In light of all of the unfair trials at the hands of the White justice system, it is easy to understand how a man like O.J. Simpson could attract such a loyal following. O.J. was not simply fighting for his own freedom. In essence, he was David against Goliath. He was a Black man, fighting the very system that had sent so many Black brothers and sisters to prison or the gallows. He was fighting in front of the whole world, and he won!

EMMETT TILL:

A prime example of the injustices that have been present in this nation's legal system is the story of a young black man named Emmett Till. Emmett came to Money, Mississippi from Chicago in 1955 to visit relatives. He was fourteen years old. He showed some young Black teens a school picture of a White girl and told them she was his girlfriend. His new friends then dared him to go into a store and speak to a White lady. He took them up on their dare.

That night two men picked Emmett up, and he was never seen alive again. His body was found in the Tallahatchie River chained to a fan from a cotton gin. He had been shot in the head. He was unclothed, and his body was mutilated. "Jet Magazine" later published the horrible photographs of Emmett's body.

Emmett's grandfather, Mr. Moses Wright, spoke out unafraid against his grandson's killers. He boldly identified them as the men who had come in the night and taken Emmett away. Yet even in the light of his eyewitness testimony, the trial in Sumner, Mississippi lasted only one hour. Both men were found not guilty.

A Black congressman attended the trial. The Sheriff remarked that they even had a nigger Congressman there. In front of TV news cameras, he told his men to let the "Boy" set with the reporters. The same Sheriff made this statement for the Newsmen before the whole nation: *"We don't have any trouble with our Southern Niggers, till they go up North and talk to the NAACP."*

Further evidence emerged, indicating the men's guilt. It was reported that, for the sum of $4,000 cash, the woman Emmett spoke with in the mercantile store had told a reporter how her husband and brother-in-law had murdered the young Black boy. She gave him all of the horrible details of Emmett's death. Still nothing could be done. The Whites had everything. Many of them believed that they were superior and that God approved and had ordained it so. This is what the Black people of the South had been taught and many had believed since the slave days. In the pre-Civil Rights era, a Black man could be arrested for not getting off the sidewalk when a White man passed by or for even looking too closely at a White man. He could even be beaten, or even worse, for staring too closely at a White woman.

Why were these kinds of things tolerated? The Whites contended that their White ancestors had founded the republic and that they must maintain tradition.

There were thousands of injustices and unfair trials like the one concerning Emmett Till. Many white murderers and rapists went unpunished without any justice for their Black victims.

INJUSTICE EXPOSED:

This kind of injustice was not new in the experience of Southern Blacks. In 1852, Frederick Douglass, one of the most renowned Black heroes of the Civil War era, was invited to give the key-note address at a Fourth of July celebration in Rochester, New York. His speech must have shocked a few folks that day. He titled his speech "What to the American Slave is Your Fourth of July?" and began by saying,

"Fellow Citizens: Pardon me, and allow me to ask, why am I called to speak here today? What have I or those I represent to do with your national independence? Are the great principles of political freedom and natural justice, embodied in that Declaration of Independence, extended to us? And am I, therefore, called upon to bring our humble offering to the national altar, and to confess the benefits, and express devout gratitude for the blessings resulting from your independence to us?

Frederick Douglass (photo courtsey of the Perry-Castañeda Library at the University of Texas at Austin)

"...I am not included within the pale of this glorious anniversary. Your high independence only reveals the immeasurable distance between us. The blessings in which you this day rejoice are not enjoyed in common. The rich inheritance of justice, liberty, prosperity, and independence bequeathed by your fathers is shared by you, not by me." [1]

Douglass' words underscored the irony of the injustice that was routinely accorded to African-Americans, both free and enslaved, in his day. He pointed out that in Virginia there were 72 crimes for which a Black man could be sentenced to death, *"...while only 2 of these same crimes will subject a White man to like punishment."* [2] What an astounding example of injustice that is based purely on race.

HOPE FOR CHANGE:

Our perception of members of other nationalities, cultures, or races is frequently clouded by assumptions, which are based on old wives' tales or biblical misinterpretations that are passed on to us by influential people in our lives, especially our immediate family. We'll look at these types of influences in more depth in a later chapter. It is very difficult to convince ourselves and other people that these perceptions do not represent reality, nor do they establish the truth about a people when, in fact, the assumptions upon which they are based are false.

The inaccurate assumptions we develop or that we inherit from the generations before us are among the greatest hindrances to breaking down the barriers between the races. Until these assumptions are identified and eliminated, our gallery of heroes will likely be limited to those of our own race or culture. When this is the case, we are unlikely to recognize "greatness" in those of other races or cultures, even though they may be true heroes in their own right.

This failure to recognize bona fide heroes among those of other races is very evident in respect to those who have served our nation in times of war. Few Americans realize that many slaves served valiantly in the Revolutionary War. Amazingly, some of these African-Americans were re-enslaved after the war was over. How ironic! Their efforts contributed to the establishment of America as the land of the free, yet they themselves were re-imprisoned in the bonds of slavery.[3]

There was a similar failure to perceive the value of the contribution that African-Americans could make during the Civil War. In fact, Blacks first had to fight for the right to bear arms in that conflict. Their outstanding performance and courage on the battlefield changed many peoples' perception of African-Americans. No longer did they question Blacks' right or ability to fight for their country as well as for their people. The concerns many had about the slaves being able to become a part of the American society were dispelled by Blacks' tenacity and courage on the battlefield.

Such enlightenment came more slowly for others. Over 180,000 African-Americans fought in the Civil War, but they were often very restricted in the areas where they were allowed to serve. Many were willing to allow them to build fortifications, cook the meals, and tend the wounded, but they denied them the privilege of bearing arms with their fellow White soldiers. Lincoln and others had to fight to ensure that the widows and orphans of fallen Black soldiers received the same benefits as those of their White comrades. Relatively few of those who did fight were given medals of honor to recognize their true heroism. [4]

RESISTANCE TO CHANGE:

The prejudice that flourished in the post-Civil War South further influenced Whites' perception of Blacks. The manner in which the Reconstruction Era was carried out did more to divide Whites from Blacks than it did to create peace and harmony between Northerners and Southerners. Segregation and Jim Crow laws grew out of the seeds of anger and bitterness Confederate supporters felt over their failed attempt to secede from the Union. The chains of slavery had been removed, but the attitudes and perceptions that Whites had developed toward Blacks were unchanged.

After World War II, there was new hope among the returning war veterans and others that things would change in the South. Many Black servicemen had fought and died **for this country**. They felt that surely their bravery and sacrifice would establish their right to equal justice. But many more Blacks would have to fight and die, battling against segregation before change would take place.

The Old South resisted change. It was believed that all of this oppression would put the Blacks in their place and keep them there! But it worked in the reverse. For every Black who died, a hundred would rise up singing, " *We shall not be moved!*" And they were not moved!

A TRUE CHAMPION:

Joe Louis, the world champion prizefighter, is another great example of a real life hero who inspired and lifted the morale of his people. Louis became a professional boxer in 1934 after winning the Amateur Athletic Union light-heavyweight title. He became the champion after knocking out James J. Braddock in 1937. He held the championship for eleven years and eight months. Louis' only loss was in 1936 to Max Schmelling of Germany in a non-title bout.

The Nazi regime saw this as the superiority of the Aryan racial faction, but Louis later defeated Schmelling in 1938 in a world-famous bout. Many sports fans saw this as a symbolic showdown between American democracy and the German dictatorship.

Louis went on to establish a record of sixty-eight victories—fifty-four by knockout with only three losses. In 1950, he returned to the ring due to financial difficulty and lost to Ezzard Charles. He lost again to Rocky Marciano by knockout the following year and retired permanently in 1951—an impressive career!

Joe Louis represented many different things to many people, but to the Black man he represented something far more significant than just being the heavyweight champion of the world. During the years that Joe Louis was champ, the Black man was enduring unbearable heartache and pain, especially in the South. The South was full of sharecroppers, who could barely survive by toiling on the White man's land. He was only one plateau above slavery, due to the fact that he was free—even if in name only.

He worked from sun up to sundown, often seven days a week, just to survive. His children went to bed hungry. He had very few earthly goods and no hope for the future. Often in those days, the landowner and overseers were unscrupulous and dishonest in their dealings with the sharecroppers, especially the Black ones. Many of these Black sharecroppers were illiterate, placing them at the mercy of the educated Whites. They had to accept the number of bushels or bales the boss said were counted. They also had to accept the unscrupulous measures their bosses often used and the accounting that was kept for items they bought on credit at the General Store.

A Black sharecropper had no recourse against the White establishment. He had to hold his peace when he felt like lashing out with his tongue. He had to suppress his anger when he felt like lashing out with his fist. And then along came Joe Louis, *The Brown Bomber!*

When Joe Louis was fighting, he was not only landing blows upon his White opponents in the ring; but he was landing blows against White oppression for his entire race. Black men would gather on street corners, in homes, bus depots and train stations to listen to the fights over the radio. Every time Joe Louis landed a blow, it was if the sharecropper himself was striking the land-owners and overseers with his own fist. Joe Louis was doing something that thousands of Black men had wanted to do for centuries. He was not only beating White men with his fists in the ring, but, in essence, he was beating them everywhere in the minds and spirit of Black America. He was indeed a credit to his race and a true American hero, because he stirred hope for true freedom and justice in the hearts of a people who had been oppressed for generations.

A BLACK OLYMPIAN:

Another hero from the Black community was Jesse Owens, the Olympic Champion of the 1936 Olympic games, who set so many world records in the track and field events. The games were held in Berlin, Germany. Adolph Hitler was present, displaying his Super-race of athletes. He had pamphlets distributed throughout the city, showing the physiological and intellectual differences between the Anglo-Saxon and the Negroid races. The brochures showed diagrams of the skull structure of the two races, highlighting the supposedly apelike skull of the Negroes.

It is doubtful that Hitler ever anticipated the arrival of this young Black man from Danville, Alabama. Jesse shocked the world by setting four world records and winning four gold medals. He won those medals not only for his race, but for all those who opposed Nazism as well. It did not matter that Hitler refused to acknowledge Jesse's victories or award him his medals. The world had seen him cross the finish line.

Barriers in Baseball Begin to Fall:

Yet another great sport's figure was Jackie Robinson. Jackie was the first Negro ball player to play major league baseball. When he stepped to the plate, tens of thousands of Black listeners across the nation were cheering for him. Many Blacks became Brooklyn Dodger fans in those days because they had someone to identify with—they had a hero! Every time Jackie went to bat against the White pitchers, he was hitting a home run for all of his brothers who had never had the chance with a professional team.

Our Motivations in Choosing Heroes:

I use these examples merely to show that there are often soul-ties and emotional needs, along with various subconscious and conscious dynamics associated with the exaltation of men. We need to carefully examine our motivations for choosing the heroes we do.

Could it be possible that O.J. Simpson is a modern type of Joe Louis? For sure it is evident that a serious racial divide was indeed manifested during and after O.J.'s trials. It is also believed by many, both Black and White, that contrary to what defense attorney Johnny Cochran proclaimed, the trial was a racial issue from day one. Robert Shapiro, a member of the defense team, expressed his disagreement with the use of the Race Card, a term he used for the strategy Johnny Cochran used in addressing the jury.

Yet it goes beyond mere courtroom tactics and penetrates the very heart and soul of America. Like Joe Louis, Jackie Robinson and Jesse Owens, O.J. was pitted against the establishment—the White-controlled, White-manipulated legal system. With all the talk of conspiracy and frame-up, racist cops, and an unfair, inequitable court system, not only was O.J. Simpson on trial, but, in essence, the entire Black community was on trial.

The appeal made to the jury was subliminal to a point, but basically it said, *"It is us against them. If you do not find this man innocent, you will not only have failed him, but your entire race as well!"* Thus the rift deepens, and the chasm of racial disharmony and division continues.

INJUSTICES, ELIMINATED OR INVERTED:

The Reader's Digest printed an article in the June 1996 issue, citing several trials after the Simpson verdict in which African-Americans were being tried. In all of the cases listed, ethnic jurors refused to render a guilty verdict even when the defendant's guilt was evident beyond a shadow of a doubt. Some even proclaimed that they would not convict one of their own. It sounds like the injustices of the past have simply been inverted, doesn't it?

There is neither an indictment nor exoneration of O.J. Simpson's guilt or innocence intended here. These are only personal observations and conclusions that lend themselves to this text as a contemporary example. This example sends a warning to the Christian community that says, *"We cannot, for personal preference or for cultural or racial identification, embrace anything but the truth. If we abide by the word of God, justice will prevail sooner or later. God is the avenger of all things."*

A FEW AMONG A MULTITUDE:

We have mentioned just a few of America's Black heroes. There are so many other great men and women of color who have made contributions to the greatness of this nation—men and women such as Harriet Tubman, Frederick Douglass, Booker T. Washington, George Washington Carver, Martin Luther King, Jr., Rosa Parks, and Colin Powell. Rosa Parks never won a gold medal, but she scored a home run for civil rights when she refused to give up her rightful place on the bus!

Let's take a moment to look at just a few of the ways these heroes have shaped our nation's history. To this brief listing of African-American heroes, we could add lists of heroes from every ethnic group in our nation. Members from each group have contributed so much to our nation's greatness. Indeed, our strength lies in part in our racial diversity. Is it any wonder that Satan has fought so hard to divide what God has been putting together in this land called America?

HARRIET TUBMAN—MOSES:

Harriet Tubman is one of the many unsung Civil War heroes. She was born a slave in Dorchester County Maryland in 1821. At a very young age, she began working in her owner's home or in other homes where he chose to rent her. As a teenager, she started working in her owner's fields. She continued this work even after marrying John Tubman, a free Black. When her owner died in 1849, she feared that she would be sold into the terrible conditions in the Deep South, so she tried to persuade her husband to help her escape. When he refused, she fled without him to Pennsylvania—a free state. [5]

Tubman settled in Philadelphia and began working as a maid and a cook, saving large portions of her earnings so she could return to Maryland and rescue her family from slavery. Her first such mission was made to Baltimore, Maryland in 1850 to rescue her sister and two children. This was the first in approximately 20 trips that she made as a conductor on the Underground Railroad—a group of courageous individuals who risked imprisonment and possible death to escort slaves to the free northern states or into Canada. The escapees traveled by night and rested by day in one of the many "safe houses" that provided refuge from the fugitive slave hunters. [6]

Tubman lead over 300 men, women, and children north to freedom on these daring rescue missions. Her work earned her the name of "Moses." She is said to have carried a gun, not so much to protect herself and her "passengers" from the slave hunters, as to keep the escaping slaves moving. If one of the fugitives grew fearful or weary and wanted to return to his/her master, Tubman reportedly said, *"Live North, or die here."* [7] She worked with the Underground Railroad from 1850 to 1860 and never lost one "passenger" either to the slave hunters or to fear and discouragement. [8]

When the Civil War broke out, the Union Army asked Tubman's assistance. In this capacity, she served as a liaison between army officials and the newly freed slaves in South Carolina. She taught the liberated slaves self-sufficiency, preparing them for a life of liberty. She also nursed wounded soldiers, and helped to organize and train a group of scouts for the Union Army. Her years of ushering fugitive slaves northward had well prepared her for this task. She even helped lead a Union raid against Confederate troops. [9]

After the war, Tubman returned north to care for her aging parents. In addition to that, she devoted much time to raising money to educate the former slaves and to provide clothes for poor children. Her heart also went out to the former slaves who were too old for manual labor. She opened her own home to the aged and the poor. With the assistance of the African Methodist Episcopal Church, she opened the Harriet Tubman Home for Aged and Indigent Colored People. [10]

In her later years, Tubman joined those working for women's suffrage. Her life was dedicated to setting free all who were held in any form of bondage. No wonder they called her Moses!

FREDERICK DOUGLASS:

Douglass was another hero, who emerged during the Civil War era. Some have called him the father of the Civil Rights Movement. He was born in 1818 on Maryland's eastern shore, the son of a slave woman and an unknown White man. We get a glimpse into the true meaning of being born a slave when we learn that Douglass only saw his mother four or five times before her death when he was seven years old. Even as a little child he witnessed slaves being whipped. The first, was a young woman. Her offense? She was being courted by one of her master's other slaves, and her master didn't approve of them seeing each other.

Douglass was twenty when he escaped to freedom. He changed his last name and settled in New Bedford, Massachusetts with his new bride and became a dynamic speaker in the anti-slavery movement. He was associated with many of the prominent abolitionists, including William Lloyd Garrison, Wendell Phillips and Abby Kelly. He was also closely associated with John Brown, but he did not agree with Brown's violent tactics. Douglass favored using words to tear down the strongholds of oppression. [11]

In a letter to William Lloyd Garrison, Douglass said, *"I am not only a slave, but a man, and as such, am bound to use my powers for the welfare of the whole human brotherhood."* [12] Douglass *"...envisioned America as an inclusive nation strengthened by diversity and free of discrimination..."*, [13] and he worked to make it so. His efforts centered on achieving freedom and justice for all Americans, particularly for African-Americans, women, and minority groups.

Abraham Lincoln once said that Douglass *was "...the most meritorious man of the nineteenth century."* [14] Lincoln conferred with Douglass concerning the enlistment of Blacks in the Union Army. When the door opened for Blacks to enlist, Douglass actively recruited volunteers—his two sons among them—for the famous African-American Fifty-fourth Massachusetts Regiment.

Douglass published his autobiography, *Narrative of the Life of Frederick Douglass*, in 1845 despite the fact that doing so might endanger his freedom. His narrative portrays the suffering and the yearning for freedom and equality he felt from an early age. Unexpectedly, Douglass also gives us a glimpse into the hearts of his enslavers; for Douglass saw the dehumanizing effects slavery had on his enslavers as well as his fellow slaves. Commenting on the character of slaveholders, Douglass said, *"The slaveholder, as well as the slave, was the victim of the slave system. Under the whole heavens there could be found no relation more unfavorable to the development of honorable character than that sustained by the slaveholder to the slave. Reason is imprisoned here and passions run wild."* [15]

The detailed documentation Douglass presented of his experiences as a slave definitely jeopardized his freedom, so Douglass opted to spend some time in England after his autobiography's publication. His sojourn there lead to speaking engagements in England, Scotland, and Ireland, which raised sufficient funds for him to start a paper—the North Star—which he used very effectively in the anti-slavery movement and in the movement for women's suffrage. [16]

Douglass continued to fight for the rights of African-Americans and women after the war was over. He was a powerful influence in the shaping of the history of our nation.

Booker Taliaferro Washington:

Washington was born a slave in 1856 and was liberated by the Union troops near the end of the Civil War. This young African-American became one of the most influential Blacks of his generation. He took a more moderate line than Douglass and other political activists. His goal as an educator was to strengthen Black solidarity and to develop self-reliance among those in the Black community. [17]

Washington graduated from Hampton Normal and Agricultural Institute (present-day Hampton University) in 1875 with honors.

Hampton was headed by General Samuel Chapman Armstrong, a White commander of Black Union troops during the war. Armstrong emphasized a strong work-based, practical education that also taught character, morality, and self-discipline. This philosophy of education was to have a profound influence on Washington. [18]

Booker T. Washington, Library of Congress, LC-USZ62-5512

In 1881, General Armstrong was asked to appoint a White educator to head Tuskegee Institute (present-day Tuskegee University), a new school for Blacks in Tennessee. Instead, he appointed Booker T. Washington. [19]

The resources available to Washington were incredibly limited. The state legislature had apportioned $2,000 to the new school for salaries, but there was not provision for buildings, land, texts, or equipment, so classes were launched in a church-owned shanty! One of the first projects the students tackled, besides their classes, was the construction of a kiln for making bricks. They used the bricks they made to build classrooms and dorms, and sold the remainder to raise funds for needed texts, equipment and staffing. [20]

Washington raised additional funds from philanthropists, most of whom were White Northerners. He assured these Whites that he was not leading his students into political activism. Instead he was training them to advance themselves through education and the economic gains it produced. He also assured Tuskegee's benefactors that his students would not leave the South after graduating but would stay and have a positive impact on the rural Southern economy. [21]

Washington's efforts were highly successful. By 1890, Tuskegee was training 500 students a year. Andrew Carnegie, one of Tuskegee's chief benefactors, praised Washington's efforts, saying, *"He is one of the greatest men...who has ever lived."* [22] Washington's efforts significantly advanced the educational opportunities available to African-Americans living in the southern states.[23]

GEORGE WASHINGTON CARVER:

Born a slave in Diamond, Missouri in 1864, Carver would become one of the greatest scientists America ever produced. Carver left home at the age of ten so he could attend a Black school in a nearby community. He earned his room and board by doing chores for a Black family. In a similar fashion, he put himself through high school and college. He earned a Bachelor's of Science and Master's degree in botany and agriculture from Iowa State College (now Iowa State University). [24]

George Washington Carver
Library of Congress, LC-J601-302

After graduating, Carver accepted an offer from Booker T. Washington to head the agriculture department at Tuskeege. Carver's accomplishments during his 50 year tenure there were many.

He essentially built the department from almost nothing—just a barn, a cow, and a few chickens. [25]

Carver's contributions to the advancement of the Black community were many. He *"...elevated the scientific study of farming, improved the health and agricultural output of Southern farmers, and developed hundreds of uses for their crops."* [26] He developed over 300 products that could be created from peanuts and over 100 products each from sweet potatoes and pecans. He developed a nutrition program for farmers' wives, teaching them how to prepare balanced meals and to preserve foods for winter. His efforts significantly raised the standard of living for many of the South's small farmers as well as profoundly impacting the science of farming itself. [27]

THE MOTHER OF THE CIVIL RIGHTS MOVEMENT:

Rosa Parks' refusal to give up her seat on a bus in Montgomery, Alabama marked a turning point in the civil rights movement in America. Up to that point, efforts to secure basic civil rights and legal justice for African-American citizens seldom made the front page of our nation's newspapers. All of that changed when Rosa Parks refused to comply with a bus driver's request that she give up her seat to a White passenger. [28]

Segregated seating on public buses was just one of the indignities African-Americans experienced in the Deep South. Not only did African-Americans have to sit in the back of the bus, they also had to pay their fare at the front and then go back outside and re-board the bus through a rear door. Drivers sometimes added to the problem by driving off before African-Americans were able to re-board. During rush hour, drivers would move the "boundary line", giving more seats for White passengers and forcing African-Americans to crowd together in the back of the bus. On December 1, 1955, Rosa decided the "boundary line" was staying where it was. Her decision catapulted both her and the civil rights issue to the forefront of American society. [29]

A PROVIDENTIAL COINCIDENCE:

Shortly before Rosa Parks' history-making arrest, Martin Luther King, Jr. moved to Montgomery, Alabama to be the pastor of the Holt Street Baptist Church. On December 5, 1955, several thousand people, outraged over Parks' arrest, gathered at King's church to create a new organization—the Montgomery Improvement Association—to fight against racial discrimination. King was elected president of the MIA. [30]

Usually when we see the initials MIA our minds would go to those who are missing in action in a military action or combat situation. There are many parallels between military actions and the battles that had to be fought to tear down the racial barriers that had been holding African-Americans captive for generations. Martin Luther King, Jr. was one of the key spokesmen for the army of African-Americans and White Americans who joined hands to take a stand for the full equality of every citizen of this nation.

Non-violent protest characterized the war that King and his followers waged against segregation. They were often met with violence in their marches and protests. Lives were lost, but the battle for freedom was never abandoned.

On August 28, 1963, King delivered his famous "I Have a Dream" speech to over 200,000 civil rights supporters, who had gathered in Washington, D.C. His words stirred hope for an America free of racism. One statement he made centered on a basic given put forth in our nation's Constitution:

"I have a dream that one day this nation will rise up and live out the true meaning of its creed: 'We hold these truths to be self-evident, that all men are created equal.' ... I have a dream that my four little children will one day live in a nation where they will not be judged by the color of their skin but by the content of their character." [31]

The slaveholders of old maintained that the founding fathers were referring only to White men when they wrote the Constitution. Lincoln and many other abolitionists disagreed. King was looking forward to the day when all men would disagree with "Whites only" advocates, a day when the barriers between the races would fall and the unity that had been established between the governments of the individual states of this nation would also be established in the hearts of the people who call themselves Americans.

In 1964 the Civil Rights Act was passed, prohibiting discrimination in employment and public education as well as making segregation in public accommodations unlawful. A major battle had been won. Non-violence had paid off.

King was awarded the Nobel Peace Prize later in 1964 for his contribution to the civil rights movement. He was the youngest man to receive this award. [32]

In 1966 and 67, King began to stress more and more the economic plight so many African-Americans were facing. He argued that economic justice was as essential to the advancement of African-Americans as legal justice, and political and social rights. His efforts in this arena were cut short, however, when an assassin's bullet ended his life on April 4, 1968. His life had been taken from him, but his voice was not silenced. His words still stir the hearts of those who oppose racism in whatever form it takes. [33]

Gulf War Hero:

In 1948, President Harry S Truman signed an executive order, making racial integration mandatory in the U. S. military. There was resistance to this move, but the implementation of across-the-board desegregation progressed much more rapidly in the military than it did in the general population. As a result, today the military offers greater opportunities for advancement based on ability alone than any other segment of society. [34]

One of the best known African-American military heroes to emerge due to this historic shift in racial policy, is Colin Powell. The list of his accomplishments is long and impressive. He earned two Purple Hearts and a Soldiers Medal in the fighting in Vietnam. One of his Purple Hearts was awarded after he was injured in a helicopter crash. Disregarding his own injuries,

Powell helped his fellow servicemen escape from the burning helicopter. [35]

Powell advanced steadily in rank. In 1989, President George Bush, appointed Powell as the first African-American Joint Chiefs of Staff, the highest rank in the military. Powell's contribution to the rapid success of the American effort in the Gulf War gained him such great popularity with the American public that many thought he would run for president. [36]

Historians must prepare to record yet another chapter in Powell's life of outstanding service to our nation. President George W. Bush has called upon him to serve as Secretary of State. He is the first African-American to hold that position, and it is one of the most crucial positions in the Cabinet.

JESUS, HERO OF ALL:

I've often said, "Jesus is my hero!" Jesus is who I want to pattern my life after. Indeed, Jesus is the example for all Christians to follow. Both as individuals and as the church, we are being conformed to His likeness and His expressed image by our Lord and Father. Therefore, let us be followers of Him. Jesus is, of course, the expressed image of the Father in us—all of us. Black, Yellow, Red or White! He appears in each of us in His Glory and Grace.

End Notes:

[1-2] Frederick Douglass, *What to the American Slave Is Your Fourth of July?* (given on July 4, 1852 in Rochester, New York), Afro-American Almanac. Available at http://www.toptags.com/aama/voices/speeches/forth.htm>, accessed in July 29, 2000.

[3-4] Christian A. Fleetwood, Sergeant-Major 4th U.S. Colored Troops, *The Negro as a Soldier In the War of the Revolution*, originally given at the Negro Congress at the Cotton States and International Exposition, Atlanta, GA., November 11 to November 23, 1895, World Book Encyclopedia. Available at <http://www.worldbook.com/fun/aajourny/html/bh116b.html>. Accessed on July 30, 2000.

[5-10] Microsoft Encarta Africana 2000, *Harriet Tubman*, Microsoft Corporation, 1999.

[11-14] National Parks Services, *American Visionaries: Frederick Douglass.* Available at http://www.cr.nps.gov/exhibits/douglass/overview.htm>

Accessed on Aug. 1, 2000.

[15] Microsoft Encarta Africana 2000, Frederick Douglass, *Frederick Douglass: Autobiography*, Microsoft Corporation, 1999

[16] Afro-American Almanac, *Frederick Douglass*. Available at http://www.toptags.com/aama/bio/men/freddoug.htm. Accessed on July 27, 2000.

[17-23] Microsoft Encarta Africana 2000, *Booker Taliaferro Washington*, Microsoft Corporation, 1999

[24-27] Microsoft Encarta Africana 2000, *George Washington Carver*, Microsoft Corporation, 1999.

[28-29] Microsoft Encarta Africana 2000, Marian Aguiar, *Rosa Louise McCauley*, Microsoft Corporation, 1999

[30-33] Microsoft Encarta Africana 2000, *Martin Luther King, Jr.*, Microsoft Corporation, 1999.

[34] Microsoft Encarta Africana 2000, *Colin Luther Powell*, Microsoft Corporation, 1999.

Acknowledgments:

The photo of Frederick Douglass is provided courtesy of the Perry-Castañeda Library, of the University of Texas at Austin. The source of this photo is : J.W. Thompson's book, *History of the Douglass Monument*, published by the Rochester Herald Press Rochester, Rochester, in 1903. Available at: <http://www.lib.utexas.edu/Libs/PCL/portraits/douglass.jpg>. Accessed on Oct. 16, 2000.

The photos of George Washington Carver and Booker T. Washington are also provided courtsey of the Perry-Castañeda Library, of the University of Texas at Austin. Available at: <http://www.lib.utexas.edu/Libs/PCL/portraits. Accessed on Oct. 16, 2000.

Chapter 5: Racial Profiling

In the last chapter, we touched on the injustices African-Americans have so often experienced in the criminal justice system of this nation. Unfortunately, this kind of injustice continues yet today, and it affects the lives of every racial minority community. Its effect on families, communities, and individuals is devastating. One aspect of the injustices racial minorities face is what is called "racial profiling." Statistics form the heart of the racial profiling system. Statistics of past criminal activity give an indication of who will commit crimes in the future. On the basis of these statistics, law enforcement officials are more likely to arrest one individual than another on the basis of their profile, because race is, of course, included in this statistical profile.

The Christian Science Monitor's May 10, 2000 issue contains an article entitled *"Will Data Make a Difference? New Facts on Racial Profiling Demand a Response from Law Enforcement."* The author, Jeffrey Prescott, Staff Attorney at Lawyers Committee for Human Rights (LCHR), presents some startling statistics that support minorities' complaints that they are more likely to be treated unfairly by the police and the criminal justice system. LCHR's May 2000 report, *Justice on Trial: Racial Disparities in the American Criminal Justice System*, underscores the need to investigate the degree to which racial profiling not only discriminates against minorities in respect to their legal rights, but it also perpetuates the statistics upon which it is based. The over-policing of minorities is going to result in a higher arrest rate, thereby affirming the need for racial profiling. [1]

The fallout from racial profiling extends far beyond the higher percentages of minorities who are arrested and convicted each year. The negative impact it has on the community must also be considered. Certainly it breeds an anger and resentment in the groups that are profiled as possible criminals, but it also engenders fear in the groups that are not. The last thing our country needs is a policy that creates greater division. [2]

The use of racial profiling is not limited to "street crimes." In May 2000, the U.S. General Accounting Office (GAO) released, which *"...showed that minorities were far more likely than whites to face intrusive searches by the U.S. Customs Service."* [3] The GAO's report indicated that the *"...racial disparities in Customs Service searches did not correlate with the likelihood of discovering contraband."* [4] In fact, the statistics showed that while African-American women *"...were nine times more likely to be X-rayed after a frisk or a pat-down in 1997 and 1998...they 'were less than half as likely to be found carrying contraband as White women."* [5]

A study of "stop and frisk" policies in New York City, conducted by New York Attorney General Elliot Spitzer, showed that African-Americans accounted for 50% of all police stops, even though this group accounted for only 25% of the population there. Based on further statistical analysis, Spitzer's study showed that even if the demographics of each police precinct and the *crime rate by race* are taken into account, African-American New Yorkers are still twice as likely to be stopped and frisked than Whites are. [6]

Such statistics are not limited to New York City. A federal court ordered a study of traffic stops conducted by Maryland State Police on Interstate 95. The results of the two-year study (1995 to 1997) showed that 70% of all the drivers who were stopped and searched were African-Americans, but that African-Americans made up only 17.5% of all the drivers using that route. A study in Volusia County, Florida, showed that almost 70% of those stopped on one of the Interstate Highways there were African-American or Hispanic, even though these two groups accounted for only 5% of the drivers on that route. [7]

JUSTICE FOR ALL:
Equal standing before the law is a fundamental right, established by the Declaration of Independence and our nation's Constitution. Racial profiling seriously jeopardizes this right for millions of American citizens today. The stability of any society depends

greatly upon how it deals with those who break the "laws of the land." It follows, therefore, that *"the system by which lawbreakers are apprehended and punished is one of the pillars of (our) democracy."* [8] In order for any system of justice to remain viable, however, *"...the public must be confident that at every stage of the process—from the initial investigation of a crime...to the prosecution and punishment of that crime by prosecutions and judges—individuals in like circumstances are treated alike..."* [9] Strong evidence is emerging that this is not the case for minorities in America today.

The fruit of this inequity is seen in many different ways. African-Americans and Hispanics make up an overwhelming majority of the mushrooming numbers making up our prison population. This fact alone has a devastating effect at the community level. In minority communities where crime rates are highest, family and friends have literally given up this generation of young men to the prison system. Many African-Americans and Hispanics believe *"...that the criminal justice system is deserving neither of trust nor of support."* [10] That kind of sentiment undermines respect for government at all levels. Unchecked, the despair and hopelessness, that inevitably result in such situations, will provide a breeding ground for extremists who advocate civil unrest or encourage the outright overthrow of the government.

Perhaps the most devastating result of racial profiling is that it contributes to *"...a perception that lawlessness is a "colored" problem, and that the disproportionate treatment of the Blacks and Hispanics within the criminal justice system is a rational response to a statistical imperative."* [11] This perception is invalid, and it does nothing to improve race relations.

A Crisis in Civil Rights:
Dramatic progress has been made through the efforts of those involved in the Civil Rights Movement in this nation. While we can rejoice in what has been accomplished, we must also recognize that there is a 21st Century crisis in the Civil Rights arena in respect to racial profiling. Some folks wonder why there is so much anger among African-Americans, especially those in the

inner cities. If you investigate their claims that they are not re-
ceiving fair treatment under the law, you will begin to see why
"Black Rage" is becoming the current "rage" among so many of
African descent. [12]

In May 2000, the Leadership Conference on Civil Rights (LCCR)
issued a report entitled, *Justice On Trial: Racial Disparities in
the American Criminal Justice System*. Translation—Racial
Profiling. (See <http://www.civilrights.org> for the full report.)
A brief review of this report gives understanding of the frustration, which so many African-Americans, Hispanics, and Asians
feel today. The report contains this profound statement: *"The
treatment of minorities in the criminal justice system is the
most profound civil rights crisis facing America in the new
century. It undermines the progress we have made over the
past five decades in ensuring equal treatment under the law,
and calls into doubt our national faith in the rule of law."* [13]
That's a difficult statement to refute when you consider the increasing numbers of cases where juries acquit minority defen-
dants even though they truly believe the evidence indicates they
are guilty.

It is imperative that we restore national faith in the rule of law.
Such faith is the cornerstone upon which the government of this
nation is founded. That faith will remain strong only as long as
every individual is guaranteed equal standing before the law.

UNDERMINING PROGRESS IN CIVIL RIGHTS:

The executive summary of LCCR's report indicates five ways
in which racial profiling is undermining the progress the civil
rights movement has made in recent decades:

- **The Civil Rights Act of 1964** prohibited discrimination in employment, but three out of every ten African-
  American males born in the United States will serve
  time in prison at some time in their lives. This lessens
  their prospects for legitimate employment and often
  prevents them from obtaining professional licenses.

- **The Voting Rights Act was passed in 1965**, but 31 percent of all African-American men in Alabama and Florida have permanently lost the right to vote because of felony convictions. Nationally, 1.4 million African-American men have been disenfranchised under similar laws.

- **The Immigration and Nationality Act was also passed in 1965.** It was intended to eliminate any remaining vestiges of racial discrimination in U.S. immigration laws, but Hispanic and Asia-Americans are routinely and sometimes specifically singled out for enforcement of existing immigration laws.

- **The Fair Housing Act was passed in 1968.** Ironically, the current housing for approximately 2 million Americans—66% of them African-American or Hispanic—is a prison or jail cell. Yet African-Americans and Hispanics combined make up only 22% of our national population.

- **Civil rights laws have abolished Jim Crow laws** and other vestiges of segregation. Minority citizens are guaranteed the right to travel and use public accommodations without discrimination, but racial profiling and police brutality too often make doing so hazardous to the dignity and health of law-abiding African-American and Hispanic citizens. [14]

These statements make it evident that, even though we have indeed made progress in civil rights issues over the past decades, in respect to criminal justice we have lost ground. In fact, *"...racial inequality is growing, not receding."* [15]

This is not intended as a blanket condemnation of our criminal justice system, but we cannot ignore the negative effects which racial profiling is having upon minorities. The statistics included in LCCR's and GAO's report alone indicate a need to reassess racial profiling's present use within the criminal justice system.

CRY FOR THE CHILDREN:

Racial disparity is evident at every level of the juvenile justice process. Generally, *"...minority youths tend to be held at intake, detained prior to adjudication, have petitions filed, be adjudicated delinquent, and held in secure confinement facilities more frequently than their white counterparts."* [16] The LCCR's report gives this example of the skewed treatment minorities receive in the juvenile justice system: In 1995, 15% of the cases nationwide, which involved White juveniles, resulted in detention, but 27% of the cases involving African-American juveniles resulted in detention.

Racial disparities such as these in respect to the arrest, prosecution, and sentencing of young people provide one of the strongest calls for reform of our criminal justice system. The whole premise for the founding of the juvenile justice system was that there is far greater possibility of rehabilitating young offenders if they are kept separate from and treated differently than adult offenders. The growing tendency to try juveniles as adults goes against this philosophy. Placing teenagers in adult facilities where they come in contact with career criminals multiplies the probability of incubating another generation of criminals. [17]

Recently the Justice Policy Institute (JPI) conducted a study of Los Angeles County juvenile justice system. The results of this study show that African-American, Asia-American, Hispanic youths are *"...far more likely to be transferred to adult courts, convicted in those courts, and incarcerated in youth or adult prison facilities than white youths."* [18] Furthermore, the study shows that although minority youths comprise *"...75 percent of California's juvenile justice population, they comprise almost 95 percent of all cases found 'unfit' for juvenile court and transferred to adult court."* [19] The study concluded that African-American, Asia-American, Hispanic youths in California's juvenile justice system are respectively six, twelve, and three times more likely to be transferred to adult court than their White counterparts. [20]

Native American youths face an added disadvantage: If they live on an Indian reservation, minor criminal offenses sometimes fall under federal jurisdiction. This means that offenses that would normally be handled by the state courts are instead subject to federal prosecution, making the offenders subject to federal penalties, which are often much more harsh than those the state courts would prescribe for the same crime. *"For this reason, approximately 60 percent of youths in federal custody are Native American."* [21]

Things don't look much better for youthful offenders in California. On March 7, 2000, California voters passed Proposition 21, the "Gang Violence and Youth Crime Prevention Act." This proposition allows prosecutors *"...to charge youthful offenders as adults without obtaining the approval of a juvenile court judge, and imposes longer, sometimes mandatory, sentences on a broader range of crimes committed by juveniles."* [22] Under this law, membership in a gang carries an automatic 6-month prison term. In addition, this law eliminates some of that state's early intervention programs. [23]

This legal action comes at a time when youth violence is actually declining in California. Notwithstanding, California voters have approved an additional $1 billion for prison construction. *"They have also voted to incarcerate 15 and 16 year olds in adult prison, despite the fact that teenagers incarcerated in adult facilities are five times as likely to be raped, twice as likely to be beaten, and **eight times as likely to commit suicide** as adults in those facilities."* [24]

Statistics like this take on much deeper significance when you go and sit in a courtroom, as my wife and I have done on many occasions in the past few years, and watch as young person after young person comes up before a judge. There are so many of them that they do not even appear before the judge in person. Instead, the judge sees these young people on closed circuit television. These young people hear the charges that have been filed against them and the penalty that can be assigned to them should they be found guilty. They don't even have a chance to

respond. It is just a necessary step in the process of the litiga-
tion of the charges against them.

I am not suggesting that the guilty should go free, but certainly
there should be equity in the prosecution of the crime or crimes
any individual commits. Above all, our legal system should be
designed to maximize the possibility of the rehabilitation of offenders of all ages, especially the youngest criminals, lest we rob
them of any hope of a better way of life.

A MATTER OF EQUITY:

Can you imagine being 14 years old and being sentenced to 46
years in prison? That's what happened to a African-American
youth living in Los Angeles, California recently. Keith did not
deny his guilt. Two of the girls he was accused of having sex
with said that it was consensual; the third girl said it wasn't and
pressed charges. Keith was tried as an adult, found guilty, and
sentenced to 46 years in prison. [25]

In another case tried in the state of Illinois, seven White youths
and one African-American youth were accused of assaulting a
young girl while she was sleeping. Five of the boys held the girl
down, and three of them sexually assaulted her. There was no
question that this was not a consensual act. These boys were tried
as juveniles and were found guilty. Their sentence? The judge
gave them a choice of community service or 60 days in jail. They
chose to do the community service. [26]

Why the disparity in the treatment these 9 young people received?
In part, it has to do with whether they were tried as an adult or as
a juvenile. But something called a Pre-Sentencing Review (PSR)
also carries tremendous weight in the decision the judge makes.
The PSR gives an indication of the stability of the situation in
which a defendant will be living when released. In the case of
the boys in Illinois, they all came from "good families." That
wasn't the case for Keith. [27]

Despite adverse circumstances at home, Keith was an "A" student and played on the sports teams. All of his teachers described
him as an excellent student. In the judge's eyes, these positive

factors did not outweigh the negative factors in his PSR. So this teenager is serving forty-six years, while eight others are doing community service. What does it say to a young person when our criminal justice system ignores the accomplishments he has achieved in spite of an unstable home life? [28]

Again, it is not a matter of guilt; it's a matter of equity. In both of these cases, the accused were guilty; but if you look at the nature of the crimes, it would seem that those who committed the greater crime received by far the lesser penalty.

God does not let the guilty go unpunished, but, in all things, He works to bring restoration in an individual's life. To be sure, some individuals will refuse His offer of grace and bring themselves under His judgement, but His desire is that all be restored. This should also be the desire, the guiding purpose, of our criminal justice system if it is to best serve our nation.

A Better Answer Needed:

Is incarceration the only answer we have for our young people, who have gone astray of the law? If we look to the world community, we will see that America *"...has the second highest incarceration rate in the world..."* [29], exceeded only by Russia. The fact is, we are losing a significant portion of a generation of young people. Surely we should rejoice in the accomplishments of so many of our nation's youth, but can we turn our backs on those young people who are ensnared in a seemingly unending cycle of "crime and punishment"? Have we nothing better to offer them?

Answers to these questions become even more urgent when you consider the destabilizing effect that high incarceration rates have on minority communities. Consider the following facts:

- An African-American male who was born in 1991 has one chance in three of spending time in prison at some point in his life. A Hispanic male who was born in 1991 has a one in six chance of spending time in prison.
- There are more young African-American men under criminal supervision than there are in college.
- One hundred African-American males are arrested

for each African-American male who graduates from college.

- African-American women are seven times more likely to serve prison time than White women.
- There was a 417% increase in the incarceration rate of African-American women between 1980 and 1995. [30]

All of these factors contribute to the destabilization of minority communities and contribute to the deterioration of family structures. The effect of these factors is, of course, felt most strongly in the inner cities. The fragmentation of the inner city neighborhoods, which results from high arrest and incarceration rates, strengthens the "crime-race" linkage which has been used to justify racial profiling. It is a vicious cycle, one which urgently needs to be broken. [31]

An additional problem emerges from the chaos, which racial profiling is fostering in families and minority communities. Arrest becomes a badge of courage for young people, who are growing up believing that the system is stacked against them. The entertainment industry supplies an abundance of negative heroes for these disenchanted youths to model their lives after. Is it any wonder we are losing a generation of young people to drugs and violence? [32]

THE CHURCH, AN ADVOCATE FOR JUSTICE:

The questions get tougher when we ask, *"Where does the Church stand in all of this?"* You can approach this question from two perspectives: (1. What is the Church doing to reverse the injustices that are pervading our criminal justice system? and (2. Is "racial profiling" practiced by the Church itself?

The Church's responsibility to be an advocate for justice is clear from the scriptures. Micah lists justice as one of the three main requirements God places on those who choose to serve Him.

[8]He hath shewed thee, O man, what is good; and what doth the LORD require of thee, but to do justly, and to love mercy, and to walk humbly with thy God? (Micah 6:8)

Justice, mercy, and humility are tied together in this passage. Where these attributes are allowed to govern the actions of men, there will be peace. Mercy compels us to see that justice is done in the lives of others. Our vigilance to maintain justice is essential to health of our community and our nation.

Amos spoke in vivid, poetic terms of the effect justice and righteousness have in the life of any people or nation:

> *²⁴But let justice roll down as waters, and righteousness as a mighty stream.* (Amos 5:24, ASV)

Justice was a scarce commodity among God's people when Amos wrote this. Judgment was certain to come if true justice was not soon restored in the land. Many are saying that America is in a similar position today. They believe that judgment is eminent, that nothing can turn God's hand aside. But, if we look at this verse from Amos within the context of the entire passage, we get a far different message from this fiery prophet. In the midst of his message of certain retribution, this passage stands as a witness to the hope that we have in God if we will humble ourselves and seek His face.

> *⁶Seek Jehovah, and ye shall live... ⁷Ye who turn justice to wormwood, and cast down righteousness to the earth, ⁸seek him that...turneth the shadow of death into the morning...⁹that bringeth sudden destruction upon the strong....¹⁰They hate him that reproveth in the gate, and they abhor him that speaketh uprightly. ¹²For I know how manifold are your transgressions, and how mighty are your sins—ye that afflict the just, that take a bribe, and that turn aside the needy in the gate from their right.*

> *¹⁴Seek good, and not evil, that ye may live; and so Jehovah, the God of hosts, will be with you, as ye say. ¹⁵Hate the evil, and love the good, and establish justice in the gate: it may be that Jehovah, the God of hosts, will be gracious unto the remnant of Joseph.*

> *²¹I hate, I despise your feasts, and I will take no delight in your solemn assemblies. ²²Yea, though ye offer me your burnt-offerings and meal-offerings, I will not accept them;*

neither will I regard the peace-offerings of your fat beasts.
²³Take thou away from me the noise of thy songs; for I will
not hear the melody of thy viols. ²⁴But let justice roll down
as waters, and righteousness as a mighty stream. (Amos
5:6-10, 12,14-15,21-24)

Justice for all is not an option if we want to continue to walk in
the blessings of God as a nation. Verses 21 through 23 tell us that
there is no substitute for justice. Indeed, there is no remedy for
the ills of our society or any society except the justice that God
mandates. Judgment can be averted if and only if justice is allowed to flow freely throughout our land as a mighty river flows
to the ocean, sweeping all that lies in its path before it. Otherwise, evil will continue to flouish in our nation, and it will bring
destruction upon us.

Unlike natural rivers, God's river of justice brings destruction
only to that which is evil. Mixed in with His justice is a mighty
stream of righteousness, which brings healing to the afflicted,
wholeness to the brokenhearted, and liberty to those held captive. The river of God restores and lifts up the downcast.

If there was ever a day that the Church needed to stand for justice
and righteousness in this nation, today is that day—not just for
"our people" but for all people. We would want nothing less for
ourselves or our loved ones. We can accept nothing less for others.

RACIAL PROFILING IN THE CHURCH:
Certainly, the Church is not in league with the criminal justice
system, helping law enforcement officials to get criminals off the
streets. That's not the kind of racial profiling we need to consider
in respect to the Church. What we do need to consider, however,
are any attitudes or unspoken policies that restrict the sinners we
want to get off the streets and into our pews. If we do let "them
folks" in, then we need to examine how we treat them once they
get there.

I noted earlier that many have said that 11:00 a.m. is the most
segregated hour in America. This should not be! It certainly won't
be that way in heaven.

One of the most disarming things about serving God is that really He believes He's in charge. We would all save ourselves a lot of skinned knees and likely a few broken noses if we would tune our ear closely to what the Spirit is telling our church, and, when we hear His voice, respond by doing what He says. But that's not human nature, especially when it comes to changing the way "things have always been." That's why when we are born again, God doesn't just dress up our human nature. He gives us a new nature, a new man. He places His life within us, and He gives us the Holy Spirit as a companion, a friend, and a teacher. Through the agency of the Holy Spirit, God works in us to transform us into the image of Jesus.

Slowly, persistently, God strips off the old way of thinking, the old way of speaking, the old way of judging others, and He teaches how to "do it His way." I do not believe that racial profiling is part of God's way of doing things. I do not believe He keeps statistics on which folks are most likely to receive Jesus and live a godly life. God's word to every man, woman, and child living today is, *"Chose ye this day, whom you will serve!"* He doesn't just speak this word and let it go at that; He sends His Holy Spirit to convict us of our sin and lead us into His righteousness. He excludes no one as a candidate for His grace, and neither can we.

When He brings newborn sheep and lambs into our congregations, do you suppose He wants us to inspect them like the priests of the Old Covenant inspected the animals that were brought for sacrifice; or do you think He wants us to receive them as the High Priest, revealed in the New Testament, received all who came to Him? Jesus opened His arms and His heart to all who came to Him. He spoke the word of God to them, He poured living water into their thirsty souls, He healed their bodies, and He set the captives free. He wasn't reluctant to be seen with sinners or tax collectors or prostitutes. Sometimes He went out of His way to talk to "them folks."

Are we willing to go out of our way to talk to "them folks" even when "them folks" are of a different race than we are? Jesus would. Can we do any less?

Many people are praying for revival today. I'll tell you this, when revival comes and the river of God begins flowing in our midst, "them folks" are going to find their way to our door. Are we going to lead them to the Lord and send them on their way to churches for "them folks", or are we going love them with the love of the Lord and welcome them into our congregation? If we don't, we may well find that the fires of revival will slowly die down and the river of life will just dry up until there is nothing but stagnant water for "us folks" to drink.

End Notes:

[1-6] Jeffrey Prescott, *Will Data Make a Difference?*, The Christian Science Monitor, Thursday, May 10, 2000. Available at <http://www.civilrights.org>. Accessed on July 12, 2000.

[7-24] Leadership Conference on Civil Rights Report, *Justice On Trial: Racial Disparities in the American Criminal Justice System,* May 2000. Available at <http://www.civilrights.org>. Accessed on July 12, 2000.

[25-28] Keith's story: Court TV, *Justice in Black and White,* August 3, 2000.

[29-30] Leadership Conference on Civil Rights Report, Ibid.

Chapter 6: The "N" Word

During the famous California vs O.J. Simpson trial, the prosecuting attorney made a reference to what was termed the "N" word. The attorney was, of course, referring to the word, *"Nigger."* The word was abbreviated because the court deemed it to be such an offensive term, both to the African-American community and to the television viewing audience at large. In recent years, the word has become common as part of the everyday vernacular and vocabulary spoken in the Black community from Black to Black. It is used in rap songs and by Black entertainers publicly. It also brings back to many of those from the older generations the reality of racial hatred and persecution.

The extreme offensiveness of this word is also reflected in some comments made by Medgar Evers' widow. Medgar Evers was the State Field Secretary for the NAACP, who was shot and killed in Jackson, Mississippi on June 12, 1963. A television special on the life of this Civil Rights leader was produced in 1994 and aired again April 12th 1996. I heard Mrs. Evers say, *"The man convicted of my husband's murder was like a beast with no heart."* It has taken thirty years for justice to be served by this man receiving thirty years in prison for the crime.

Mrs. Evers made another statement that I believe to be so profound. She said, *"When I hear the word "Nigger," it still does something to me! It is as horrible today as it was in the past. It still has the same effect it did when we saw it printed on signs and heard it shouted at us during the freedom marches."*

In a lot of ways this word has inflicted deeper wounds in the spirits of African-Americans than the chains of slavery ever did in their bodies. I wonder if part of the reason for the depth of the offense the "N" word stirs in the hearts of African-Americans isn't that this racial slur was not only spoken; it was written out publicly. Often at the city limits of towns during those days there were signs stating, *"Nigger, Don't Let The Sun Set On Your Head In This Town."* And they weren't joking.

As I've listened to older African-Americans, who had to endure the name calling, the slander, and various other forms of verbal abuse and physical abuse as well, I have found that they are not readily inclined to use the "N" word. This is not true, however, of the younger generations that have not experienced the suffering associated with this word.

DEFINING THE "N" WORD:

Let's look at the definition of the "N" word. The Webster Dictionary defines the term "Nigger" as follows: *Nigger, "ni-ger" Noun (alter. of early "neger" the French word "negre", also from the Spanish and Portuguese "Negro" from "Negro", Black, and from the Latin word "niger" (1700). (1. A black person-a term usually taken to be offensive. (2. A member of any dark-skinned race-usually taken to be offensive. (3. A member of a socially disadvantaged class of persons.* [1]

Nigger was used in senses 1 and 2 in the works of such writers as Joseph Conrad, Mark Twain and Charles Dickens. What was "acceptable" then is not acceptable now. This word ranks as perhaps the "Most Offensive" and "Inflammatory" racial slur in the English language. Its use by and among Blacks is not always intended or taken as offensive, except in sense 3. It is otherwise a word expressive of racial hatred and bigotry.

It is evident by the above definitions that this word is no doubt an extremely demeaning and derogatory term. It is also evident that it has a dual meaning or represents a double standard in the Black community.

Let us take a look at the use of this word from an outside perspective—from the view of non-Blacks. Let us also consider other equally slanderous word usages in our society. Identifying and eliminating such words will do much to bridge the chasm between the races.

In another chapter of this book, I have shared my experiences concerning my own personal roots in the totally segregated South.

One of the results of inefficient training and knowledge of the races was, of course, the usage of the word, *"Nigger."* Children in the South were seldom taught respect for people of color or people of other races. In fact, many children were inculcated with the bigotry and hatred typical of earlier generations. This hatred was spawned during the Civil War and in the years after the war—the *Reconstruction Days.* Many Southern families, who had lost all of their wealth and prosperity as well as their Anti-Bellum way of life, became embittered against the North during the *Reconstruction.* They blamed the Negro and the abolishment of slavery for the South's destruction.

The people of the South failed to realize that the Glory had departed because of the cruel enslavement of the Africans, among other factors. They were determined that they would not give up so easily. Hence, appeared the *Night Riders, a.k.a., the Ku Klux Klan.* These people called themselves *Freedom Riders.* They viewed themselves as purveyors of justice. They were determined to not allow the newly freed Blacks to experience any enjoyment or fulfillment of the equal rights the Emancipation Proclamation had given them. Unfortunately, there are many, both in the North and in the South, who still share this twisted and perverted, and no doubt, ungodly sentiment today.

The term, *Nigger,* was commonly used as an everyday word for Black people or *colored people,* as they were often referred to. It was not only used in the second person, but was also used to address Black individuals personally.

There was no remorse or embarrassment attached to the use of the word, because no one was taught that it was derogatory or slanderous. On the contrary, it was an acceptable part of conversing. In fact, we were taught that it was descriptive of Black people. We were taught that they were the lowest of the low on the socio-economic scale and the educational strata of society; that they were people who did not marry, but only lived in common-law relationships; a people who birthed numerous children, most not knowing the identity of their real father. Blacks were dope addicts, gamblers, whoremongers, and thieves. They were too lazy to work and would not pay their bills. We were told they had no moral values whatsoever and that Blacks were violent by nature, void of natural affection and that shooting and cutting each other on Saturday night was their only way of life.

When a Black person approached the house of a white family, he was required to knock at the door, then step down from the porch into the yard with hat in hand. A White child answering the door would commonly exclaim, *"There is a niggerman at the door."* If the back-door was accessible, a Black person was required to go there first. It was often impossible to reach the back-door, due to the fact many people had vicious dogs that would not allow passage by anyone to the rear of the house.

You may ask, *"How could anyone in this modern, sophisticated, educated and civilized society in which we live practice such narrow-minded ignorance and racial discrimination?"* The answer is quite simple: We were taught respect for parents, teachers, and all adults in early childhood. We were taught to say, "Yes, Ma'am and No, Ma'am." You never addressed an adult by their first name. You always had to refer to them as "Mr." and "Mrs." or "Aunt" and "Uncle." But we were not taught to respect people of color.

The myths and old wives tales concerning the races were passed from one generation to the next generation as the absolute truth. We were taught these "truths" from our earliest years. As I said, it wasn't until I joined the military that I began to question these basic "truths."

INCREASING USE OF THE "N" WORD:
There has been a shift in the usage of the term, "Nigger," in recent years. After having spent a great deal of time in the Black community, both in ministry and in close relationships with so many Black friends, I have come to realize that this offensive term is no longer used exclusively by White racists. Blacks addressing other Blacks also very commonly use it. In fact, the "N" word is used extensively in the movies and in the Rap style of music that is so popular with the younger generation today. Black comedians readily use the term *Nigger* to elicit laughs from their audience.

I often wonder at the validity of using derogatory remarks about your own people as a means of entertainment. You seldom see people of other races, especially entertainers, telling jokes at their race's expense.

Since the 1930s the ethnic entertainers have worked to replace Hollywood's *stereotyped* portrayals of Blacks. They have made such great strides in eliminating the *step-and-fetch-it* mentality that permeated the movie industry for so many years. Today great Black actors and actresses, as well as other performers of various ethnic groups, receive the honor they deserve for their own merits in the entertainment field.

It is this writer's opinion that the movies that are being produced today, which depict life in the Black community—especially in the ghetto—are reversing the progress that has been so painstakingly fought for over the last forty years or so. These movies invariably depict the young Black male as a gun-toting, kill-crazy, dope-dealing whoremonger—one who is profiting from the misery and addictions of his own community and people. In addition, it depicts the young Black females as promiscuous, scantily clad and lust-filled sex objects, only to be referred to as, *"Bitches" and "Whores."* In fact, in one popular movie, one of the music sound tracks was titled, *Nig'ahs and Bitch'ahs.*

Depicting life-styles that are all too common in urban settings and in the ghettos, as well as the lyrics used in the Rap music, is doing exactly what the Ethnic community has tried so hard to eliminate in the entertainment business. It is stereotyping people of color.

So often in the past, the Mexican was depicted as the slow and lazy peasant or bandit with the big sombrero. The more current portrayals show them as the killer Chicano gang members in LA's East Side. The same kind of stereotyping has occurred with Puerto Ricans in New York and the Chinese Charlie Chan or the *"No-tickie-No laundry"* roles. The painted-savage portrayal of the Native American, the "bone-in-the nose" African witch doctor or chief, and the beret-wearing, effeminate Frenchman are all derogatory and demeaning stereotypes that should by all means be eliminated from the entertainment world.

I am sure that most of the movies today have a much deeper meaning than merely portraying young Blacks as gangsters and murders. However, this deeper meaning may be often overlooked because of the obvious and explicit presentation of the nature of the Ghetto. Maybe the producers of these movies should ask the question, *"What kind of message is being sent to the young people and the next generations?"*

RETALIATIONS AND "BLOOD FOR BLOOD":

A good example of the negative effect of these movies and songs is the outbreak of violence that occurred in so many movie theaters across the country following the showing of *Boys in the Hood.* This was one of the first movies to show gang violence in the Black neighborhoods. News reports told of young Black men, running from the theater, assaulting people on the street.

So often there seems to be an overlapping message in these movies that says, *"Yo, this is the way it is, and nothing is going to change that! You know what I be say'in?"* Some of the dialogue even expounds, *"You ain't nothing but a nig'ah, and that's all you are ever going to be!"* Consequently, in many of these movies, the good die young, and the individual who is struggling to rise above his or her environment often succumbs to the evil of "the hood." There is also the element of vengeance, which makes the violence appear justified. In essence, there is a message that is saying loud and clear, *"There is NO way out!"* Is this the kind of message we want to send to young people and to the next generations? Absolutely not!

ARTISTS' RESPONSIBILITIES:

I have heard some of the Rap music artists on television, debating the pros and cons of the lyrics on their albums. Some of them say that they are singing about who they really are. In other words, they are saying, *"Indeed, we are gangsters."* The lyrics often state, *"If you come into our neighborhood, we will shoot you."* These Rap music artists went on to say that they were indeed gun-toting gangsters. Too often this macho image creates a "hero worship" by the younger boys when they see these street-tough gang member portrayals.

Unlike these "Street Rappers", there is a group of musicians known as "Studio Rappers." These artists sing about what is happening in the street, but they do not live the life-style they are portraying in their music. The message they bring is the same, however.

There are many that argue the point that seeing these kinds of portrayals does not have a negative effect on the younger children. Some older individuals in the inner city, who grew up streetwise and tough, told me just the opposite. They said, *"The younger boys are always 'acting out' the shootings and killings as they listen to rap music."*

Some of the leading Rap artists have been arrested and charged with very serious crimes. Some have even been shot down on the street, possibly as a result of their violent life-styles. *Snoop Doggie Dog* was accused of being involved in a drive-by shooting, and the popular rap artist *TuPac Shakur* was killed in a gang-style killing. His death is believed to have been a result of a dispute between the West Coast Rappers and the East Coast Rappers and the gangsters who control the Rap recording industry. Articles that appeared after his death quoting those close to him state, *"TuPac lived the life he sung about, and died who he was."* His demise was so in keeping with his character portrayals, like the movie *Above the Rim.* In the conclusion of this movie, he was shot to death. Biggy Smalls, another popular rap artist, was murdered in a similar manner.

It is believed among many young people today that TuPac is alive. Unauthorized CDs are being sold on the street, proclaiming him as the Black Messiah. His young followers are waiting for his return. They may have to wait for eternity.

It is interesting how other rap music artists and public officials became so concerned about the message of their music after the deaths of TuPac and Biggy Smalls. It is a shame that there was not more concern sooner about the effect it was having on their teenager audiences. These young people have been killing each other in our cities by the hundreds for a decade or so with their "gang banging." The mass killing of students in Columbine, Colorado in 1998 and the shooting of fifteen students and adults by a fifteen year old gunman in Santee, California in 2001 shocked America. Yet hundreds of teens, the majority of them people of color, die by violence in our cities each year.

STEREOTYPING'S EFFECT:

It is important to consider the effect that this stereotyping has not only on the Black community, but also on the public at large. For example, I have witnessed young Black and Hispanic teenagers walking down the street in the Bronx in New York City. They were dressed in Bomber jackets, with their caps on backwards, strolling down the sidewalk. Some out of town visitors were immediately fearful and uneasy in their presence. They assumed they were a New York street gang. The truth of the matter is that the youths were just a group of Christian teens on their way to church. Why then would anyone jump to such rash conclusions? That is not difficult to answer when you see the image of young Blacks and Hispanics that is presented to the White community by the entertainment media.

THE CHURCH'S RESPONSIBILITY:

In our many years of cross-cultural ministry, we have had the opportunity to minister to almost all races and nationalities. We have ministered to West Indians, Chinese, Japanese, Koreans, East Indians, Europeans, Africans, Latin Americans, and Hispanics of almost every Spanish-speaking nation. We have ministered to French-speaking people as well. In all of these years I have very seldom heard the Orientals refer to their brothers as "Chinks," or the Hispanics refer to their brothers as *"Spics."* The French do not refer to their brothers as *"Frogs,"* nor do the Irish refer to their brothers as *"Mics."* The Italians do not call each other *"Wops, Ginnys, or Dagos,"* nor do the Whites call each other *"Honkies or Crackers."* Why then does the Black community so readily use such a slanderous term in addressing one another?

What is the Church's responsibility in all of this? First of all, young people must be taught what it means to be *Christ-like*. He is their role model. They must also be taught that there is a way out of poverty, and it is not the way of crime, but it is through Jesus.

Philippians 4:13 declares, *"I can do all things through Christ Jesus that strengthens me."* Notice that it says <u>ALL</u> things. <u>All</u> things means overcoming every disadvantage in life, including being born in the Ghetto and having little promise of success in the future. God gives us a simple principle that says, *"That which has no promise of success in the beginning can and will glorify God in the end if we will summon Him into our life and situations."*

Each generation has an awesome responsibility to the generations that will follow. Therefore, we must tell the young that, indeed, God is no respecter of persons, that He will see us through all our difficulties, He will bring us out of the darkness into His marvelous light!

Secondly, there needs to be a public denouncing of any media production that presents a role model that is demeaning of any race of people. Statistics show that in 1996 there were approximately 200 radio stations that were owned by African-Americans. There were over 300 African-American journalists who wrote for major newspapers and publications in the U.S. All of these sources of media influence in the Black community, including the Black church, should take a stand against any and all productions that bring racial defamation.

Black producers, actors, and actresses should continue to get achievement awards for their work, but only if that production is not detrimental to the community. This same standard should be applied to White producers, actors, and actresses or those of any other race.

Thirdly, the church in the Black community should institute a boycott of *"Gang'sta Rap"* and movies that continue to portray the African-American youth or any other ethnic people in such a derogatory light. Cultural pride can be an asset unless that which produces the pride violates the principles of God's word. At that point it must be rejected as detrimental, and the church has no choice but to denounce it openly.

It has been said, *"We can not criticize that which we ourselves allow."* This simply means that, if a word or term is so derogatory and defaming as the word *Nigger* when it is used by those outside of the Black community, why should the Black community be comfortable with the use of it within their own ranks? Many a White child has had their mouth washed out with soap for using that word. It is not an acceptable word in any Christian home in most of the White community. Therefore, shouldn't it be eliminated from the Black community as well?

Indeed, if we want racial remarks to cease by others, should we not want it to cease within ourselves? After all there are enough other "N" words that plague our community. Words like narcotics, neurosis, neurological, needles, nothing, nowhere, and nobody. All of them, negative. It is the church's responsibility to change the negative to the positive, to give hope to the hopeless.

It is the sincere prayer of this writer that the "N" word, which Webster defines as the most slanderous word in the English language, will be eliminated from the vocabulary of both Whites and Blacks and readily replaced with words of encouragement and self respect.

Each generation has an awesome responsibility to the generations that will follow. Therefore we must tell the young, *"You can do all things through Christ Jesus that strengthens you."* The blood of Jesus breaks the curse, and you can enjoy life more abundantly through Him.

End Notes:
[1]*The American Heritage Dictionary, Second College Edition,* Houghton Mifflin Company, Boston, 1985

Chapter 7: Raising Awareness

Different factions of our society view slavery in various ways. Some see the atrocity of it, and others see the immorality involved in owning slaves or "keeping slaves," as it was referred to in those days. Yet, there are others who either do not see the wrong that was perpetrated upon those enslaved or are too ignorant (unknowledgeable) to understand it.

It is not difficult to perceive the frustration and exasperation this causes many African-Americans, who are attempting to raise the consciousness level and cultural awareness associated with slavery. Their attempts to stimulate an Afro-Centric historic awareness among the populace of the United States at large has been successful to a point. It is, of course, much more prominent in the Black community than in the non-ethnic segments of society. Why? Is it because White people have no interest in that part of our nation's history? Or could they care less about the plight of the Black man, past or present? The answer to those questions may be, "Yes," but with some reservations. We must be careful to not generalize and start classifying or grouping segments of people in any manner without proper documentation. Too often statements are made in a rash manner that places people in a particular classification unjustly.

But, it is a commonly known fact that there are those who are disinterested in the slavery issue or who simply don't care about it, especially those in the Southern part of the country. Why is this? I believe this is true mainly because White people, especially Southerners, see slavery from an entirely different viewpoint. This viewpoint has been handed down from generation to generation. Most Southerners' historical knowledge of slavery is very limited. In many cases it is restricted to oral tradition—that is, what the "old folks" have told them down through the years. Most Americans view slavery as an issue that ended in 1865 at the conclusion of the Civil War. Therefore, slavery is not a current issue to them. So they ask, *"Why should we be concerned with something that does not concern us as a people or a nation today?"* Of course, there is also a certain amount of denial when it comes to dealing with the issue of slavery—certainly one of the darkest areas of American history.

A similar example of such denial, can be seen in the Neo-Nazis' refusal to accept the Jewish Holocaust as factual. Regardless how much evidence is provided, whether films showing the Nazi death camps with thousands of dead bodies or eyewitness accounts and sworn testimony of Jews who suffered there, they refuse to believe that the Holocaust ever happened. They even accuse the Jews of perpetrating a hoax. Racial prejudice and hatred easily becomes a blinding force to the truth of a matter.

I don't believe that it is callousness or lack of sensitivity that blinds the majority of White people to the nature of the slavery issue. I believe it is ignorance—a lack of education and, in this instance, a lack of cultural awareness—that helps to maintain this attitude. Ignorance certainly plays a major role in fueling what seem to be racial and biased attitudes. If you have ever listened to people, who are involved in hate group organizations like the K.K.K. and other White militants, it is evident that they are ignorant of the facts concerning race and slavery. Unfortunately, false beliefs often attract more ardent followers than the truth.

When reflecting on the lack of education among Whites concerning the slavery era and its ramifications, we ask, *"Why isn't there a greater emphasis on this section of our nation's history?"* The answer certainly must lie in a differing priority between the races. In other words, there is a greater emphasis on the slavery issue among African-Americans than among non-Blacks for obviously painful reasons.

In the minds of non-blacks, slavery ended 135 years ago, but this issue is kept alive and current in the Black educational system and arts community. From kindergarten through college, numerous books, dramas, songs, and school plays on slavery are provided to the Black community each year. Political forums and church sermons devoted to this issue also help to create an awareness of the slavery issue, as well as maintaining a memorial to it. From generation to generation the knowledge is kept fresh and the wounds tender, with a *"lest we forget"* attitude. All of this helps to maintain a quickening to the remembrance of slavery among those in the Black community.

But despite all of this cultural production, the desired awareness level is not always reached, even in the Black community. This is especially true among the youth. Equally discouraging to proponents of increased cultural awareness, these efforts have very little effect in the White community at large.

I believe that if a simple ten-point questionnaire concerning Black History were handed to White adults or young people, many of them would have difficulty answering the questions. It might astonish many Black educators who teach cultural awareness if they saw how poorly many African-Americans would score on the same exam.

Confusion or Lack of Education:

Often what appears to be a lack of education can be simple confusion on the part of the Whites. Let me sight a prime example of this. For example, what terminology is correct when describing those of African descent? First of all, we know that the "N" word is taboo. (We covered this subject quite extensively in the previous chapter.) Negro is no longer an acceptable term, yet according to the Dictionary, it is correct when describing a Black person. Negro has been used by Mr. Farrakhan as an insult, as in *"You scared Negro preachers",* to chide his Black brothers, who follow the teachings of Jesus instead of Mohammed.

"Black is beautiful" was "in" for a couple of decades. The word *"colored"* was widely used for centuries, but it also has become offensive. Yet, today most writers, educators, and public spokespersons for the ethnic community use the term *"people of color."* This seems to be a logical use of the term. That which has *color* is *colored* by definition. But the term *colored* can also be used to describe that which is *biased.* The term *coloring* describes skin tone especially of the face, complexion, etc.

For a short time, *Afro-American* became the "politically correct" phrase, but it has now given way to *African-American,* which probably leaves those outside the ethnic community just as confused as ever. Many people now prefer to be called a Black American.

Maybe we could simplify the whole process, not by doing away with our social clubs or cultural holidays, but for the sake of unity just all be called AMERICANS. In the same sense that Italian-Americans, Irish-Americans, Spanish-Americans, Polish-Americans, Asian-Americans, Chinese-Americans, etc., etc., etc. are called Americans, so those of African descent could simply be called Americans.

It's a shame that a month has to be set aside to recognize any group of people in this country for their contribution to this great nation of ours. I am not against a Black History Month, but I am not sure it should be necessary, just as a German or Chinese History month is not necessary. After all, there are hundreds of nationalities represented in the Untied States and only twelve months in the year.

Each individual should take their place in American history as they have earned the right to be there. For example, George Washington Carver should have an equal position with George Washington. It is another indictment on this nation when any people has to force recognition of their accomplishments. Rather, we should willingly honor all of our heroes equally. The history of Africa and all its nations should be included as a part of the courses taught on World History. In the same way, African-American contributions to the history of our nation should be taught as a part of American History.

Praise God for those who work to insure that ethnic children learn of their culture's contributions to the society in which they live. The word of God says to give honor to whom honor is due.

Cultural Awareness Raised Through the Media:

Many negative things are said about the media's impact on our society, and rightly so. But the media is a valuable tool for bridging the gaps between our various cultures. This is especially true of television and the movie industry. These media sources are able to present historical truths in a graphic manner that gives viewers the opportunity—at least vicariously—to walk in another person's shoes for a few moments.

An example of the media truly touching the heart of America with a vivid portrayal of a sensitive issue is Alex Haley's *Roots*. A production like this gives a wake-up call to America. Night after night, Americans of all races had an opportunity to see the realties of life as a slave played out on their television screens. These were not words in a text that could be hurriedly read. Instead, for five evenings viewers followed the steps of one unwilling African immigrant from his capture in Africa to his grave in the New World. As dramatic as these productions are, there seems to be no lasting effect, however. The awareness they create is often short-lived.

Hollywood has attempted to present some truthful aspects of other racial subjects, but it often seems to be a case of too little too late. *"Dances With Wolves"* was an attempt to depict the suffering and injustices White settlers perpetrated upon the Native American Plains Indians. It was really moving and enlightening, to say the least, but I wonder how much impact it had on the average viewer. After all, since the start of motion pictures, viewers have seen the American Indian as the painted-face savage, riding around and around wagon trains, being killed. When it seemed that the Indians were getting the upper hand, along would come the hero with his white hat and trusty steed. A bugle would sound in the distance, and the U.S. Calvary would ride to the rescue. At this point, the theater would erupt with applause.

These movies glamorized a very negative portion of our national history. Unfortunately, they never showed the bloody scalps of Indian women and children taken for bounty. Nor did they show smallpox-laden blankets being given as "gifts" to an eastern tribe. Why was this done? Oil had been discovered on their land. That tribe was almost totally annihilated as this dread disease swept through their ranks.

Certainly we have never heard a script that included a priest telling the settlers that the indigenous people of the Americas were heathens and possessed no soul. *"So,"* the priest reasoned, *"the killing of an Indian was no different than killing a wild animal."* Incredible as it may seem, this "truth" was actually taught from many pulpits in 19ᵗʰ Century America. Teachings such as these, coupled with the White man's greed, allowed him to take any measures necessary to obtain what was never rightfully his.

These and other false teachings made slavery and the oppression of Native Americans the accepted norm for many, but not all, Americans. Then, as now, there were those who worked for the abolition of slavery and for the just treatment of Native Americans.

Another reason for disinterest in the slavery issue is the dramatic change that has taken place in the cultural makeup of America since the Civil War era. Much of today's population is comprised of third and fourth generation Europeans, as well as Asian, East Indian, Hispanic, and Middle Eastern factions. Their ancestors had not yet migrated to the United States when slavery was at its height. As a result, many of these groups know little or nothing about this portion of American history.

Examining the underlying causes of this low awareness of the slavery issue is essential. Otherwise, this lack of interest is easily interpreted as indifference. Presentations such as *Roots* have shown us that people are not indifferent to the great suffering slavery caused; rather they are uninformed.

Undoubtedly then, education is the key to racial understanding. There must be a combined effort on everyone's part and on the part of our educational system to increase awareness of all of the issues related to slavery. This will not happen by just teaching American History from an Afro-Centric perspective to African-Americans. Instead, we must teach American History in a multi-racial context to everyone.

Chapter 8: Who's Going to Pay?

Hand in hand with efforts to raise awareness of the slavery issue is a widely supported movement to obtain reparations for all that African-Americans have suffered because of the institution of slavery. We need to examine the case for reparations carefully. This issue is one with great significance to all races, especially within the Church.

The dictionary gives this definition for the word reparation: *"Reparation implies giving compensation to satisfy one who has suffered injury, loss, or wrong at the hands of another; in the plural form it applies to the compensation a defeated nation must make for damage to the enemy, especially to civilians."* [1] Unquestionably, African-Americans who were enslaved suffered injury, loss, and wrong during the time of their enslavement. Reparations, therefore, are due to them—or, in this case, to their heirs. The question is *"Who should pay these reparations?"* The answer to this question requires that we identify those guilty of inflicting harm on this group of people.

This is not as easy a task as it might seem. As we saw in the second chapter of this text, wave after wave of immigrants has come seeking a new life in America. As a result, the population of America has changed dramatically since 1865. The majority of these groups had little or no representation in America during the time slavery was allowed under the law. It is difficult, therefore, to place any measure of blame for the atrocity of slavery on the descendants of Italian, Irish, German, French or other European immigrants simply because they are White. Many of these peoples' fathers and mothers and grandparents arrived in the 1920s and 30s. Many others came in the 1940s to escape the war that was ravaging Europe. They took no part in slavery, nor did their forefathers.

Likewise, the Civil War era ancestors of many White Americans neither owned slaves nor condoned slavery. In fact, many of these forefathers were abolitionists and anti-slavery activists both in the North and the South! Many Christians in the South—true Christians, that is—helped to free the runaway slaves. They assisted the Underground Railroad in transporting them North. Many risked their lives in doing so. Some subsequently lost their lives in the process.

Many White Americans' ancestors never wore a sheet or burned a cross. It is likely that some of the Black political activists of today are the descendants of slaves whose very lives were spared by some of these God-fearing White Abolitionists. Being White, therefore, does not automatically place you in the "enemy's camp" in terms of the slavery issue.

Another factor that complicates the resolution of who must pay reparations to the descendants of America's enslaved is the basic principle that you cannot indict an entire nation or race of people for the undesirable acts of some of its citizens. A good example of this point is Nazi Germany. After World War II, war crime courts were held in Nuremberg, Germany to try Nazi war criminals. These criminals were tried and many were executed for their part in the annihilation of Jews and for committing other torturous acts. Those who were guilty represented only a small percentage of the German population. Those convicted had to bear the punishment for their crimes, but the entire country was not indicted because of the acts of these few citizens.

There is, however, a principle of accountability that dictates the necessity for a nation to be aware of certain acts of tyranny. This principle does not allow a nation's people to turn a blind eye or deaf ear to the plight and suffering of any of its citizens. This is true especially in the Christian community.

At this point the question, *"What is the answer?"* is indeed valid. First of all, rectifying any given situation requires an objective search for the truth. It is difficult to affix any measure of guilt until the truth is first established. Once the absolute truth is present, then all parties involved can bear the burden of their portion of guilt and/or innocence, whichever the case may be.

Often it is very difficult to establish guilt or innocence on current issues. It is even more difficult to establish guilt or innocence when the incident in question happened so very long ago. In the case cited earlier concerning Nazi war criminals, the search is continuing today to find and try any of these criminals who are still alive. The search will soon end because all of the participants will have succumbed to death in their old age. The memory of the atrocities and the effects of them, however, will live on in the lives of those who suffered as a result. Likewise, the unjust suffering they experienced will continue to have an effect in the lives of their descendants long after the guilty are deceased.

Adjudicating guilty those who are the apparent heirs of those individuals who held or dealt in slaves is a very similar issue. How do you properly affix guilt when the crimes were committed from 135-350 years ago? Certainly all of those present at that time and directly responsible for transporting and for buying, selling, and owning slaves have passed on into eternity.

Spokespersons for many organizations make public statements, demanding restitution from the Whites for the enslavement of the Africans. Others speak of the White race asking for forgiveness of the Black race for slavery. This is certainly understandable, but wouldn't justice and fairness dictate that we must include all the participants in the slave trade?

I heard a Black brother at a Promise Keepers meeting in Harlem say to his Black brothers, *"We must accept the White brother's plea for forgiveness, and forgive them."* For sure that is true, but this act of forgiveness cannot be limited to the Black/White factions of this issue.

For example, is there a demand for apology and contrition on behalf of the African-American community from the African tribesmen who initiated the West African slave markets? These Africans were enslaving and selling their own countrymen to the Arabs and North Africans for centuries prior to the development of the Atlantic Slave Trade. As we will see in a subsequent chapter, this practice continues even today!

But let us continue this search for truth on which we have embarked. A historical look at slavery should assist the reader to gain a greater understanding of this issue and provide a stronger basis from which to make judgments concerning those involved.

The first slaves were brought to America a few short years after the settlement of the New World began. These slaves were not brought here against their will. They were indentured slaves, sometimes referred to as bondservants, from Europe. These people chose to sell themselves into slave labor for a time in exchange for an opportunity to redeem themselves at a later date and begin a new life here in America.

As the settlers began to develop this fertile new land and agriculture began to flourish in North America, the Caribbean and South America, there was a tremendous shortage of labor. About that time, the Spanish and Portuguese mariners discovered the slave markets in West Africa. Some of the West African chiefs were actually capturing their own countrymen and selling them into slavery.

As was stated earlier, this practice had been going on for centuries before the Spanish and Portuguese exploited this degrading form of commerce. The Spanish and the Portuguese saw these West African slave markets as the apparent answer to the labor shortage in the New World. Soon the British, who "ruled the waves," made the shipping of human cargo a profitable and lucrative business. This business would eventually transport over twenty-five million Africans to the West.

Soon the cane fields of the Caribbean and the cotton fields of the South were stocked with slave labor. Over the next 365 years, many would be born and die in the same fields, having never experienced freedom. Like the children of Israel who were in bondage in Egypt for 400 years, their cries would go up for generations until God delivered them from the tyranny of human bondage.

WHO IS GOING TO PAY?

By this time you must be saying, *"I want to know WHO is going to pay?"*

There is a custom in the United States, often used when dining out, that is called *Going Dutch*. I am not sure of its origin, but I do understand the principle. It goes somewhat like this. You can order anything you like and eat as much as you want. However, when it is time to pay the check, everyone pays for his or her individual meal. It does not matter what you ate or how much you ate, because you are paying for your share and your share only. In fact, everyone present at the table pays for themselves.

But how does this principle apply to slavery? It is very simple. If there is going to be a just restitution by the current generation for the acts of past generations, then we must fix the rightful responsibility to each faction that was involved in the slave trade. Every person or group of persons whose ancestors were directly responsible should pay their rightful share, beginning with the African Chiefs who captured and sold their own countrymen into slavery.

The complicity of Africans themselves in respect to the slavery issue is a delicate subject, but it needs to be addressed if we are to come to the whole truth about this matter. Professor Chinweizu considered the role Africans played in the slave trading, in a paper, which he read at the second Plenary Session of the First Pan-African Conference on Reparations that was held in Abuja, Nigeria on April 27, 1993. It should be noted that Professor Chinweizu was not disputing the justice of seeking reparations, but he was urging his listeners to explore the factors within the existing African societies that might have aided the massive enslavement and export of so many of their countrymen.

Twenty years prior to this historic Pan-African Conference, Professor Chinweizu wrote a paper entitled *The West and the Rest of Us.* He subtitled this paper *White Predators, Black Slavers and the African Elite.* *"The purpose of this paper,"* Professor Chinweizu said, *"was to serve notice that we cannot overlook our complicity, as Black Slavers and as the African Elite, in what happened, and is still happening to us. We must, therefore, change ourselves in order to end our criminal complicity in perpetuating our lamentable condition."* [2]

His point is well taken. West African chiefs and members of the elite were routinely kidnapping and enslaving members of other tribes as early as the 1400s. Other slaves were taken as the "spoils" of war, just as the Romans did with the nations it conquered. Many of these African slaves were exported via the same trans-Saharan trade routes that caravans had used for centuries. The slaves were then sold to buyers in North African, Middle Eastern, and Mediterranean countries. [3]

From the early 15th century until late in the 19th century, Africa's elite amassed great wealth from this well-developed network of slave trading. Pre-colonial empires such as the Dahomey (present-day Benin) and the Ashanti (present-day Ghana) were among the kingdoms whose economy and subsequently their military, was based heavily on the slave trade. The abolition of slavery and the subsequent collapse of the North Atlantic Slave Trade meant the loss of a major portion of the slave market. Some nations, such as Dahomey, never recovered from this financial setback. [4]

A VITAL ROLE:

As hard as it might be to believe, Africa's leaders played a key role in the development of the North Atlantic Trade Route, especially in the early years of its development.. A writer, Zayde Antrim, pointed out that *"...Europeans often acted as junior partners to the African rulers, merchants, and middlemen in the slave trade along the West African coast..."* [5] She indicated that there were two reasons for this dependence: West Africa's rough coastal geography and diseases such as malaria. West Africa had few natural harbors. In addition, the seasonal wind patterns that were typical along the Atlantic Coast produced heavy surfs and dangerous cross-currents. Offshore reefs and sandbars added to the hazards ships had to negotiate. As a result, international trading vessels usually anchored off shore and waited for the skilled African canoemen to bring goods and slaves out to them. [6]

Even where the natural ports were good, tropical diseases restricted the effectiveness and expansion of European trade efforts. Many Whites who lived and traded in these ports were in a constant state of ill health. Hence, Africa became known as the "White man's grave." In addition, Africa's elite coastal leaders and merchants were very much in control of the coast and any traffic on the rivers. European military technology was not highly developed enough at that point to allow them to overrule the Africans' dictates. In this kind of environment, European merchants and slave traders were rarely in a position to call the shots until the 19th century. [7]

This is by no means an excuse for Europeans' victimization of millions of African slaves, but, if our historical analysis of this ignoble chapter in America's history is to be accurate, we need to recognize that the slave trading wasn't initiated by the European traders. It would be reasonable, however, to assume that European's eagerness to purchase slaves accelerated the Africans' efforts to take more slaves.

It is important to note that *"...Europeans...encountered well-established and highly developed political organizations and competitive regional commercial networks..."* [8] when they first came to Africa. This continent's coastline and treacherous ocean currents might have restricted her peoples' interaction with the people of other continents, but it did not impair the development of their social order.[9] Makes you wonder how Blacks ever got the reputation of being "barbaric heathens," doesn't it? Perhaps this lie made it easier to justify enslaving millions of them.

WHY?

Some might ask, *"How could Africans sell their own countrymen?"* To answer this question, we need to understand something about the cultural norms at that point in Africa's history. West African societies, for example, did not consider the land as their private property. Personal wealth was determined by the number of people who were dependent upon you, whether they were family members, those who had joined themselves to your household, or slaves. The larger your household, the wealthier your were. [10]

We also need to remember that Africa was not one huge, harmonious nation then anymore than it is now. Conflicts and wars occurred between tribes and nations there just as on the other continents. Divisions and strife, it seems, are the common human experience. Africans, like other people groups, divided along the lines of religion, class, language, gender and ethnicity. It was along these lines of division that some, but certainly not all, Africans participated in the slave trade. [11]

Arab Involvement in Slave Trading:

Having considered the role Africans themselves played in enslaving so many of their own people, we must now call upon the Arabs, who not only were the most prominent slave traders then, but who continue to engage in African slavery today. Many historical writers on the subject of slavery tell us that not only did the Arabs initiate the export of slaves from West and Central Africa, but they also continued that trade after the emancipation and discontinuation of slavery in the Americas and Europe. Earl Parvin, in his book *Mission USA*, confirms this fact. Parvin indicates that additional slave markets opened up on Africa's eastern coast until the late 1700s. Multitudes of Black Africans were sold to Arabs in neighboring countries, creating a slave trade that was even worse than the existing West Africa slave trade. [12]

After we call on the Arabs, we must address the Portuguese, Spanish, French, British, as well as other European nations who not only dealt in the Atlantic slave trade, but who also imported slaves into Europe. Of course, we must include the slave buyers and sellers and all those who owned slaves—both Northerners and Southerners—in the United States, as well as the slave owners in Central and South America.

I believe that Africa will never be totally healed of the gaping wounds left from the slave trade until all of the European nations, who took part in wounding, begin to be part of the healing process. The same thing would apply to the Arab nations who were or who are currently involved in the enslavement of Africans. (We will address present-day slavery in a later chapter.)

Tracing Our Ancestry:

Now comes the task of tracing our ancestry in each of these nations to see whose forefathers dealt in slavery and whose did not. After all, I think we have established already in this chapter that you cannot indict an entire nation, a family, and certainly not an entire race for the acts of some of its individuals. Tracing each individual's ancestry would be a daunting task, even in this age of computers. Some families' records are more complete than others, and some may not even know who their birth families are.

How then do we set the record straight? Perhaps we should also ask, *"What is our purpose in setting the record straight?"* Will determining who should pay how much bring healing among the races? Will it bring about the respect and acceptance African-Americans so richly deserve?

GOING BEYOND APOLOGIES TO FORGIVENESS:

We talk about a lot of rights today—Civil Rights, Equal Rights, Human Rights, Women's Rights, etc. When I became a Christian, one of the first things I learned was that I had to give up my rights—my rights to unforgiveness, hatred, bitterness, stubbornness, bigotry, racial prejudice and the like. It is the same for all men everywhere.

How is it possible to forgive when the wrong is so great? Only Jesus can give us grace to forgive when we've suffered so unjustly.

I have heard many leaders of predominately White denominations making public apologies for what the White race has done to the Black race. I think that is a wonderful start in healing the wounds.

We must understand that as individuals, as well as a race, there needs to be a personalizing process in all of this. In other words, you and I need to deal with our own individual prejudices and racist attitudes—both Blacks and Whites—if true healing is to take place between the races.

It is wonderful to see thousands of men in stadiums across the country hugging each other and asking forgiveness, but it cannot stop there. We must bring it home with us and incorporate it into our everyday lives. It is easy to say, *"Forgive me"* in the midst of fifty thousand men and then go home with the attitude, *"But I don't want your son to date my daughter."*

I pray that the voicing of apology and the asking of forgiveness by national leaders of many White organizations has been a true and heartfelt contrition and not for any other reason, especially for mere convenience's sake. But the voicing of apology and asking of forgiveness is only one aspect of what is needed to bring healing and unity in our nation and in the church. An apology must be accepted and forgiveness must be granted for either to have an effect.

THE CHURCH'S ROLE:

With all of the growth in the Black church of America and the progress made in the last decade, it would be easy for Black leaders to say, *"Where were you when we needed you?"* While justified from man's perspective, such an attitude will do nothing to heal the race-based divisions in the body of Christ.

A popular camp meeting song from the 70s contains these lines: *"We will walk with each other; we will walk hand in hand...and we'll pray that all unity may one day be restored..."* This is really the bottom line for us as believers. The question is, are we promoting healing and unity within our local congregation, our local community, our nation and the Christian community worldwide?

Consider this question before answering it. Lay your heart before God and ask Him to reveal any vestiges of racism or prejudice that have not yet been removed. You don't need them, and neither does the body of Christ.

IMPERFECT MESSENGERS:

Certainly there was much in the ministry and missions outreach conducted by Whites that was far from the ideal pattern that Jesus exemplified, but we will benefit from their errors more if we learn from them than if we simply condemn them as racists. Despite their imperfections, Whites did respond to the call to take the gospel to other nations. To their credit, White church organizations around the world have sent countless millions of dollars to the continent of Africa alone and are continuing to do so. It is a fact that I do not personally have knowledge of the numbers of Black missionaries who have been sent to Africa or the amount of dollars that have been invested there by Black organizations. I do know, however, that it takes more than kente cloth and Swahili songs to meet the many political, economic, social, and spiritual needs of that great continent.

The litmus test of any movement is its impact on today's people. If God is in a thing, it will bring wholeness on all levels of man's existence—political, economic, social, and spiritual—and not just for one race, but for all races.

Have those in the reconciliation movement become so involved in resolving the injustices of the past, that they are overlooking the injustices of the present? Slavery is not an issue of the past. There has been a dramatic resurgence in slavery in Africa during the past decade. This present-day slavery is not case of Whites enslaving Blacks, but of Browns and Blacks enslaving Blacks.

Even assuming that Whites and Blacks in America could reach a settlement of all the issues put forward by those in the reconciliation movement, what impact would that settlement have on present slavery situations? Would it halt the slave raids on southern Sudanese villages? Would it free young Asian children from the brothels that are proliferating on that continent? Would it stop the genocide that is taking countless lives because timeless tribal conflicts have never been resolved? Would it reach into the inner cities of America and bring restoration in the ethnic families that are being devastated by drugs, crime, and hopelessness? Would it stamp out the roots of pride and ignorance (lack of knowledge of the simple truth that God created all men equal, that no race was meant to serve another race, but that people of all races were meant to serve God) that allow slavery to be practiced in the first place? Will it address the present day injustices that are happening because of racial profiling?

While we should not discount the need to resolve the injustices of the past, neither should we dwell on what is past to the exclusion of what is presently happening. Over two million southern Sudanese have died in the past two decades in that nation's efforts to convert all of its citizens to Islam. Four and a half million others have been forced from their land and are presently living in concentration camps that are passed off as "peace camps." Countless others—most of them women and children—have been forced into slavery to their Arab captors or sold into slavery in other nations. Where is the outcry for these oppressed people? This is just in Sudan—not to mention the tribal wars and "ethnic cleansings" that have taken place in the last decade in dozens of African nations, claiming millions of lives.

FORGIVENESS, AN OPTION OR A RESPONSIBILITY?

What is the Christian's responsibility in regard to forgiving atrocities committed against him or against his race? The Holy Word of God is quite plain to all of us in the response that Jesus gave His disciples when they asked Him to teach them how to pray. In Matthew, chapter 6:9 Jesus said, *Pray, "Our Father which art in heaven, Hallowed (Holy) be thy name.* The word OUR meaning, "OUR" as in Father to ALL of us!

In verse 12, Jesus said, *forgive us our DEBTS as we forgive our debtors.* The word that is translated *debts* is the Greek word, *of-i-lay-mah*, which means *something owed.* In other words, we are to pray, *"Lord, forgive my faults and what I owe to you, as I forgive the faults of others and what they owe to me."*

In verses 14-15, Jesus says, *"For IF you FORGIVE men their trespasses, YOUR heavenly Father will also forgive YOU! BUT IF YOU forgive NOT neither will YOUR Father forgive your trespasses."* The word forgive in this passage is the Greek word *af-ee-ay-mee* which means, *to send forth, lay aside, to leave, to forsake, or to give up.*

These two verses that Jesus added to his instructions concerning forgiveness show the importance He attached to it. It also shows the necessity of forgiving others. This is essential, not only so that we can be blessed, but also so that our relationship with God will not be hindered. Jesus makes it very plain: **If we want to be forgiven, we must first forgive.** Forgiveness, therefore, is not an option, but a necessity for our own forgiveness from God.

In light of this definition of forgiveness, it is indeed time for all sides of this racial division "to give it up" and "let it go!" Forgetting that which is past on all sides and pressing on towards the mark of the high calling—shoulder to shoulder, side by side in this war to advance the Kingdom of God on earth—we will be able to work together to further the gospel of Jesus Christ if we not only say, *"I love you,"* but we are also willing to demonstrate the kind of love God freely gives to each of us.

I believe that we can implement a *Forgive and Forget Policy* in this country, especially in the church. This does not mean that we sweep everything under the rug and act as if none of it ever happened. But for the sake of healing the wounds—both past and present—we must stop looking back and start looking forward toward a brighter future—a future free of racism and bigotry in the body of Christ.

It has been my experience, when confronted with someone who says, *"I am willing to forgive, but I will not forget it!"* that if we do not want to forget it, is possible that we really do not want to forgive it.

We realize that, in order for us to forget some things, God would have to give us brain damage. Forgetting doesn't change the fact that something happened, but it does change the effect. When God has truly healed the wounds, the hurt is no longer there when we think about an incident.

Jesus' first words on the cross were, *"Father, forgive them, they know not what they do."* Ignorance is not an excuse for racism. We need to help each other gain the necessary knowledge to overcome our prejudicial ideas. Forgiveness opens up the channels of communication so that an impartation of knowledge can take place.

End Notes:

[1] *The American Heritage Dictionary, Second College Edition*, Houghton Mifflin Company, Boston, 1985, pg. 1047.

[2] Professor Chinweizu, *Reparations and a New Global Order: A Comparative Overview*, A paper read at the second Plenary Session of the First Pan-African Conference on Reparations, held in Abuja, Nigeria, April 27, 1993, the Africa Reparations Movement web site. Available at <http://www.arm.arc.co.uk/NewGlobalOrder.html. Accessed on July 29, 2000.

[3-11] Zayde Antrim, *Slave Kingdoms: The Trans-Saharan Trade Route*, PBS Online. Available at <http://www.pbs.org> Accessed on July 29, 2000.

[12] Earl Parvin, *Mission USA*, Moody Press, Chicago, 1985, pg. 81.

Section 2: The Theological Foundations of Racism

Chapter 9: Biblical Misinterpretations and Old Wives' Tales

By far the majority of Whites and Blacks do not accept the radical teachings of today's vocal, racial supremacists. But error—biblical misinterpretation and old wives' tales, handed down from generation to generation—has tainted the theology that guides many ordinary Christians' lives. Identifying and eliminating these distortions and misrepresentations of God's perfect nature will play a vital role in drawing all races into the oneness that God desires for His Church. Often these misinterpretations of scripture deal with the origin of all the races, with God's purpose for racial diversity, or with God's dealings with various people throughout the Bible. Because these misinterpretations have been used to support racism, we need to consider some of these scriptures carefully.

We'll concentrate on three of these misunderstood scriptural accounts. The first account concerns the origin of the Black man. Many believe that Noah cursed his son Ham and turned him Black. Proponents of this fallacy contend that not only did Noah pronounce this curse of "Blackness" on Ham, but that he also included in this anathema the eternal servitude of the Blacks to the other races of the earth. This, they say, gives rise to the justification of slavery as a God-created institution.

The second account concerns Moses' marriage to an Ethiopian woman. (She is sometimes referred to as a Cushite, because Cush is the ancient name for Ethiopia) Those who misinterpret this passage believe that this union displeased God. They therefore believe that God prohibits biracial marriages.

The third account concerns Jesus' words to his disciples in John 4:35—*"Lift up your eyes, and look on the fields; for they are white already to harvest."* The term "White" here was believed to mean that the Anglo-Saxon—the Caucasian—race was to be given a priority for evangelization. It doesn't get much more absurd than that, does it?

NOAH'S CURSE:

I have already spoken of my early childhood experiences in the Deep South concerning things that have been taught that are not the truth of God's Word. Often in my life when the question was asked, *"Where did the Black man come from?"*, the answer given by clergy and layman alike was, *"Noah cursed his son and turned him Black!"* This is supposedly where the Black race came from. We were also taught that, because of Noah's "curse", all the descendants of Ham were destined to be "servants" to the descendants of Shem and Japheth. Unfortunately, if you asked many Southern Black Christians where the Black man originated, they would give similar answers, because this is a widely accepted misinterpretation of the scriptures.

One white pastor of a large church did compensate in one way by saying, *"In the rapture, God is going to turn all of the saved Black people, White!"* I know of an African Pastor in the West who today is teaching the idea of Blacks being servants, according to God's decree through Noah.

So hurtful has this misinterpretation been that in 1993 one church actually staged a trial of Ham. In this mock trial, powerful evidence was presented from the Word of God that Ham's Blackness was not the result of a curse, but that he was Black from birth.

THE TRUTH ABOUT HAM:

Let's look into God's Word to see exactly what Noah said and to whom he said it. Genesis 9:20-27 proclaims:

> *20And Noah began to be an husbandman, and he planted a vineyard: 21And he drank of the wine, and was drunken; and he was uncovered within his tent. 22And Ham, the father of Canaan, saw the nakedness of his father, and told his two brethren without. 23And Shem and Japheth took a garment, and laid it upon both their shoulders, and went backward, and covered the nakedness of their father; and their faces were backward, and they saw not their father's nakedness.*

*²⁴And Noah awoke from his wine, and knew what his younger son had done unto him. ²⁵And he said, **Cursed** be **Canaan; a servant of servants shall he be unto his brethren.** ²⁶And he said, Blessed be the LORD God of Shem; and Canaan shall be his servant. ²⁷God shall enlarge Japheth, and he shall dwell in the tents of Shem; and Canaan shall be his servant.*

Most commentators believe that this incident reveals a number of different things. First of all, it is believed that Canaan, the youngest of Ham's sons, did what he did with a disrespectful attitude. In other words, instead of covering Noah's nakedness, he revealed it. The Hebrew for *nakedness* is *gâlâh* (pronounced gaw-*law*), which means *to de-nude, to strip as a slave is stripped naked or to shamelessly uncover.* In other words, in this context, neither Canaan nor Ham showed any respect when they revealed the shame of Noah.

One theory is that the term *uncovering nakedness* in Hebrew speaks of the father's wife, making it possible that Canaan committed incest with his grandmother. Having explored this possibility, I find very little that validates such an assumption.

Gâlâh is in the Hitpael verb form in this verse. Therefore it means *to uncover oneself* or *to be uncovered.* The implication in this verse is that Noah became overheated from the wine he imbibed and he uncovered himself in his tent. Ham's downfall was that he revealed what he saw when he walked into his father's tent. [1]

Some translators say this verse implies that Ham "had sexual relations with" Noah, and that this was the reason his line was cursed. "However, the expression 'see nakedness' usually refers to observation of another's nakedness, not a sexual act." [2] In Genesis 42:9, this same word is used to indicate vulnerability:

⁹And Joseph remembered the dreams which he dreamed of them, and said unto them, Ye are *spies; to see **the nakedness of the land** ye are come.*

There are instances when the expression "see nakedness" implies having sexual relations, but there is no indication of this either in verse 22 or 23. Noah uncovered himself, and Ham merely saw his father while he was naked. Shem and Japheth took Ham's word for it, and respectfully covered their father up.

Part of the difficulty we have with this passage is that nudity is much more accepted or at least tolerated now than it was in Noah's time. We tend to think that something else had to be going on in Noah's tent for him to get that upset. It couldn't have been that Ham just saw him naked.

This is where the principles of hermeneutics come into play. We have to understand the culture within which a given text was written in order to understand what the text meant to them. In the patriarchal society within which this passage is written, *"...seeing another's nakedness was a major offense."* [3] We also have to remember that Ham was not a little boy running into his father's tent at an inopportune moment. He was likely about 100 years old and had sons of his own. [4]

THE NATURE OF NOAH'S CURSE AGAINST CANAAN:

This gives us some insight into why Noah cursed his grandson Canaan. Now we need to look at the nature of his pronouncement against Canaan. The first question most people raise is, *"Why did Noah curse Canaan? Ham was the one who revealed Noah's nakedness!"* The text itself does not give us a definitive answer, but there are some reasonable assumptions that we can call upon to explain Noah's response. Canaan may have been with his father. Today we would call him an accomplice. That still doesn't explain why Canaan and not Ham took the brunt of Noah's wrath.

A more plausible explanation is that Noah saw something lacking in Ham's character that had been passed on to his grandson Canaan. In the case of this incident, Ham had failed to show respect for his father. This characteristic may have shown up many times in the year the family spent together on the ark. Ham's actions may have been the proverbial "last straw." Noah's response was to prophesy what may have been a generational type of curse. A review of the descendants of Ham reveals that many of them were some of the most cruel and vicious people in Biblical history.

So what is the actual nature of Noah's curse? In verse 25, we hear Noah saying, *"Cursed (arar, pronounced Aw-rar) be Canaan..."* *Arar* means *to curse bitterly or to execrate,* which gives us a graphic picture of the type of curse Noah intended to place upon Canaan. One meaning of the word *execrate* is *to invoke a curse upon.* [4] *Execrate* comes from the Latin word *execrari.* The root word is *sacrare,* which means to consecrate. The prefix *ex-* means to take away, giving us the word *execrate. To execrate,* therefore literally means *to take away consecration.* Ham's actions took away the consecration that rested upon him as a result of his election as one of the eight people to be spared from the flood. Ham was destined for honor, but his actions robbed him of his inheritance. Instead of being honored along with his brothers, he would be one who served his brothers.

Noah indicated this when he said, *"Cursed (arar, pronounced Aw-rar) be Canaan; a servant of servants (ebed, pronounced eh'-bed) shall he be unto his brethren."* In the Hebrew, this phrase is written *arar canaan/eved avadim yihyeh l'echav,* which literally translates, *a slave of slaves shall he be to his brothers.* It should be noted that *Eh-bed* can also be translated, *"a servant of servants."*

What was the nature of the service Noah prophesied for Canaan? *Eh-bed* means *to be in bondage* or *to enslave.* It also means *to be a bondman, a bondservant, a manservant, or a worshipper. Eh-bed* comes from the word *'abad,* which means *to work* in any of several different senses. Some of the different types of work *'abad* refers to are *to serve, to till, to enslave, to keep in bondage, to bring to pass, to (cause or to make) serve, to (set a) work, to be wrought, and to be a worshipper.* [5]

One of the most interesting meanings of *'abad* is *to be wrought.* Is it implausible to assume that Noah's purpose in this curse was not to place Canaan and his descendants in a perpetual state of slavery, but that the flaws in his character might be transformed by what they experienced during their season of servitude? God's refining fire is seldom pleasant.

Even though the curse placed on Canaan was unquestionably a Divine condition of servitude, it was by all means a temporal one, not a perpetual one. It did not apply to all of the descendants of Ham for all time—and there is certainly no indication that it has anything to do with race or color. Noah says nothing about either of these factors. What we do see is that Noah's curse, in fact, contained a prophecy concerning the conquest of Canaan or The Promised Land, rather than a pronouncement of the eternal servitude of the descendants of Ham to the descendants of Shem and Japheth.

One thing is indisputable in this passage: Noah didn't kick Canaan out of the family. Certainly his relationship with the family was changed for a season, but he was still very much a part of the family. We need to remember this when we are dealing with difficult "sheep" and "lambs" in our churches.

Prophesy in Noah's Words:

It is believed that there was no personal resentment in Noah in regard to his proclamation, although there may well have been great personal sorrow. Any parent can identify with the pain of seeing a child walking in ways that do not please the Lord. The same applies to friends seeing friends choose paths that will lead to destruction. Noah's proclamation was not the vindictive statement of an enraged father; it was a perfectly symmetrical prophecy that included all three of his sons. First, we see the curse of Canaan. Secondly, we see the blessing of Shem, and thirdly, the enlargement of Japheth, giving somewhat of a prominence to the doom of Canaan.

Let's look at each of these prophecies for a moment. The curse that Noah placed on Canaan is the second curse that the Bible records being placed on man. It is generally believed that this second curse was not an imprecation—like the curse pronounced on Cain—but a prediction of the future subjection that would come when the Shemites would possess the Promised Land. The dictionary defines an *imprecation* as *to curse*, or *to invoke evil upon*. [6] Noah's intent was not to invoke evil upon Canaan and his descendants. Rather, it was a recognition of the things that were lacking in Ham and Canaan's character were going to cause them problems—translation, lead them into sin. Sin will get you into bondage every time, but, praise God, Jesus sets us free!

It must be noted that this curse was confined to Canaan alone. It did not apply in any way to Ham's other sons—Cush, Mizraim, and Phut. Nor did it apply to Ham himself. This shows that this curse was indeed limited in its scope and <u>not</u> a Divine "cursing" of an entire race or its progenitors.

The prophetic nature of Noah's statement becomes clear when you see that most of the tribes, that the Israelites had to conquer and destroy before they could possess the Promised Land, were descendants of Canaan. Some of these tribes are mentioned in the Book of Joshua, chapter 3, verse 10:

> *And Joshua said, Hereby ye shall know that the living God is among you, and that he will not fail to drive out from before you the Canaanites and the Hittites, and the Hivites, and the Perizzites, and Girgashites, and the Amorites, and Jebusites.*

Genesis 10:15-17 gives an account of the descendants of Canaan:

> *¹⁵And Canaan begat Sidon his firstborn, and Heth, ¹⁶And the Jebusite, and the Amorite, and the Girgasite, ¹⁷And the Hivite, and the Arkite, and the Sinite, ¹⁸And the Arvadite, and the Zemarite, and the Hamathite: and afterward were the families of the Canaanites spread abroad. ¹⁹And the border of the Canaanites was from Sidon, as thou comest to Gerar, unto Gaza; as thou goest, unto Sodom, and Gomorrah, and Admah, and Zeboim, even unto Lasha.*

From this we can see that Canaan was the father of the Jebusites, Amorites, the Girgasites, Hivites, Arkites, Sinites, Ardadites, the Hamathites, (not to be confused with the Cushites, the ancient name for the Ethiopians). Canaan's descendants continued in his ways. They were known for their cruelty and viciousness, not for their worship of God. Many of them had to be dispossessed in order for the Israelites to possess the Promised Land.

So, was there prophecy in the words of Noah? I believe that is exactly what he was doing—prophesying the conquest of the Promised Land. Noah certainly was not placing a curse of color or perpetual servanthood on a race of people.

THE GOD OF SHEM:

In verse 26, he says, *"And Noah said, Blessed be the Lord God of Shem; and Canaan shall be his servant."* The word translated blessed here is *baw-rak*, which means *to kneel, to bless God as an act of adoration; or in reversal, that man might curse a god as well.* Notice that Noah speaks of the God of Shem. Why not the God of Ham or Japheth? First, because the Shemites would be in the lineage of Jesus, beginning with Seth to Abraham and continuing on to the Messiah. This lineage would produce the true Son of God. Second, because the offspring of both the Hamites and the Japhethites would produce idolatrous and paganistic societies.

In verse 27, Noah said, *"God shall enlarge Japheth, and he shall dwell in the tents of Shem; and Canaan shall be his servant."* Japheth means *expansion or roomy.* Certainly when we see how the Anglo-Saxon world has expanded throughout history through all of Europe and in the Western Hemisphere, we see that indeed God has enlarged Japheth just as Noah predicted.

But what about the prophecy that Japheth would dwell in the tents of Shem? The Messiah and Christianity would come through the lineage of Shem. The New Testament Church would begin by and with the Jews, but it would not be limited to the Jews. God made provision for the grafting in of the Gentiles as well. We see reference to this in what the Apostle Paul wrote in Romans chapter 11, verses 17-18:

> *And if some of the branches be broken off, and thou, being a wild olive tree, were grafted in among them, and with them partakest of the root and fatness of the olive tree; Boast not against the branches. But if thou boast thou bearest not the root, but the root thee.*

What is he saying? He is speaking of the Gentiles—the descendants of Japheth and Ham—becoming worshippers in the tent (or Tabernacle, as the word translates from the Hebrew) of Shem. Noah was foreseeing the Gospel message being taken not only to the Jews, or the lost sheep of Israel, but also to the Gentiles, **causing them to dwell in the tent of Shem.**

It certainly appears that Noah did indeed prophesy the conquest of Canaan and the disposition of the Hamites and Japhethites. This eliminates any scriptural grounds for justifying slavery in the West on the basis of the curse Noah placed on Canaan. It also shows that there is no basis for believing that Black skin was the result of this curse.

MOSES' MARRIAGE TO THE CUSHITE WOMAN:

Another area of scripture that always seems to find its way into discussions on race is the Biblical account of Moses marrying a Cushite woman. In Numbers 12, verses 1-2, the Word says,

> *¹And Miriam and Aaron spake against Moses because of the Ethiopian woman whom he had married: for he had married an Ethiopian woman. ²And they said, Hath the LORD indeed spoken only by Moses? hath he not spoken also by us? And the LORD heard it.*

These and other similar scriptures often give rise to the idea that interracial marriage is prohibited by God. **Well, nowhere in the Bible can I find such an ordinance.**

First of all, Miriam and Aaron did not oppose Moses' decision to marry an Ethiopian because she was Black (if indeed she was Black), but because she was not of the tribe of Levi. Secondly, we observe in Numbers 12 that, when God rebuked Miriam, He did not speak of Moses' marriage to an Ethiopian.

> *⁴And the LORD spake suddenly unto Moses, and unto Aaron, and unto Miriam, Come out ye three unto the tabernacle of the congregation. And they three came out. ⁵And the LORD came down in the pillar of the cloud, and stood in the door of the tabernacle, and called Aaron and Miriam: and they both came forth. ⁶And he said, Hear now my words: **If there be a prophet among you, I the LORD will make myself known unto him** in a vision, and will speak unto him in a dream. ⁷My servant Moses is not so, who is faithful in all mine house. ⁸With him will I speak mouth to mouth, even apparently, and not in dark speeches; and the similitude of the LORD shall he behold: wherefore then were ye not afraid to speak against*

my servant Moses? ⁹And the anger of the LORD was kindled against them; and he departed. (Numbers 12:4-9)

This proves that Moses' marriage did not displease God. What God did say in this passage pinpoints the heart of the conflict between Moses and his siblings: Moses' standing as a prophet of God. This also shows that God was not displeased with Moses' selection for a marriage partner.

God made it very clear that Moses was still a prophet "in good standing" before Him. Numbers 12:10 shows us that God's judgment was directed at Miriam, not Moses.

¹⁰And the cloud departed from off the tabernacle; and, behold, Miriam became leprous, white as snow: and Aaron looked upon Miriam, and, behold, she was leprous. (Numbers 12:10)

Aaron was very quick to repent when he saw what happened to Miriam. He turned and appealed to Moses to intercede for their sister:

¹¹And Aaron said unto Moses, Alas, my lord, I beseech thee, lay not the sin upon us, wherein we have done foolishly, and wherein we have sinned. ¹²Let her not be as one dead, of whom the flesh is half consumed when he cometh out of his mother's womb. (Numbers 12:11-12)

Aaron's attitude toward Moses did a complete 180 degree turn when he saw the effect sin had on Miriam. God had made His point. Moses was still His prophet, and Aaron appealed to the man of God for mercy.

Moses' response was gracious. He ...*cried unto the LORD, saying, Heal her now, O God, I beseech thee* (Num. 12:13). He could have asked God to zap Aaron, too. Isn't that our flesh's first reaction when we are offended or falsely accused? But Moses' response preserved unity in his family and brought healing and restoration to Miriam. The same thing will happen in the body of Christ if we ignore the suggestions the flesh is so quick to offer and follow the Spirit's promptings to forgive and be an agent of reconciliation.

Moses' prayer was heard. Miriam was restricted to "Sick Bay" for seven days. Her sin was not against Moses, but against God the Father. In essence she was saying, *"God, you made a mistake when you set Moses up as prophet over us."*

[14]And the LORD said unto Moses, If her father had but spit in her face, should she not be ashamed seven days? let her be shut out from the camp seven days, and after that let her be received in again. *[15]And Miriam was shut out from the camp seven days: and the people journeyed not till Miriam was brought in* again. (Numbers 12:14-15)

Miriam's sin affected not only herself, but the entire nation of Israel. Their journey to the Promised Land was put on hold until Miriam got things straight with God.

The final verse in this chapter speaks volumes concerning the power of being agents of reconciliation:

[16]And afterward the people removed from Hazeroth, and pitched in the wilderness of Paran. (Numbers 12:16)

Where racism is permitted to continue unchallenged, whether in the Church or in the world, a wilderness of prejudice, hatred, pride, sorrow, and pain will block mankind from experiencing the righteousness, peace, and joy in the Holy Ghost that God desires to make available to each of us.

It is interesting to note that, as a descendant of Canaan, the Ethiopian woman Moses married was very much a part of the nation of Israel. God created racial diversity, but He never indicated there should be any segregation of the races that made up His holy nation.

I do wonder, however, why, if Moses was Black, as some believe, that Miriam and Aaron were opposed to him marrying a Black woman. They were Moses' sister and brother, so they would also have been Black. If that were the case, it seems more likely that they would have been upset if Moses had married a White woman. *"Guess who's coming to dinner?"*

MARRIAGE OUTSIDE THE NATION OF ISRAEL FORBIDDEN:

Marriage outside the nation of Israel was clearly forbidden, however. The Bible is quite plain concerning God's perpetual conservation of a people who would inherit the promise. These things have nothing whatsoever to do with race or color but simply the preservation of a holy nation, a nation from which the Messiah would come forth.

God's command regarding marrying "outsiders" created strong sentiments against those Israelites who did so, especially when the "outsiders" were members of nations that conquered and occupied Israel at various points in her history. These strong sentiments were the root of the aversion the Jews of Jesus' day had against the Samaritans. The Samaritans were descendants of "half breed" Jews.

SPIRITUAL ISRAEL:

When we speak of racially mixed marriages, it must be from the standpoint of a born-again believer. Members of all the races make up the Church—spiritual Israel—today. Just as there was no reference to race in the guidelines God gave to the Israelites—only a restriction that they were to marry within their nation—there is no restriction placed upon us except that we are to marry a fellow believer. Paul addressed this issue in II Corinthians 6:14 where he said,

> *14Be ye not unequally yoked together with unbelievers: for what fellowship hath righteousness with unrighteousness? and what communion hath light with darkness?*

It is commonly believed that this text is referring only to business relationships or friendships. Not so! It applies to marriage relationships as well.

If we examine this passage, we find the following: The words "unequally yoked" are translated from one Greek word, *het-er-od-zoog-eh-o*, which means *to yoke up differently* or *associate discordantly"* with an unbeliever. Unbelievers is the translation of the Greek word *ap-is-tos*, which means *disbelieving* or *without Christ*. It has absolutely nothing to do with race. The principle emphasized here is the need for one believer to marry another believer, first to produce Godly offspring. Whether the believers are of the same race or not is not an issue.

There are many sociological factors that should be considered by both partners prior to a biracial marriage: for instance, the effect it may have on both families and on the racially mixed children that will issue from it. There are various other sociological and cross-cultural considerations that must be addressed as well. However, the Word of God posts no prohibition on marriages between members of different races, only on those between believers and unbelievers. From a biblical perspective, **there are no inter-racial marriages in the context of the Christian community today except those between believers and unbelievers.** Just as the Israelites could not marry outside the nation of Israel, we can not marry outside the Kingdom of God.

An understanding of God's attitude toward mixed marriages draws us closer to His view of His Church. He sees this issue with unclouded spiritual vision. He sees us as one in Christ—a supernatural race, which transcends all cultures, nationalities, and physical characteristics. Each of us is cleansed by the blood of Jesus, each is born of Holy Spirit, each is seeking to walk in His ways. We are one in Christ! What God has joined together, man is ill-advised to try to separate.

AVERTING ANOTHER TOWER OF BABEL:

Over the years, some have opposed mixed marriages in order to prevent another Tower of Babel. They site the passage in Genesis 11:5-9, which speaks of the dispersement of the races to prevent mankind from uniting once again in ungodly pursuits. They contend that this is a basis for forbidding inter-racial marriages. We will address this passage in more depth in a later chapter. For now it is only necessary to note that the Word does not indicate that God was upset about inter-racial marriages among the Israelites. He was angry because they had joined together to accomplish their own will.

> *5 And the LORD came down to see the city and the tower, which the children of men builded. 6 And the LORD said, Behold, the people is one, and they have all one language; and this they begin to do: and now nothing will be restrained from them, which they have imagined to do. 7 Go to, let us go down, and there confound their language, that they may not understand one another's speech. 8 So the LORD scattered them abroad from thence upon the face of all the earth: and they left off to build the city. 9 Therefore is the name of it called Babel; because the LORD did there confound the lan-*

guage of all the earth: and from thence did the LORD scatter them abroad upon the face of all the earth.

God's intent was for mankind to fill the whole earth, not to prevent the races from inter-marrying.

THE FIELDS WHITE TO HARVEST:

The final biblical misinterpretation we want to consider is the belief that Jesus' statement, *"...the fields are white to harvest,"* indicates that God places a priority on the evangelization of the Anglo-Saxons—the Caucasians, the descendants of Japheth.

> *Say not ye, There are yet four months, and then cometh harvest? behold, I say unto you, Lift up your eyes, and look on the fields; for they are white already to harvest.* (John 4:35)

If you consider John 4:35 within the context of the rest of scripture, there is no basis for assuming Jesus was espousing a "Whites first" approach to evangelism. When Jesus said, *"...the fields are white to harvest,"* He had just finished sharing the "good news" with the Samaritan woman. He had broken strong cultural barriers in doing so. As I said earlier, the Jews despised the Samaritans because they had inter-married with their captors during times when Israel was under foreign occupation. Jesus ignored this traditional prejudice. He placed no racial distinction on the harvest He would gather or the world harvest yet to be gathered. In fact, He was striking at the very roots of racism with His statement to the disciples.

Even as Jesus spoke, the Samaritan woman was returning to her village, carrying the precious "seed" He had planted in her heart. When she arrived, she told everyone about Jesus and asked, *"Can this be the Messiah?"* Many believed that He was. The "seed" was beginning to take root in their hearts as well. They came out to see and hear Jesus for themselves. Hearing His words, many of them believed. The harvest was ripe, and Jesus gathered it in.

Jesus was clearly not instructing them to be exclusive in their harvest gathering, but inclusive! In fact, Jesus had gone out of His way to bring the "good news" to these "outcasts." The Word says, *And he must needs* (had to) *go through Samaria.* (John 4:4) The verb *had to* (δει', *dei*) can be interpreted as *a logical necessity*, but it was not a geographical necessity for Jesus to travel through Samaria. The normal route the Jews would take—the Transjordan route—ran up the east side of the Jordan River.[7] This would have been a far easier route to Jerusalem than over the mountains of Samaria. Had Jesus taken the easier route, He would have missed His appointed meeting with this little woman in the town of Sychar. Her life would have continued its downward spiral, and the people of Sychar would not have heard the "good news."

Chance does not rule our lives when we follow the leading of God's Spirit. If you look at the way John typically uses the verb *dei* in his gospel, it involves God's will or plan (3:7, 3:14, 3:30, 4:4, 4:20, 4:24, 9:4, 10:16, 12:34, 20:9).[8] It was neither by chance nor out of necessity that Jesus went to Samaria. It was simply part of God's plan to gather in **all** of His harvest.[9]

Jesus' statement was directed at the fields of grain. When the wheat is ripe, the grain is white and therefore ready for harvesting.

SOME ROOT MEANINGS OF THE WORD WHITE:

It is worth noting that the term *white to harvest* does not occur anywhere else in the Word. If Jesus intended this to be a guiding principle in the expansion of the Kingdom of God—if He was giving the disciples a "White" priority for their evangelistic outreach—He would have expanded upon this term, as He did on other key facets of our faith.

Let's go to the scriptures and see how the word *white* is used there. "Vine's Expository Dictionary" tells us that the Greek word *leukos* is one of the words that is translated as *white*.[10] It is from this word that we get the word leukocyte—a white blood cell that is primarily involved in cleansing the blood of harmful bacteria that invade the body. What we see in the natural has a parallel in the spiritual. One of the key uses of the word *white* in the scriptures is in reference to cleansing of sin. For example, God's invitation in Isaiah 1:18 for the Israelites to come to Him for cleansing of their wicked ways:

Come, let's consider your options," says the LORD.
"Though your sins have stained you like the color red,
you can become white like snow;

though they are as easy to see as the color scarlet,
you can become white like wool."(Isaiah 1:18 The NET Bible)
The phrase, *become white like snow*, is not referring to the color of
the peoples' skin, but rather to their needed purification from sin. The
translators of the New English Text version of the Bible note that the
imperfects in this verse *"...must be translated as modal (indicating
capability or possibility) to bring out the conditional nature of
the offer. This purification will only occur if the people repent
and change their ways."* [11] God is not concerned about the color of
our skin; He's concerned about the presence of sin in our lives. Like
the leukocytes that course through our blood stream, searching for
harmful microbes, God is ever-vigilant to make us aware of the things
that invade our heart; and He is ever-faithful to call us to repentance
and cleansing.

This verse from Isaiah does not imply that God simply covers over
our sins. Rather, it speaks of God removing our sin and replacing our
old thought patterns, our former *modus operandi*, with an ethical
purity that reflects His nature. God is saying, *"Your sins, that are
now as obvious as the color red, will be washed away and the
ones who are sinful will be transformed."* [12]

God's statement here is revolutionary if you look at it in context. In the
verses prior to verse 18, God was telling the Israelites that He'd had
more than enough of their burnt offerings. He says emphatically that
He will not even hear their prayers as long as they continue in sin:

*And when ye spread forth your hands, I will hide mine eyes
from you: yea, when ye make many prayers, I will not hear:
your hands are full of blood.* (Isaiah 1:15)

The import of what God said through the prophet Isaiah is lost if we
do not remember that under the Old Covenant sacrifice was the only
means by which forgiveness for sin was granted. Had the Israelites
had ears to hear, they would have heard God telling them of a new
way to obtain both forgiveness of sin and the removal of the roots
from which sin "grows." He was calling them to a new way of life, to
God-directed transformation. He was exhorting them to cease doing
evil and to learn to do good.

Wash you, make you clean; put away the evil of your doings from before mine eyes; cease to do evil; [17]Learn to do well; seek judgment, relieve the oppressed, judge the fatherless, plead for the widow. (Isaiah 1:16-17)

"Come to Me," God was saying. *"Let's talk this thing over. Your sins are so obvious that anyone can see what you are doing, just as anyone can see the blood of the sacrificial animals. Come to Me and learn to do right."*

Again and again, throughout the scriptures, when the word *white* is used in relationship to spiritual matters, it is in reference to the need for purification from sin. There are no racial overtones attached to this word, and we bring division and hurt to the body of Christ when we add them.

ADDITIONAL USES OF WHITE IN THE SCRIPTURES:

Leukos, white, is used as an adjective in reference to clothing in Matthew 17:2; 28:3; Mark 9:3; 16:5; Luke 9:29; John 20:12; Acts 1:10.[13] In some instances, *white* in this sense refers to the brightness of the clothing. For example, in Matthew 17:1-2 where Jesus was on the Mount of Transfiguration:

And after six days Jesus taketh Peter, James, and John his brother, and bringeth them up into an high mountain apart, [2]And was transfigured before them: and his face did shine as the sun, and his raiment was white as the light.

In other instances, *leukos* is used symbolically. We see this in Rev. 3:4, 5, 18; 4:4; 6:11; 7:9, 13;19:14 (2nd part)[14] In Rev. 3, Jesus is speaking of the saints who will walk with Him in glory:

Thou hast a few names even in Sardis which have not defiled their garments; and they shall walk with me in white: for they are worthy. [5]He that overcometh, the same shall be clothed in white raiment; and I will not blot his name out of the book of life, but I will confess his name before my Father, and before his angels. (Rev. 3:4,5)

Note that white has no reference to the skin color of the saints, but only to the robe of righteousness Jesus gives to each person who comes to Him. The word *leukos,* then, is not symbolic of any superiority inherent in man or earned by the works man accomplishes. Rather it refers to an election in Christ, made sure by a life lived to God's glory.

Leukos is also used symbolically in the 18th verse of this chapter:

> *I counsel thee to buy of me gold tried in the fire, that thou mayest be rich; and white raiment, that thou mayest be clothed, and* that *the shame of thy nakedness do not appear; and anoint thine eyes with eyesalve, that thou mayest see.* (Rev. 3:13)

O' that we might anoint our eyes with eyesalve that we might look not upon the skin, but upon the hearts of our brothers- and sisters-in-Christ and see Jesus seated upon the throne of each heart—the same Jesus that is seated upon the throne of our heart.

Leukos is also used in Revelation 2:17 where Jesus is speaking of the special delight He has in overcomers. To those who overcome, who continue to walk steadfast in their faith in Him, He will give a white stone upon which is written a new name.

> *The one who has an ear had better hear what the Spirit says to the churches. To the one who conquers, I will give him some of the hidden manna, and I will give him a white stone, and on that stone will be written a new name that no one can understand except the one who receives it.'* (Rev. 2:17, The NET Bible)

No racial significance is attached to this white stone. Its significance lies solely in Jesus' delight in and love for those who overcome by the word of their testimony and by the blood of the Lamb. (Rev. 12:11)

Leukaino is the verb form that is translated as *white*, meaning *to whiten or to make white.*[15] We see it used figuratively in Revelation 7:14.

> [13] *Then one of the elders asked me, "These dressed in long white robes—who are they and where have they come from?"* [14] *So I said to him, "My lord, you know the answer." Then he said to me, "These are the ones who have come out of the great tribulation. They have washed their robes and made*

them white in the blood of the Lamb! (Rev. 7:13-14, The NET Bible)

The purity we seek as believers lies not in our race, as the racial supremacists believe, but in the power of the poured-out blood of the Lamb.

The Greek word *koniao* means *"to whiten, whitewash."* It is derived from *konia*, which means "Durst, lime" and refers to the "paint" used on tombs. [16] Jesus used this word in His terse comments to the "lawyers" and Pharisees of His day:

> [27] *"Woe to you, experts in the law and you Pharisees, hypocrites! You are like whitewashed tombs that look beautiful on the outside but inside are full of the bones of the dead and of everything unclean. [28] In the same way, on the outside you look righteous to people, but inside you are full of hypocrisy and lawlessness.* (Mat. 23:27, The NET Bible)

The word *white*, in this case, is referring to a covering for that which is dead. Remember Miriam? She was turned white with leprosy—a disease which brought death—because of her rebellion against Moses. Neither of these are very flattering usages of the word *white*.

DICTIONARY DEFINITIONS OF WHITE AND BLACK:

We can gain further insight into God's view of the Black and White races by looking at the dictionary definitions of these words. White is defined as *"an achromatic color of maximum lightness, the complement or antagonist of black, the other extreme of the neutral gray series. Although typically a response to maximum stimulation (of the retina), **white appears always to depend upon contrast."** [17] Black is defined as *"an achromatic color value of minimum lightness or maximum darkness; one extreme of the neutral gray series, the opposite being white. Although strictly a response to zero stimulation of the retina, **the perception of black appears to depend on contrast with surrounding color stimuli."** [18]

An interesting fact emerges from these definitions: both white and black are dependant upon contrast to reach their highest expression. There is a richness in both of these colors that does not become evident without the presence of other colors. The same is true in the body of Christ. The highest expression the body of Christ can present to the world occurs when we dare to cross cultural barriers and walk as one in Christ.

Do we have to eliminate all of the "White" churches, "Black" churches, or the other ethnic churches that are flourishing in this land? No, but we do need to tear down the walls that divide us, that keep us from worshipping together and working together for the advancement of the kingdom of God.

A final definition of light that we need to consider comes to us from our physicist friends. These scientists tell us that objects that appear *white* or *colorless* are in fact reflecting back to our eyes all the colors of the rainbow! On the other hand, objects that appear *black* or *colored* are not reflecting any of the colors of light back to our eyes! Just goes to show that things aren't always what they appear to be.

THE LIGHT OF THE WORLD:

Jesus said, *"I am the light of the world."* Revelation 21:22-23 speaks of the glory of God lighting the new Jerusalem. Any child with a prism in his hands can show us that light contains all of the colors of the rainbow. There is a spiritual truth that is evident in this observation about light: those of every color are included in Christ! In Him, we are joined together, fashioned into one dwelling place, one holy temple.

That statement shouldn't surprise anyone. After all, Jesus told us that *"...God so loved the world that He gave His only beggotten Son that whosoever believes on Him might not perish, but have eternal life."* (John 3:16) This and other passages affirm God's intent to make His house available for all who would come—all races, all nationalities; none preferred, none excluded. If our traditions run contrary to God's desire to have a harmonious, glorious, "blended" family, we need to examine the "truths" we are accepting as fact in the light of the Word of God.

SOURCES OF BIBLICAL MISINTERPRETATION:

What are some of the sources of biblical misinterpretation? Certainly there have been many instances of people deliberately distorting the message of the scriptures to suit their own purposes. Hitler's persuasive rhetoric convinced countless Germans that it was necessary to exterminate their fellow citizens simply because they were Jews or were guilty of harboring Jews. Gradually others—handicapped adults, Gypsies, Jehovah's Witnesses, etc.—were added to his list of "untouchables." Eventually, even little children, who were mentally handicapped, were targets of his blanket extermination policies.

It's interesting. Hiltler's goal was the same as God's, i.e., to establish a perfect race. The only problem was Hitler was looking on the exterior, while God considers only what is on the interior, in the heart. Hitler chose to use extermination to accomplish his goal; God uses transformation. Hitler's method uplifted one race; God's method uplifts all races, fashioning them into one family, one people, one nation—a supernatural race.

Perhaps the key source of biblical misinterpretation, however, is a bad hermeneutic—an inaccurate interpretation of God's word. The proper interpretation of a passage of scripture requires more than an accurate translation of that passage from the original language in which it was written. We must also attempt to learn as much as we can about the author of a given text and the characteristics of the society in which he lived. God's message to His people is always relevant to what is going on in their lives and/or in the life of the community or nation in which they are living. We need an understanding of the cultural setting and the historical circumstances in which the author was living to be able to understand more fully what God was zeroing in on when He inspired him to write a particular passage. For instance, the temple prostitutes in Corinth commonly had their hair cut short. It was reasonable for Paul to exhort Christian women to keep their hair long to avoid any connection between them and their less-than-noble "sisters".

We can't exclude demonic sources of error. Paul warned us about preaching a different gospel even though it comes to us by angels of light. Just because something comes to us from the spiritual realm, it does not mean that it is from God. We must test the spirits.

EFFECTS OF BIBLICAL MISINTERPRETATION:

We must guard against biblical misinterpretation for several reasons:

It distorts our understanding of God. The Word has been given to reveal the Father. It is intended to given us understanding of His character, His will, His ways. If we misinterpret God's Word, we will misrepresent His desires for and directives to His Church.

It deters us from fulfilling His purpose. To the degree that our understanding of God is flawed, our ability to know His will in any particular situation will be impaired. The works we do may be good by default, but they still may not be the works God planned for us to do. Without the clear guidance of the Holy Spirit, there remains the possibility that the works we do will be evil—actually causing harm rather than good to ourselves or others.

It divides us from others who do not agree with our interpretation of the Word. Regardless of the basis for the division, whether it is racism or any other misinterpretation of God's Word, error separates those God has called as co-heirs in Christ. Every military officer knows the effectiveness of a *"divide and conquer"* strategy. It certainly has caused its share of havoc in the Church.

In the case of racism, **it blinds us to the infinite worth each person has in the eyes of God.** How can we convince the lost of other races that God loves them and highly esteems them, if we do not do so ourselves? How many have rejected Christ simply because the person witnessing to them did not fully accept them?

John spoke very effectively to this last point in I John 2:9-11, when he said,

> *He that saith he is in the light, and hateth his brother, is in darkness even until now. [10]He that loveth his brother abideth in the light, and there is none occasion of stumbling in him. [11]But he that hateth his brother is in darkness, and walketh in darkness, and knoweth not whither he goeth, because that darkness hath blinded his eyes.*

Often racism's influence upon our attitudes and actions toward others is so subtle that we would be indignant if anyone labeled them hate. But when we experience racism first hand, the veil of tradition, which makes these "social realties" seem acceptable, is quickly stripped off. Racism, like any other form of hate, will cause us to stumble in our walk with Christ. For when we practice racism or tolerate it in any form, we fall short of the unconditional love God calls us to have for one another.

End Notes:

[1-3] *The NET Bible: Study Notes*, (Dallas, TX: Biblical Studies Press) 1998.

[4] *The American Heritage Dictionary, Second College Edition*, Houghton Mifflin Company, Boston, 1985, pg. 474

[5] Spiros Zodhiates, Executive Editor; Warren Baker, Assistant Editor; Joel Kletzing, Assistant Editor, *The Hebrew and Chaldee Dictionary of The Hebrew-Greek Key Study Bible: NSBA Edition*, AMG Publishers, Chattanooga, TN 37422, 1977, pg. 84

[6] *The American Heritage Dictionary*, Ibid, pg. 647.

[7-9] *The NET Bible*, Ibid.

[10] Merril F. Unger and William White, Jr., Editors, *Vine's Complete Expository Dictionary of Old and New Testament Words*, Thomas Nelson Publishers, New York, 1985, pg. 674

[11-12] *The NET Bible*, Ibid.

[13-16] Unger and White, Ibid.

[17] *The American Heritage Dictionary*, Ibid, pg. 1378

[18] Ibid, pg 183.

Chapter 10: Black Theology Vs. White Theology

As previously stated, history is usually written in favor of those who are writing it. This appears to be true when we look at how various writers have interpreted the Word over the years. Such cultural bias can easily fashion the Word of God into an instrument that divides rather than unifies the body of Christ. Two examples of this are "White Theology" and "Black Theology".

The term "White Theology" denotes a theology written in favor of the Caucasian race. It is written with an exclusivity that alludes to the racial supremacy of Anglo-Saxons. The term "Black Theology" must, no doubt, mean exactly the opposite, or a theology written in favor of people of Color, alluding to their racial supremacy.

To explain this concept more fully, first let us define Theology. Theology can be defined as *that which is thought and said concerning God.* True theology is given by the bible itself. The bible then is a revelation of God in human terms.

In addition to the theology presented in the bible, there is a theology that is developed within the church. This theology develops as man seeks to understand the truths contained in God's word. It is essential that the Church carefully assess what it embraces as its theology. Otherwise there is a danger that our theology will not conform to biblical norms.

Over the centuries the various humanistic approaches to Biblical truths have indeed distorted the message presented in the bible, creating a need for an accurate apologetic. The dictionary defines apologetics as *"The branch of theology that is concerned with defending or proving Christian doctrines. 2. Formal argumentation in defense of something, such as a position or system."*
[1] It is necessary to develop an accurate apologetic because our theology shapes our understanding of God and provides a standard for relating to our fellow man.

RELEVANT TO EVERY BELIEVER:

Sometimes we view theology as an esoteric subject, one with which only the ultra-scholarly need be concerned. In reality, theology is an issue which should command the attention of all who submit to the doctrines and teachings it produces. This becomes evident when you study the development of theology throughout the history of the Church.

Henry Clarence Thiessen, in his book *Introductory Lectures in Systematic Theology*, addresses the cause and effect relationship between the theology that a group of believers espouses and the nature of the religion they practice. Thiessen says that *"...in theology a man organizes his thoughts concerning God and the universe, and in religion **he expresses in attitudes and actions** the effects these thoughts have produced in him."* [2] We can see from this statement that the theology we embrace has a profound influence on us, our church or denomination, and ultimately upon society itself.

Theology organizes the facts that we accept as true about God and His relationship to all of His Creation. Theology shapes the character of the religion we practice, which is to say, it dramatically influences the attitudes and actions that typify our relationship with God and with others, both within the church and within the world in general. Our theology, therefore, defines our understanding of God, our daily walk with Christ, and our relationship with those around us. It is imperative, therefore, that we have a basic understanding of the theology we are embracing when we join ourselves to any denomination, local congregation, or other organization in which our faith plays a key role. [3]

THE DIVISIONS OF THEOLOGY:

Four common divisions of the field of Theology are as follows:

> Exegetical Theology
> Historical Theology
> Systematic Theology
> Practical Theology. [4]

Exegetical Theology concerns the study of the Sacred Text (the original manuscripts). A number of disciplines are required to preserve the message contained in these texts and still present it in a way that makes its message relevant to us today. A knowledge of biblical languages, biblical archeology, and biblical hermeneutics is essential. A study of the socio-political climate in which each text was written, a knowledge of manners and customs typical of the people to whom a particular portion of the text was written gives greater insight to basic truths it is intended to convey. The theologian must also consider the character of each writer and the historical context in which he ministered. [5]

Historical Theology investigates the history of God's people as it is recorded in the Bible and the history of the Church since the time of Christ. It addresses the origin of true religion, its development, and its growth throughout the ages. It considers the branches of the Church that have developed and the basic doctrines and practices each branch has embraced. This requires a study of Church History, the History of Missions, Biblical History, and the History of Creeds, Doctrines, and Confessions of the Church. [6]

Systematic Theology organizes the information gathered by the Exegetical and Historical theologians and organizes it in a logical order, addressing each facet of our faith. It is important to remember that there is an intrinsic difference between the contributions of Exegetical and Historical Theology. The former provides the only real and infallible source information, but the latter provides a perspective of the progressive development of the Church's understanding of the basic doctrines of the faith. This perspective enhances understanding of the Biblical revelation. [7]

Systematic Theology often encompasses Dogmatic Theology today. Strictly speaking, Dogmatic Theology entails *"...the systematization and defense of the doctrines expressed in the symbols of the Church."* [8]

Practical Theology entails the application of what is learned in Exegetical, Historical, and Systematic Theology to practical Christian living. Preparation for this field requires a study of Homiletics, Church

Organization and Administration, Christian Education, Missions, Worship, and Liturgics. [9]

THE HISTORICAL DEVELOPMENT OF THEOLOGY:

There are four main historical groupings in theology: the Patristic, the Scholastic, the Reformed, and the Modern. The **Patristic** grouping refers to the portion of the Church's history when the teachings and writings of the fathers of the early Christian church served as a norm for the development of doctrines and practices and as a guide for everyday Christian living.

Even in the early Church there was a need to ensure that error did not distort the basic gospel message. Within the Scriptures themselves we see many occasions where the writers would present basic truths in a way that would identify and correct erroneous practices and beliefs. For instance, Paul's letter to the Galatians, who were yielding to the Judiazers' demands that they submit to circumcision. *"Otherwise,"* the Judiazers insisted, *"you cannot be saved."* While Paul did not dispute the importance of circumcision to the Jews, he left no doubt that salvation is available on the basis of the shed blood of Christ alone. Nothing needs to be or can be added to the finished work of Christ.

The dominance of the Patristic "school of theology" extended into the second century. In 1050, followers of the **Scholastic** "school of theology" began to replace the Church fathers as the main guardians of biblical truth. One of the causes for the development of Scholasticism was the rediscovery of—or reemphasis upon—the philosophy of Aristotle. Men such as Alexander of Hales embraced Aristotle's teachings and attempted to relate them to theology. Under Scholasticism, theology was addressed from a philosophical perspective rather than from a biblical perspective. One of the greatest challenges for Scholastics was to harmonize the new discoveries of science with the basic tenants of our faith. To do this, they had to reconcile Aristotle's general natural philosophy, which is arrived at by rational processes, with the theology that is revealed in the Bible and which must be accepted by faith. [10]

Scholasticism was embraced by the mendicant orders of the Roman Catholic Church. Thomas Aquinas was perhaps the greatest of all the

Scholastics. The expansion of the university system accelerated the growth of the Scholastic movement. Under its influence, the universities began to center their curriculum around the study of theology, arrived at through the use of logic and reason. The University of Paris became one of the leading centers of Scholasticism. [11]

Earle E. Cairns, the author of *Christianity Through the Centuries: A History of the Christian Church,* said *"...Scholastics were not so much seeking truth as they were trying rationally to organize a body of accepted truth so that truth, whether it came by faith from revelation or by reason from philosophy, might be a harmonious whole."* [12] Harmony of thinking in the political, ecclesiastical, and intellectual realms was of prime importance in the medieval era. This undergirded the power of the Roman Catholic Church, because it placed an emphasis on the institution rather than on the individual. For example, Aquinas taught that the sacraments were the only channel of grace. This strengthened the hold of the Roman Catholic Church on individuals, because it meant that there was no salvation apart from the sacraments that were dispensed by the hierarchy of the church. [13]

The oppression, which this kind of teaching fostered, was one of the factors that caused reformers to challenge Rome's power. Had the leadership of the Roman Catholic Church responded positively to requests of sincere men, like Wycliffe and Hus, for needed reforms, change might have come without division. [14]

Many factors contributed to the development of the Reformed "school of theology." The abuses of the Roman Catholic Church gave rise to a desire to bring the doctrines and practices of the Church back to the purity of the Christianity described in the New Testament. Dramatic changes in the political, economic, intellectual, and religious character of medieval society, that began to take place in 1500, made the Protestant Reformation inevitable. [15]

MODERN THEOLOGY:

In this brief overview of the first three historical periods of theology, a gradual shift is evident in the way the church leaders regarded the Word of God. Most of the earliest Church fathers (disciples) had been with Jesus during the time of His earthly ministry. They saw Him walk on the water, cleanse the lepers, raise the dead, cast out devils, and feed the multitudes. Following Jesus' crucifixion and resurrection, this mantle and the power to do these works was passed on to the New Testament Church. Those who believed in Jesus inherited what Jesus purchased on Calvary. It was something new, something fresh, something different.

As a result, the early Church fathers' understanding of the Word of God was built on their personal experience with Jesus, what He had taught and done, and what they themselves had done by the power of His Spirit. Their doctrine, therefore, was built on nothing less than their experiences with Jesus—the revealed Word of God—and the penned Word of God that had been breathed out by the inspiration of God on the writers of the Old Testament. This same inspiration of God guided those who wrote the New Testament, providing instruction in doctrine, pastoral care, and just simple, Christian holy living.

The foundation of belief was very simple in those early years of the Church. The 66 books of the bible provided an authoritative source for answers to any questions that might arise. If you had a question, God had the answer. If you were confused, you could rest in the assurance that God is not the author of confusion. He is the author and finisher of our faith, and if we hear His Word and adhere to it, it is a faith-builder. As it builds faith in us, we can understand what God is saying. Even more important, we come into an understanding that God said what He meant and meant what He said. The walk of faith was a very simplified thing.

As the Church expanded and began to draw in the whole world, the world began to come into the church structure, bringing questions with them. This was especially true of those who came from other nations, other cultures, and other belief systems. It was no longer enough to just listen to the voice of the Church fathers anymore.

Theology became very scholastic at that point. It became more exegetical than historical. Theologians began a more in-depth interpretation of the Word of God from the original language. Based on what they learned, they began to write their doctrines and dogmas, saying, *"This is what I believe, and this is the way I understand the*

Word of God." As a result, believers divided up into different theological camps.

As time marched on, more and more people were drawn into the Church, bringing with them more questions about fundamental beliefs and doctrines established by previous generations. As people debated various issues, reforms came in their understanding of the Word. Some theologians began to question accepted interpretations of the Word and put forward their own doctrines and teachings. So the splits and divisions began in the Church. The foundation became more and more divided. The answers weren't so simple anymore— or at least not so simply believed.

By the time of the 20th century, man became much more advanced in respect to his technological development, and the evangelization of the world continued to draw more and more people into the Church. People were becoming more technical in nature, more educated, more intellectual, and they had more questions regarding faith in God. People began to question the basic tenants of the Christian faith, demanding more apologetics and desiring a greater "free will" in drawing their own conclusions.

The era of modern theology was upon us. People were no longer quick to simply believe. Theologians began to say, *"We have to change some of our methodology. We can't be as dogmatic as we used to be. We can't just say, 'God said it, and that's it!', and just go with it and not question it. We need to change our methodologies to meet the needs of modern man."* As a result, a little more diluting—a little more watering down, if you will—of the basic teachings of the Word took place.

Now we have moved through that modern era, and there is really a fifth era of theology. We've moved into a whole new century, a new millennium, and we are now in the post-modern theological era. There are more questions; there are more ideas. There are more questions concerning abortion, premarital sex, common law marriage, situation ethics, and even the validity of the Word of God itself. Many believers in the new generation refuse to be called fundamentalists, and they refute the inerrancy of the Bible. There's more new age thought and different methodologies.

We are living in a time when people just really don't know what they believe, in a time when we're allowed to believe anything we want to believe. No one wants to be put in a box. No one wants to adhere to anything. We want to eliminate dogmatism or any dogmatic statement of belief. We want to make an apologetic for what is said in God's Word, saying, *"There's no doubt what the Word says, but we want to make it more palatable for the world."* So we start to blend all of these worldly things into the Church, and the nature of our theology begins to change.

The democratic system has done a lot to erode the strength of the Church. We have gone from a theocratic system where God's Word was the foundation of the truth that was to guide peoples' lives, and we have come down to this democratic system where people are saying, *"You have the freedom to believe and do whatever you want to believe and do."* But I'm telling you, there is a danger in that. We want to reach the world, but we do not want our methodologies to become so pragmatic in nature that we start leaning more toward cause and effect and what we can do to blend the world into the Church instead of standing firm on the foundation of holiness that God has laid down for us.

We may differ in the details of our theologies, but we cannot compromise the holiness of God and the fundamental truths that are presented in His Word.

Guarding Against Heresy:
If we do not have a correct revelation of God's word, our theology will be built around error. This is how heresies develop. Because man is imperfect, heresies have plagued the Church from its inception. Often these heresies have been based on racial prejudice. It was not uncommon for Jews, who were new converts to Christianity, to want to retain the requirements of the Law and to force all Gentile converts to conform to them as well. The bible records many confrontations on this issue. Even Peter did not understand that God was willing to accept the Gentiles "just as they were" until he had his "housetop experience" and subsequently saw the Holy Spirit fall on all the Gentile folks who had gathered at Cornelius' house. When Cornelius greeted Peter, the Word says he *...fell down at his feet, and wor-*

shipped him ²⁶*But Peter took him up, saying, Stand up; I myself also am a man.* (Acts 1:25-26) Today we might say, *"...I am a man, just like you."*

When Peter addressed those who gathered at Cornelius' house, he immediately tackled the chief issue that divided them—race. Peter, with his characteristic boldness/bluntness, said, *"Ye know how that it is an unlawful thing for a man that is a Jew to keep company, or come unto one of another nation; but God hath shewed me that I should not call any man common or unclean."* (Acts 10:28-29) This was an astounding statement for a Jew to make. It contradicted the teachings—the biblical misinterpretations and old wives' tales—that had been "canonized" in Jewish tradition for generations.

Instead of glossing over the dramatic revelation God had given him concerning the races, Peter allowed it to form the heart of his message that day. As he continued speaking, he said, *"Of a truth I perceive that God is no respecter of persons:* ³⁵*But in every nation he that feareth him, and worketh righteousness, is accepted with him* (Acts 10:34-35)."

Peter's message was brief by today's standards, but it got results! When Peter said, *"To him give all the prophets witness, that through his name whosoever believeth in him shall receive remission of sins,"* (Acts 10:43) the Holy Spirit came upon **all** who were listening.

The circumcised believers who had accompanied Peter were amazed! You can almost hear them thinking, *"They're never going to believe this when we get back to Jerusalem! The Holy Spirit, poured out on the Gentiles!?"*

Peter's companions could not deny what they were witnessing though; *"...for they heard them speak with tongues, and magnify God* (Acts 10:46)" The evidence of God's grace being poured out on the Gentiles broke down the barriers which racial prejudice and resentment had created between the Jews and the members of the Roman occupation.

Peter ended the service that day by asking, *"Can any man forbid water, that these should not be baptized, which have received the Holy Ghost as well as we?* (Acts 10:48)" How could his companions object? God had clearly accepted the Gentiles into His family!

Peter still had some explaining to do when he got back to Jerusalem. Some of the party of the Pharisees insisted that Gentile converts must be circumcised and required to obey the law of Moses. (Acts 15:5) Peter's response was simple:

> *And God, which knoweth the hearts, bare them witness, giving them the Holy Ghost, even as he did unto us; ⁹And put no difference between us and them, purifying their hearts by faith. ¹⁰Now therefore why tempt ye God, to put a yoke upon the neck of the disciples, which neither our fathers nor we were able to bear? ¹¹But we believe that through the grace of the Lord Jesus Christ we shall be saved, even as they.* (Acts 15:8-11)

Peter's words brought understanding. His listeners saw that it is on the basis of what people allow God to do in their hearts that they are saved, not on the basis of circumcision or any other outward act or work of man. Likewise, they saw that it is not on the basis of race that believers are accepted into God's family. Race always has to bow to the **g-race** of God.

If Peter had not acted upon the revelation God gave him on the rooftop, Cornelius and all of those gathered in his house would have been denied an opportunity to accept Jesus. Had Peter yielded to the demands of the Pharisees, unnecessary requirements and restrictions would have been placed upon Gentile converts, and error (heresy) would have come into the teaching and doctrines of the Church. The stand Peter took was not an easy one. Undoubtedly a few believers left the Church because "those people" were allowed to join. Courage is sometimes necessary to preserve the purity of the gospel message.

CUSHITE THEOLOGY:
Race is a key area where misunderstanding and serious error has come into the teachings and doctrines of the Church. For years, those of European descent preached a White gospel. The fruit of this heresy was the oppression of the other races by many Whites.

In recent years, some of our African-American brothers and sisters have embraced their own version of racially-based doctrine. The Cushite Theology is one example of this. Followers of this theology insist that the Church has moved into a new era, that it is now time for the descendants of Ham—the Cushites—to exercise dominion. They advocate a reversal or inversion of racial discrimination and oppression, such as what was imposed upon their ancestors by the ancestors of today's Whites. But while many may seek to reverse discrimination, we, as Christians, must seek to abolish it. Two wrongs will not balance the scales of justice; they will only add to the injustice already present within our society.

The scriptural basis given for Cushite Theology is found in II Samuel 18. This chapter records the death of Absalom in his attempt to prevent David's return to reign in Jerusalem. Despite Absalom's treachery, David had asked his men to spare Absalom's life, but Joab and his men ignored David's request. News of Absalom's death had to be taken to King David. The main premises of Cushite theology rests upon the messengers who bore this news, so let's take a look at the passage that recounts this event:

> *19Then said Ahimaaz the son of Zadok, Let me now run, and bear the king tidings, how that the LORD hath avenged him of his enemies. 20And Joab said unto him, Thou shalt not bear tidings this day, but thou shalt bear tidings another day: but this day thou shalt bear no tidings, because the king's son is dead. 21Then said Joab to Cushi, Go tell the king what thou hast seen. And Cushi bowed himself unto Joab, and ran. 22Then said Ahimaaz the son of Zadok yet again to Joab, But howsoever, let me, I pray thee, also run after Cushi. And Joab said, Wherefore wilt thou run, my son, seeing that thou hast no tidings ready? 23But howsoever,* said he, *let me run. And he said unto him, Run. Then Ahimaaz ran by the way of the plain, and overran Cushi.* (II Samuel 18:19-23)

Ahimaaz started later, but he outran the Cushite. Some commentators in the past suggested that this was due to a superior intellect possessed by the Hebrew. Certainly there is no scriptural basis for assuming that was the case. However, I believe this "race" between Ahimaaz and Cushi can serve as a type or shadow of one race outpacing another simply because they have embraced the God of Israel, Elohim, rather than on the basis of any greater intrinsic worth of their race over all other races.

The best case in point is how the Japhetites progressed beyond the other races and people of color. The Japhetites settled in the northern sections of the world, populating the various nations of Europe, Eastern Europe, and Russia. They were a fierce and very barbaric people. When the Anglo-Saxons were converted to Christianity from their barbaric ways, they began to prosper beyond any other people's progress. This prosperity did not come because of any innate advantage, either psychologically or physiologically, inherent in the Japhetites, but only because they received Jesus Christ as Lord and Savior. When they did, the promises to Abraham immediately became theirs. (This is covered in more depth in another chapter.)

This is not to say that the descendants of Shem and Ham did not develop great kingdoms as well. They did. The history of mankind records the rise and fall of many great kingdoms, for example the kingdoms of the Babylonians, the Romans, the Grecians, and the Egyptians. Each of these kingdoms extended over much or all of the known world at that time—at least over the portion that was known to them. Yet what remains of these kingdoms today? None of them are dominant players in the present global order. All that remains of their former glory are archeological remains that attract thousands of tourists each year.

Why did each of these powerful kingdoms fall? Of the four, only the Grecians were not primarily a militarily oriented people. Alexander the Great did succeed in world conquest from 315 to 330 BC, but he would die at 33 years of age.

The influence of the Greeks (known as "the Fathers of Democracy") is still evident in drama, the sciences, philosophy and the arts, but they did not embrace the gospel message when it came to them. Remember Paul standing on the Areopagus—the Hill of Mars meeting place—proclaiming the nature of the unknown God the Greeks had been worshiping along with all of their other gods? The majority of the

Greeks refused to abandon their many, traditional gods and serve God alone. Instead the Graeco philosophies and beliefs would continue to out distance the teachings of Christianity and belief in Jesus. In doing so, the Greeks excluded themselves from the promises that were to come to all the descendants of Abraham, and their empire never regained the prominence it had once had.

The Egyptians ruled over vast kingdoms for centuries. Their power enabled them to hold millions of God's people in bondage for 450 years, but when God heard the cries of His people and sent a deliverer to lead them back to the Promised Land, the gods the Egyptians worshiped could not prevent their exodus. The Egyptian Pharaoh had experienced the power of Moses' God Yahweh, yet they rejected Him. In doing so, they lost far more than the millions of slaves whom Moses led to freedom.

Like the Egyptians, the Romans enslaved those they conquered. The Grecians tried to tell the Romans that the people would prove more profitable to them if they gave them a measure of freedom and did not tax them too heavily, but the Romans did not listen. They imported countless slaves from among those they conquered—a policy which undermined the middle class Romans. How could the small shop keepers and businessmen compete with slave laborers? Rome's policies generated many of the slums of Europe. The Romans sought the council of soothsayers and false gods, and in the end ancient Rome fell. Moral decay from within and the attacks of the hordes of barbarians from without brought Rome to her knees. The great Roman dominators of the world never recovered. Certainly the wrath of God was upon them in retribution for the horrendous persecution of God's people which occurred under Caesar Nero.

The Babylonian Empire was perhaps the greatest of the ancient empires. Their rule extended over most of the known world. They built extensive road systems and aqueducts that still serve people today. The Babylonians exercised a much more benevolent rulership over those they conquered than their Romans counterparts did. As long as the people lived in peace with them and paid the reasonable taxes the Babylonians required, the occupation forces did not oppress them.

The Israelites were deported only because they repeatedly refused to comply with the Babylonians requirements.

Even though the Babylonians built a great empire, they never fully embraced the God of Israel. Nebachadnezzar did meet the God of Daniel as the fourth man in the fire (Daniel, chapter 3), and he did declare His glory, but Nebuchadnezzar's faith in Jehovah was short-lived. His pride in the kingdom he had established blinded him to the fact that God had allowed, even ordained, his success. God warned him in a dream that such pride would bring judgment, but Nebuchadnezzar ignored the warning.

Twelve months later, as Nebuchadnezzar was walking around his palace, when he said, *"Is not this great Babylon, that I have built for the house of the kingdom by the might of my power, and for the honour of my majesty?"* (Dan. 4:30) Whether Nebuchadnezzar realized it or not, God was listening when he said this. Even as Nebuchadnezzar was still speaking, a voice spoke from heaven, saying, *"...O king Nebuchadnezzar, to thee it is spoken; The kingdom is departed from thee."* (Dan. 4:31), and, as the dream had predicted, Nebuchadnezzar became as one of the beast of the field and was driven from the palace. He remained tethered to the stump of a tree for seven years until his mind was restored. At that point, he acknowledged God's eternal reign over all the earth, saying, *"...I blessed the most High, and I praised and honoured him that liveth for ever, whose dominion is an everlasting dominion, and his kingdom is from generation to generation."* (Dan. 4:34) He also acknowledged that God is able to abase those who walk in pride. (Dan. 4:37)

Nebuchadnezzar's son Belshazzar did not heed what had happened to his father and instead turned back to the worship of idols and desecrated the house of God. He threw a great feast at which he and his guests used the gold and silver vessels, which his father had taken from the temple in Jerusalem, to drink a toast to *"...the gods of gold, and of silver, of brass, of iron, of wood, and of stone."* (Dan. 5:5) Moments later, the hand of God, writing on the wall, spelled the end of Belshazzar's kingdom. He had inherited a great kingdom, but he had not embraced the God of Israel. As a result, both the kingdom and his life was taken from him. The Babylonian empire was taken over by the Medes and the Persians. Modern day Iraq and Bagdad are all that remains of this great world empire.

Similar accounts emerge from the histories of the kingdoms of Africa, although, because of Africa's geographical isolation from the other centers of population in the ancient world, we are less aware of the accomplishments of these powerful leaders. Our African-American brothers and sisters' desire to learn more about their African heritage has blessed the other races as well, because it has enriched our understanding of the great civilizations that developed in their ancestral homelands.

Even though great civilizations developed on the continent of Africa, idolatry predominately characterized their worship. The majority of ancient Africans failed to embrace the God of Israel, the God of Ham. This was true despite the conversion of the Ethiopia eunuch and Philip's missionary journey to Nubia (Sudan). This was long before the barbarians of Europe were tamed by the truth contained in the gospel message. Yet none of the nations of Africa rose to be global powers as did the kingdoms founded by the descendants of Japheth. Neither did the nations of Asia—and remember the apostle Thomas was sent to India to share the gospel. But let me say again, the dominance of the Japhetites was not due to their greater intrinsic worth; it was due to the fact that they embraced Jesus as Savior and Lord.

Students of history can readily tell you that some of the kingdoms that the Japhetites built also fell. Does that invalidate the hypotheses that accepting Jesus as Savior and Lord causes a people to prosper? No, it doesn't. The key is accepting Jesus as both Savior and Lord. It is not sufficient to accept the salvation Jesus provides and not embrace the life-style He lived. His sinless life enabled Him to become our Savior. His salvation enables us to lead a life that glorifies Him. Will we ever fail? Will we ever sin? Yes, but when we do, we have an advocate with the Father, who is able to understand our weaknesses and who is willing to forgive our sin and cleanse us of all unrighteousness.

It is God's grace working in a people that makes them great. Nothing else. If the Cushites would be great, they must run the race Jesus puts before them; and that race must be defined and guided by the Word of God. Just as I do not believe that the Word of God validated the enslavement and oppression of the descendants of Cush, I do not believe that it validates a redirection of those grievous excesses against the descendants of Japheth. Pursuing such a goal, will accomplish only one thing ultimately: securing revenge for the atrocities the Cushites' ancestors endured. But God said, *"Vengeance is Mine..."*

In my humble opinion, pursuing something that God has staked out as His own is dangerous business. Doing so is not only dangerous, it is unproductive in the Kingdom of God. The world may embrace such a philosophy, having nothing to tell them that the course they are pursuing is wrong. They may succeed in building a temporary kingdom, as did the Egyptians, Grecians, Romans, and Babylonians, but it too will fall if it is not built on godly principles. One of the foundational principles that guides God's rule over His people is a policy of mercy toward those who have done nothing to merit mercy.

THE 10/40 WINDOW:

What was true of the ancient kingdoms is true of the various nations today. Those nations that embrace Jesus as Lord and Savior will stand the tests that come against them and in the end will prosper; and those that chose to serve other gods will not stand. That sounds harsh, but God has made a way for blessing to come to each of us. That way is Jesus. There is none other.

The truth of this statement is evident if you review just the recent history of nations where Buddhists, Hindus and followers of Islam or other religions make up the majority of the population. Many of these nations lie in what is called the 10/40 window. Within this 50° window covering Africa and Asia, less than 50% of the people have ever heard the gospel message. Christians living in these nations typically suffer great persecution. Is it a coincidence that this 10/40 window is also plagued by more poverty, natural disasters—famines, earthquakes, etc.—than any other region? Remember Jesus' answer to His disciples when they asked Him *"...what shall be the sign of thy coming, and of the end of the world?"* (Mat. 24:3)

⁴And Jesus answered and said unto them, Take heed that no man deceive you. ⁵For many shall come in my name, saying, I am Christ; and shall deceive many. ⁶And ye shall hear of wars and rumours of wars: see that ye be not troubled: for all these things must come to pass, but the end is not yet. ⁷For nation shall rise against nation, and kingdom against kingdom: and there shall be famines, and pestilences, and earthquakes, in divers places. (Matthew 24:4-7)

When liberation theologians cry out for justice for the oppressed, for relief of their suffering, they seek a good thing; but they must join that cry with a faithful proclamation of the sovereignty and saving power of Jesus Christ. For apart from Jesus, nothing we secure on earth will be lasting.

A HEART OF COMPASSION:

Every work that is done in the kingdom of God is judged by the fruit that it produces. In the case of Cushi and Ahimaaz's race, we need to look at the effect their message had on David as it is recorded in II Samuel 18.

²⁴And David sat between the two gates: and the watchman went up to the roof over the gate unto the wall, and lifted up his eyes, and looked, and behold a man running alone. ²⁵And the watchman cried, and told the king. And the king said, If he be alone, there is tidings in his mouth. And he came apace, and drew near. ²⁶And the watchman saw another man running: and the watchman called unto the porter, and said, Behold another man running alone. And the king said, He also bringeth tidings. ²⁷And the watchman said, Me thinketh the running of the foremost is like the running of Ahimaaz the son of Zadok. And the king said, He is a good man, and cometh with good tidings.

²⁸And Ahimaaz called, and said unto the king, All is well. And he fell down to the earth upon his face before the king, and said, Blessed be the LORD thy God, which hath delivered up the men that lifted up their hand against my lord the king. ²⁹And the king said, Is the young man Absalom safe? And Ahimaaz answered, When Joab sent the king's servant, and me *thy servant, I saw a great tumult, but I knew not what* it was. *³⁰And the king said* unto him, *Turn aside,* and *stand here. And he turned aside, and stood still.* (II Samuel 18: 24-30)

Ahimaaz was concerned about David's feelings. He knew that, regardless of all that Absalom had done, David still loved him greatly. He knew that David would be deeply grieved when he heard of Absalom's death. Out of his love for the king, Ahimaaz only gave part of the news.

Cushi, on the other hand, was apparently a slave. He had no affection or concern for the King. Who would expect him to? The message he brought was very different—

> *³¹And, behold, Cushi came; and Cushi said, Tidings, my lord the king: for the LORD hath avenged thee this day of all them that rose up against thee. ³²And the king said unto Cushi, Is the young man Absalom safe? And Cushi answered, The enemies of my lord the king, and all that rise against thee to do thee* hurt, be as that *young man is.* ***³³And the king was much moved, and went up to the chamber over the gate, and wept:*** *and as he went, thus he said, O my son Absalom, my son, my son Absalom! would God I had died for thee, O Absalom, my son, my son!* (II Samuel 18:19-33)

It was a fact that Cushi was bringing a message of truth, and it is possible that he took no thought concerning David's feelings. He readily spoke of Absalom's death. It was indeed the truth. However, the truth, purveyed in a manner void of compassion, can often have a very negative effect on the hearer.

I believe that we are living in a time that the absolute truth is a necessity. If we are going to see a united body and a non-racially biased church, we must teach, receive, and live God's truths. Yet the truth must be spoken with the guidelines that are evident in Galatians 6:1— *Brethren, if a man be overtaken in a fault, ye which are spiritual, restore such an one in the spirit of meekness; considering thyself, lest thou also be tempted.*

The truth must be spoken by those called and filled with the spirit, and it must be spoken in a spirit of gentleness and meekness. Then and only then will the gospel message of God's love reach the heart of both speaker and hearer—both White and those of Color—and have the impact that God has purposed in this age of unity.

A BASIS FOR RULERSHIP:

The key issue for advocates of a White Theology or a Black Theology is who has the right to dominion over all the other races. On the basis of II Samuel 18:18-33, the developers of the Cushite Theology say that the White man has had his chance to run—to exercise leadership in the Kingdom of God. They contend that now leadership—dominion—has passed to the Black man.

I do not really understand how they get that kind of concept from what is said in this passage. The only change of rulership that took place was that Absalom—the usurper of David's throne—had been put to death, and David—God's anointed king—had been returned to power. Neither Ahimaaz nor Cushi had been vested with any power, dominion, or authority. They were simply message bearers, and the message they had to carry was not the good news David wanted to hear. Furthermore, the Word does not indicate that David honored either Ahimaaz or Cushi for bringing him this message.

Perhaps Ahimaaz and Cushi expected to be honored. After all, the king's enemy was dead; the rebellion was ended. But the king's enemy was also the king's son. David had not withdrawn his love from Absalom. David's continuing love for his wayward son is a beautiful picture of God's unconditional love for each of us.

There is an inherent danger in taking a passage of scripture and stretching it to fit our personal or political agenda. We have seen how Whites did this to justify slavery and the Jim Crow laws that followed the Civil War years. It also gave support to the doctrine of Manifest Destiny—a philosophy which justified an unbridled expansionist policy adopted by our national government during our nation's early history. This philosophy brought error into the theology of the Church and negatively influenced America's missions outreach for decades. Considering the bitter fruit that grew out of slavery practices and Manifest Destiny, it is difficult to imagine why anyone would want to imitate them. If it was wrong when Whites followed these doctrines—and unquestionably it was—it will be wrong if Blacks adopt similar doctrines.

LOVE ONE ANOTHER:

The Cushite Theology or any other push to establish the supremacy of one race over another violates Jesus' basic, unchanging command to the Church: *"Beloved, love one another!"* Love perpetuates healing, restoration, wholeness. Racial supremacy, regardless of its hue, perpetuates hatred, pride, and oppression. Love establishes peace, while racial supremacy readily incites war. At "best," racial supremacy inspires prejudice, oppression, and verbal abuse of others.

One old adage is true—two wrongs don't make a right. No amount of apologies or acts of contrition will erase the wrongs that White racism have perpetrated upon the other races. Likewise, no amount of apologies or acts of contrition will erase the wounds Black racism will create if Cushite theology is embraced.

CULTURAL THEOLOGY:

Just as we do not want to repeat the errors of the past, making one race or culture dominate over all others, we also do not want to eliminate cultural differences. God created cultural diversity. Our race, our culture identity, is one of God's gifts to us. In God's hands, these gifts are a source of blessing.

It would be such a simple matter if printing an Afro-centric bible would really be the answer to racial equality. If depicting every character in the Bible as a Hamite would be the answer, how easy it would all be. However, if they were not all Hamites, then we would have done the same thing the Europeans did when they depicted them as all White.

We would then have to create a bible for all other races and nationalities to achieve some measure of equality in all of this. Red hair and freckled faces for the Irish, and slant eyes and yellow skin for our Oriental brothers, and so on. There would have to be hundreds of different versions of the bible, one for each of the world's races and cultures.

We must realize that God is spirit and that He is to be worshipped in spirit and in truth. He must appear as an <u>individual God</u> to <u>all</u> <u>men</u> in the circumstances of their individual lives and in the midst of their crisis and needs.

Is God BLACK? Absolutely! Is God WHITE? Without a doubt! What about RED? YELLOW? BROWN? Yes, Yes, Yes!

In the mind of the individual, God must be a God who is not only aware of his personal plight or the plight of his people, but a God who can relate to them in their own tongue, culture and language, according to their needs both as individuals and as a race. In all of this, we must remember that we are not fabricating a God in our likeness. Rather we are being created in His image. His likeness is not manifested in the color of our skin, but in His character, seen in us.

The "theos-logos" of theology must not be written in the context of any particular race. It must be applicable to all races.

The Peril of "Designer-Gods":
There is a caution in all of this: We must not create a god of servitude, a god designed to fulfill our own desires and ideological structures. Mohammed, for example, created Allah as an alternative to Jehovah. His hatred for the Israelites motivated him to design a god for the Arabs—one who would invoke the Jihad, or holy war, and demand the destruction of all infidels or non-believers of Islam.

Mohammed's "designer god" bore no resemblance to Jehovah. He was nothing like the God who gave His only begotten son to save fallen mankind. Allah was not a God of love; he was a god of war, a god of destruction. He bears the image of the one who created him.

In the hour we live, some racially motivated political movements are filling auditoriums, street corners, and even some churches with the same vehement hatred that has fueled the fires of religious war for centuries. Black skinheads, like their White skinhead counterparts, are spewing venomous hatred and racial unrest. They speak with such hatred and vilification of the Jews, referring to them as hook-nosed, bagel-snapping Kikes. In their ignorance, they must not realize that God made a proclamation that states, *"Those who Bless you I will Bless them and those who curse you them also will I curse."* (Gen. 12:3) I don't know what this scripture may say to a lot of people, but what it says to me is that I do not want to be part of any movement, organization, individual who curses the Jews. For indeed God will curse those who curse the Jews.

If you listen to these debates by both Black and White racists you will hear them speak of the Jews as though they were the scourge of the earth. It appears that none of them know that in order to be a born-again Christian you must be washed in the blood of a Jew. Likewise, none of them seem to know that the bible was written by Jews and to Jews originally. They also seem to ignore the fact that Jesus was a Jew, plain and simple.

The bible declares that Jesus was circumcised on the eighth day, that He was in the synagogue at 12 for His Bar mitzvah, and that He attended the synagogue on the Sabbath, as was His custom. You cannot make Jesus anything different than what He was—a Jew.

I am stunned when I see the Klansmen on television with a cross on their robes, declaring their "White Christianity" and hear how they speak against the Jews. As I said earlier, I remember, as a child growing up in the South, seeing the racial signs that read, *"No Niggers or Jews allowed."*

Of course, the Muslims have a different agenda. They do not believe in the deity of Jesus but believe that He was only a prophet.

THREE CONSIDERATIONS:
From this discussion, we can identify two errors we must avoid: We must not clothe the gospel with our culture, and we must not restrict other cultures from the promises in God's Word. That said, a third consideration is necessary when we present the gospel message: We need to relate the truths of God's word culturally, i.e., within the context of the cultural setting of the people we are addressing. In other words, the recipient of the Gospel must be able to relate it in a practical way to his own cultural needs and understanding.

Unfortunately, over the centuries this aspect of the evangelization process has not always been understood by mission organizations or by foreign missionaries. Many times missionaries would try to duplicate their own culture in the nations where they were serving. As the church history was written for each of these nations, it would appear that the indigenous church was merely a continuation of the mother church.

Consequently, the indigenous church's history would not be written with its own historical foundation but with that of the founding organization. This meant that often the local church's history would be recorded in a European context, neglecting the efforts of the indigenous believers.

In light of this, it is evident that the Word of God has been used to support various principles of *"White Privilege,"* reinforcing the idea that, from the beginning, God's plan for man included some form of racial superiority. These heretical interpretations of scripture have been used to foster a theology that excludes the people of color from the equality that the Kingdom of God provides for all. Supporters of these theologies have propagated doctrines that have given place to curses and eternal servanthood. They used these doctrines to provide a biblical justification for slavery.

This underscores the importance of receiving a correct revelation from the Bible. Otherwise heresy—an incorrect revelation—may get our theology off-track. Heresies are demonically inspired sometimes, but more often they are just a matter of simple human ignorance. The term ignorance here is not intended to be derogatory. Actually, ignorance is defined *as "the condition of being uneducated, unaware, or uninformed."* [16] The great danger of ignorance is that it leaves us vulnerable to error.

If there is error in our understanding of God's word, we will build our theology around a mistake. Great harm can be done to the Body of Christ when errors—misinterpretations—are accepted as truth.

LIBERATION THEOLOGY:
The African-American writer, James H. Cone, says that "Black Theology" is a theology of liberation. In actuality, the *Theos-logos* of God's Word and the Gospel of Jesus Christ has always been a theology of liberation for <u>all men</u> for <u>all time</u>. Unfortunately, it has not always been represented as such because of the many prejudices that have permeated the church. These prejudices have produced a lack of understanding and compassion for the plight of people of color and their struggles for freedom.

But just as there have been problems with the theology presented by the church in the past, there are also problems with the White and Black Theologies racial supremacists are espousing today. When someone makes a statement that a people must be made free, *"By ANY means possible,"* they are making a very dangerous statement. Does, *"By any means possible,"* mean by physical violence and destruction; or does it mean only that which is contained by and within the parameters of God's Word? After all, God's Word is not humanistically inspired. It is the unadulterated Word of God. It cannot be altered or manipulated by the personal preferences of men in order to justify their own brand of racist attitudes, regardless of which side they represent.

So what do we do when we, as individuals or as a people, suffer oppression in any form? We must simply continue to believe and hold to the truth that God cannot, nor will not, fail us in time of trouble. It took over 400 years for a deliverer to come to the Israelites in Egypt, but—according to the prophecy and the promise of God to Abraham—in due season, He heard their cry, and He delivered them.

GOD-GIVEN DELIVERANCE:

If we take a closer look at Israel's deliverance from Egypt, we will see something very significant that illustrates God-given deliverance. We know that **only one man died as a result of the arm of flesh** in the entire episode of the exodus. The book of Exodus, chapter two, details the story of Moses killing the Egyptian soldier. Even prior to having an encounter with God, Moses was moved by the inhumane way the Egyptians were treating the Israelites. One day, when he saw an Egyptian soldier beating an Israelite, he killed the soldier and hid his body in the sand. When what he had done was discovered, Moses was expelled from Egypt. Years later after having the burning bush encounter with God, Moses was sent back to Egypt as a deliverer.

As we read Exodus from chapter four through chapter twelve, we see that God sent ten great plagues upon Egypt to force the liberation of the Israelites. The firstborn of all the Egyptians—from the house of Pharaoh to the least of the kingdom, as well as all of their beasts—were slain in the last great plague. The night of that first Passover, God did indeed smite their firstborn. Through all of these plagues, not one Israelite raised his hand to strike an Egyptian to insure his freedom.

The Egyptians finally consented to let the people of God go, but later they pursued them in vengeance. With their backs to Pharaoh's army and facing the Red Sea, it would appear to the natural mind, that all was lost. Yet the God of Abraham, Isaac, and Jacob had given the Israelites a promise in Genesis chapter fifteen. **Now it was time** for that promise to come to pass! God opened the sea for his people to pass to safety. As the Egyptians pursued them, God closed the waters, destroying Pharaoh's mighty army. Not one Israelite was slain, and not one Israelite raised his hand against the Egyptians. They came out of Egypt, carrying the riches of their oppressors—four hundred years of back wages. The prophecy was fulfilled. This is true liberation by God and God alone.

PERSECUTED, BUT PERSEVERING:

Especially in the face of oppression, we must maintain the knowledge that we are spiritual beings, subject to and led by the Holy Spirit of God. *"Vengeance is mine, sayeth the Lord!"* (Romans 12:19) Many Christian martyrs' blood has soaked into the soil of many nations, but it does not alter the fact that God is on the throne and prayer does change situations.

Christians were crucified, tortured, and butchered, fed to the lions and burned, but they did not smite the Roman persecutors with the sword. Why? Because as the Apostle Paul wrote in Ephesians 6:12-13, *"We wrestle not against flesh and blood, but against principalities, and against powers, against the rulers of the darkness of this world, against spiritual wickedness in high places. [13]Wherefore take unto YOU the whole armour of God that ye may be able to withstand in the evil day and having done all, to stand."* It says, the WHOLE armor of **God**, not of the FLESH.

Unquestionably, there is wickedness in high places today just as there always has been throughout the ages. Wicked politicians and rulers, bigots and racists, false brethren and false teachers abound, yet God is sovereign. He will bring them to judgment while He liberates His very own.

One of the main characters in the book "Roots" by Alex Haley is Kunta Kinte. He was a young West African, who was captured by African tribesmen and sold to slave traders. He ended up in the United

States as a slave. His slave owner named him, Toby. When they asked him, *"What is your name?"*, he answered, *"Kunta."* And they beat him.

Again they asked, *"What is your name?"* Again he answered, *"Kunta."* And they beat him. They beat him and beat him and beat him until finally his mouth said, *"Toby,"* but his spirit was screaming, "Kunta!"

He ran away so many times, they finally chopped off all the toes on one of his feet with a hatchet so he couldn't run anymore. But, in his spirit, he was still free! His White slave owner had forced him to be "Toby" on the outside, but he would remain "Kunta" on the inside forever.

No man is truly totally free until his spirit is free. Then, at that point, he can never be totally imprisoned again. Once the inner-man has undergone a change, then his outer-man can be changed as well.

True Freedom for All:

Those who advocate a White or Black Theology are seeking a freedom which man establishes—a freedom that ensures the rights of a few. The freedom God offers, on the other hand, has been made available to all on the basis of Jesus' blood, not the color of our skin.

If we are going to achieve true unity, we must put all of our theology into the right perspective and not over-culturalize it beyond God's intent. If we insist on maintaining a distinct dichotomy of Black/White theology, what will be the difference in the premise of both or either? Due to the inequities and untruths purveyed by those of the White theology, is a Black theology going to advocate a Good/God-Bad/God philosophy? In other words, has White theology stood only for racial exploitation and bigotry? If so, will a Black theology help a Black man discover who he really is in God and enhance his own personal life through the blessings and promises of God, or will it simply widen the racial gap that already is a chasm in the Kingdom of God?

An Apologetic Needed:

Unquestionably, an apologetic is necessary for the theological flaws that have permitted the existence of or formed the basis for racism or slavery. Clearly neither White Theology nor Black Theology is the answer. **White Theology perpetuates an old wrong, while Black Theology creates a new one.** Neither of them will bring the liberty that adherence to the pure theology which is presented in the scriptures can bring.

Like Kunta Kinte, our external circumstances may not change, but the freedom that God accounts to us on the basis of the blood of His Lamb imparts a freedom, dignity, and worth that no chains can shackle nor any slave master take away.

Should we be concerned about liberating the oppressed? Yes! Jesus was. That's why He came and suffered for the sins of all mankind.

How precious is the freedom that God provides. It is on the basis of this freedom that we are truly accounted equal.

The equality our God offers draws people together, rather than dividing them. It calls us to love our enemies and inspires us to hope that they will become our friends and companions in Christ. This kind of liberation theology will break down walls that seem impenetrable, rather than building new walls that a new class of "oppressed" will have to fight to demolish.

End Notes:

[1] *The American Heritage Dictionary, Second College Edition*, Houghton Mifflin Company, Boston, 1985, pg. 64.

[2-3] Henry Clarence Thiessen, *Introductory Lectures in Systematic Theology*, Wm. B. Eerdmans Publishing Company, Grand Rapids, Michigan, 1968, pg. 26

[4-9] Thiessen, pg. 46.

[10-12] Earle E. Cairns, *Christianity Through the Centuries: A History of the Christian Church*, Zondervan Publishing House, Grand Rapids, Michigan, 49506, pg. 231-233.

[13-15] Cairns, pg. 234

[16] *The American Heritage Dictionary*, Ibid, pg. 675.

Chapter 11: What About This Man Called Adam?

Today it seems that everyone with their own, personal brand of "racial axe" to grind is determined to identify Adam as their own racial progenitor, presumedly giving their race dominion over all the earth. Therefore, let's take a close look at this first man, Adam.

If we do an etymological study on the word Adam, we find the following translation from the Hebrew: *Aw-dawm*, meaning *"ruddy," a human being, an individual or the species, or mankind.* It also means *hypocrite, low or of low degree. Aw-dawm* comes from the word *Aw-Dam* which means *to show Blood in the face, flush or turn rosy.* Another derivative of this word is *Aw-dome,* which also means *red or rosy.*

Because Adam's name translates as *"Red,"* many writers believe that indeed he was a man of Color. It is a fact that some people of African decent have light skin that often has a reddish tone. They are, therefore, often called by the nickname "Red."

The translation of the word, *earth*, gives further proof that Adam was a man of Color. Earth means *"red clay."* God made Adam from the earth, from *"red clay."* Therefore, some say that it is only logical to conclude that Adam was a man of color.

On the other hand, the Neo-Nazis and White supremacist groups contend that the term *"ruddy"* also translates *"pink"* and describes only those of the Caucasian race. Their argument is based upon the fact that when a White man is of very fair skin or extremely white, he often has a very flushed or reddish skin tone—especially in the face. Their contention is not only reinforced by the definition of the term *"ruddy,"* but is also based on the fact that the Hebrew word *Aw-dam* means *"to show blood in the face."*

This reminds me of some of the dialogue in the movie, "Cry Freedom," a portrayal of Steven Biko, a political activist in South Africa.

When a Judge Advocate asked him, *"Why do you call yourself Black, when indeed you are Brown?"* Biko answered, *"Why do you call yourself White, when indeed you are Pink?"*

In reality, it is very difficult to pinpoint the exact physical characteristics of Adam and Eve. Nevertheless, both sides of the argument are eager to establish the racial makeup of our first parents. The people of Color are attempting to find their roots in a man of Color, while the Whites are trying to establish the fact that a White man was God's preference.

Why is there so much contention concerning the racial characteristics of the first man and woman? It is an issue of dominion. Genesis 1:26 proclaims that God gave dominion to Adam. White supremacists contend that, if Adam was White, then ultimately God gave the world's rulership, or at least that which the Garden of Eden encompassed, to the White man. Black supremacists, on the other hand, contend that if Adam was of Color, then God gave dominion over the world to people of Color.

If we choose to join in on this debate—no matter which side of the argument we are on—we must not lose sight of one major fact, and that is simply this: Whether Adam was Black, Yellow, Red, or White, "He Blew It!" Regardless of his racial makeup, Adam did a very poor job of being the federal head and ruler of the human race!

THE ADAMIC COVENANT:
Let's take a close look at the nature of the covenant relationship between God and Adam. First of all, Adam was given a <u>promise</u> and a <u>condition</u> for the continuation or fulfillment of that promise. God also gave a <u>penal</u> <u>sanction</u> for failing to meet the contingencies of the promise.

Secondly, we see in Genesis 1:26 that God indeed gave dominion to Adam over all of creation regardless of his racial makeup:

> [26]*And God said, Let us make man in our image, after our likeness: and let them have dominion over the fish of the sea, and over the fowl of the air, and over the cattle, and over all the earth, and over every creeping thing that creepeth upon the earth.*

God also gave Adam what we would refer to as eternal life. In Genesis 2:16-17, God instructed Adam on the contingency for maintaining his eternally secure position. He told him, *"Of every tree of the garden you may freely eat:* ¹⁷*But of the tree of the knowledge of good and evil, you shall not eat of it: for in the day that you eateth thereof you shalt surely die."* A better translation of the last portion of this verse is, *"...you shall cause me to have to kill you."* God made it as simple as possible, as if to say, *"Listen Adam, I don't care how, when, or in what order you want to partake of the fruit of the garden. If you want apples on Monday, peaches on Tuesday or bananas every other Friday, go for it! But DON'T ever eat of the fruit of this tree!"* Guess what? He did!

In verse 18, God observed that it was not good for Adam to be alone, and God stated His intent to make a helpmate for Adam. God had brought all of the animals in the garden to Adam and allowed him to name them. Whatever Adam called them, that was their name. It declares this in Gen. 19-20.

THEN in verses 21-25, God put Adam to sleep, took one of his ribs and made Adam a companion, a wife, a helpmate. Adam awoke from his sleep and, lo and behold, there was a new creature in the garden—like none he had ever seen before. Not long thereafter, trouble would come to paradise.

Adam and Eve were the federal heads of the human race. They had total dominion. They had charge of the garden and were responsible for tending it and caring for it forever. Whatever they had would belong to the human race, and whatever they lost would be lost to the human race forever apart from divine intervention.

THE FALL:

In Genesis, chapter 3—*Thus enters the snake!* Eve was deceived, tempted, and fell, and so was Adam. They disobeyed the one commandment that they had to keep in order to maintain this *Heaven-on-earth* existence. They forfeited their God-given dominion as a result of three things:

- *the lust of the eye*—the fruit was appealing,
- *the lust of the flesh*—it was good to the taste,

- the *pride of life*—Satan promised them knowledge. *"You will know all that God knows,"* Satan said. *"You will be like God."*

THE CONSEQUENCES OF THE FALL:

The consequences of the fall were many. First of all, death entered the human race. When our first parents were expelled from the garden, the dominion of the garden was lost, eternal life was lost, and a curse overshadowed the entire human race. One of their sons would be the first murderer. Women would travail in childbirth. Man would now sustain himself with the sweat of his brow and with backbreaking toil. The earth itself was cursed, covered with thistles.

What have we learned from all of this? Well, one thing is a sure fact: As I said earlier, Adam, regardless of his racial makeup, did a very poor job of being the federal head and ruler of the human race. In fact, he did a terrible job. Had it not been for Adam's miserable failure, we preachers would not be giving altar calls, inviting people to receive the gift of eternal life through the last Adam, Jesus Christ. If Adam had not disobeyed God, death would have not entered the human race.

In light of these facts, it is surprising that all of these different racial factions are trying so hard to establish that Adam was of their race. It is sort of like proudly claiming relationship to someone in your family tree who was hung as a horse thief, or identifying yourself with a great Uncle or Aunt that no one else in the family wishes to talk about because of one indiscretion or another.

Every family seems to have some *"family skeletons"* hanging around in the closet somewhere. It appears that Adam and Eve are the *"family skeletons"* of the entire human race. It also appears that the only thing God created in the garden that didn't turn out to be good would be the people He placed there and left in charge.

ADAM FAILED:

Regardless of Adam's color, he failed! As a result of his failure, dominion was lost and sin entered the human race. Because of sin's influence, just a few generations later everyone on the face of the earth would be destroyed except the eight people of Noah's family.

If Adam was a man of Color, he failed. If Adam was White, he failed. Regardless of Adam's racial makeup, this first man, who had received so much—the mandate of God and the dominion over the earth— failed, and he caused all men to suffer greatly. If dominion was given to the White man or to the man of Color, we know that there is nothing to be proud of concerning Adam's accomplishments or the accomplishments of his descendants prior to the flood. God's commentary on the record of their accomplishments is pretty clear:

> *⁵And God saw that the wickedness of man was great in the earth, and that every imagination of the thoughts of his heart was only evil continually. ⁶And it repented the Lord that He had made man on the earth, and it grieved Him at His heart. ⁷And the Lord said, "I will destroy man whom I have created from the face of the earth; both man, and beast, and the creeping thing, and the fowls of the air; for it repenteth Me that I have made them."* (Genesis 6:5-7)

The word *repenteth* in Hebrew is *Naw-Kawm*, which means *sorry.* What is God saying? He is saying that these guys, starting with Adam and continuing until Noah's time, have made such a mess of civilization, that they are so evil that *"I am sorry that I ever made them!"*

The important thing for Christians to grasp in all of this lies in one of the first statements made in the beginning of this chapter: the translation of the name of Adam is from the Hebrew *Aw-dam;* which means, *"blood in the face."* Brothers and Sisters, as Christians we must realize that when we are washed in the blood of Jesus, we receive *"The Blood in the Face"* of the Lamb of God. At that point, our race and culture must take a position of lower priority. Our racial differences must diminish, and we must realize that indeed we have become members of a *supernatural* race of people—one family with one heavenly lineage, joint-heirs with Jesus, sons of Abraham—entitled to the heritage of Jacob. Through Jesus, the dominion God granted to Adam and Eve in Eden was restored and made available to all who accept Jesus as their Savior. This dominion, therefore, is based on **our relationship with God, not on our racial makeup.**

What should this say to the Black supremacists who believe that it is the Black man's time to rule, that it is time to turn the tables on the Whites, for the Blacks to oppress the Whites? What should it say to the White supremacists who believe that God made Blacks forever to be the servants of Whites?

Remember this, a house divided cannot stand. Neither can a people, a church, or a nation.

Chapter 12: Eve Or Lucy?

Scientific debates over the origin of the human race provide another point of contention among racists. Racial supremacists have literally "left no stone unturned" in their attempts to prove that their race was the "mother race" of all the races!

In the last few years, there has been much discussion about an archeological discovery in Africa. The debate has centered on skeletal remains that scientists discovered in Ethiopia. Many Black militants, religious leaders, and educators have spoken from various forums around the world concerning this discovery. They believe that these scientists' findings establish that the "mother of all humankind" was indeed Black.

The scientists involved in this discovery are paleo-anthropologists. They believe that the theory of evolution is the key to understanding the origin of life. This fact alone brings up a problem for the believer. The scriptures do not point us to a "missing link" as our common ancestor. They point us to Adam and Eve, who were sovereignly created by God.

It is interesting that these scientists are looking for **a** "missing link", rather than **many** "missing links." If the origin and development of life on this earth were indeed a random process, wouldn't it be reasonable to expect that the human race evolved through many different links? If evolution were an ongoing, random process, wouldn't it be logical to expect to see all of the stages of man from the "original" human to present-day man evident among us?

This line of thinking gives rise to the possibility of multiple origins of man, rather than one origin. But, scientists would reject this possibility. Why? Because, despite all of our external differences, we are one people—or as the scientists would say, we are one species. So, although race divides us emotionally, politically, and socially, it does not divide us in regard to most of our basic physical attributes. Inter-racial marriages would not be possible if this were not the case.

The bottom line is, we are one! We are all created by God, all intended to be included in one family—His. This "oneness" seldom sees its full expression in the world. Sadly, often it doesn't see its full expression in the Church either.

DEFINING RACE:

Given the amount of controversy race has created over the centuries, it would be profitable to take a moment and look at what race truly is. The dictionary offers four definitions: *(1. A local geographical or global human population distinguished as a more or less distinct group by genetically transmitted physical characteristics. (2. **Mankind as a whole**. (3. A group of people united or classified together on the basis of common history, nationality, or geographical distribution: the German race. (4. A geological line; lineage.* [2] From these definitions, we can see that, while race reflects our physical characteristics, but, in a broader sense, race also reflects our culture, our heritage and our nationality. In the broadest sense, however, the concept of race joins all the races together as a whole. We are all part of the human race.

There are both exclusive and inclusive aspects of race. Racial supremacists, whether Black, White, Yellow, or Red, concentrate upon what divides us. **God concentrates on what makes us one.** It's another case of man looking on "the external" and missing "the eternal."

TWO WARNINGS:

Two warnings need to be posted to the Christian community at this point: (1. We cannot, for the sake of our culture or cultural identity, embrace anything that does not line up directly with the Word of God no matter how learned the scholars may be who present their findings. (2. It is important that, as Christians, we do not compromise the Word of God when faced with scientific issues. We are, indeed, Creationists and must maintain that position in light of all the supposedly scientific evidence the secular scientists may produce.

It is equally important that we do not retreat into a cloak of ignorance or run in fear from the various theories of the origin of life on this planet. We should not fear any scientific discovery or shy away from Archeology. To my knowledge, no archeological discovery has ever disproved any portion of the Bible. In fact, there have been archeological discoveries have accomplished the opposite.

For instance, there has been a consensus among archeologists that the ruins of the ancient city of Jericho do not match the chronological time line used by Theologians. This theory was based on physical evidence found at Jericho. It was accepted as true by most archeologists for a century and a half. But recent discoveries have disproved the validity of this theory. After digging below the level of earlier discoveries, archeologists have indeed found the burned remains of Jericho. These burned remains validate the date of destruction as the date when Biblical scholars say Joshua and his army conquered the city!

Another example of archeology validating biblical accuracy concerns the Hittites. For many years archeologists regarded the belief that the Hittite army had ever inhabited the city of Jericho as mythical. There was no physical evidence to prove that these people ever existed except that they were named in the Book of Joshua. But in more recent "digs" the necessary evidence was found. One of these artifacts was a shield that was uncovered in the geographical vicinity of Jericho. It had the word, Hittite, etched on the inside of it, and Hittite was spelled exactly the same way as what is found in the Hebrew text, recounting the fall of Jericho. From the Tower of Babel—or the Ziggurat, as the towers were called—to the recent possible discovery of Sodom and Gomorra under the Dead Sea, archeology is helping to prove to the world that the Word of God is true, both historically and scientifically.

GENESIS' RECORD OF CREATION:

The Genesis account of creation tells us that God first created all living things; then He made Adam from the clay of the earth and breathed His life into him. Finally, God created the first woman from one of Adam's ribs. This sovereign, creative miracle is described in Genesis 2, verses 20-25:

²⁰ And Adam gave names to all cattle, and to the fowl of the air, and to every beast of the field; but for Adam there was not found an help meet for him.

²¹ And the LORD God caused a deep sleep to fall upon Adam, and he slept: and he took one of his ribs, and closed up the flesh instead thereof; ²² And the rib, which the LORD God had taken from man, made he a woman, and brought her unto the man. ²³ And Adam said, This is now bone of my bones, and flesh of my flesh: she shall be called Woman, because she was taken out of Man. ²⁴ Therefore shall a man leave his father and his mother, and shall cleave unto his wife: and they shall be one flesh. ²⁵ And they were both naked, the man and his wife, and were not ashamed.

The Hebrew word for rib is *tsal-aw*, which means literally, *the curved, side of a human, or the ribs.* Adam's helpmate is called *Ish-shaw* or *naw-shemm* here, which means *a woman* in Hebrew (This is the generic for female.) In Genesis 3:20, we see that after the fall Adam gave his wife a proper name: *Now the man called his wife's name Eve, because she was the mother of <u>ALL</u> the living.* In Hebrew Eve's name is *Chavvah (Khav-vaw)* which means "life-giver." From her, all life would originate. Dominion was given to her, as well as to Adam. This is why racial supremacists are so anxious to prove that Eve was of their race.

Claims Concerning Lucy:

Let us leave the Genesis account of creation for a moment and take a serious look at what scientists and evolutionists have discovered in Africa and what scientific claims they have made on the basis of this discovery. To do this, we will examine information contained in the March, 1996 issue of *The National Geographic Magazine*. One of the articles in this issue indicates that in 1974 Donald Johanson—a paleo-anthropologist—and his archeological team discovered 40% of the skeletal remains of what they determined to be a hominid while they were working in Hadar, Ethiopia. (A hominid is supposedly a distant ancestor of the human race.) In 1978, the hominid they discovered was classified as *Australopithecus afarensis*, or the common ancestor of all humans. The scientists named it *"LUCY"* because the Beetle's song, *"Lucy in the Sky with Diamonds,"* was popular at the time.

Although some of Lucy's bones were found as much as 200 feet apart and 9 feet below the surface, the scientists determined that they were all of the same creature. They determined that Lucy was approximately 3.18 million years old, and they believed that the remains had existed virtually unchanged for approximately 900,000 years. Initially, only Lucy's elbow was discovered. Immediately identifying it as the elbow of a hominid, the archeological team came roaring back into camp with horns blowing! This was a great discovery!

On later expeditions, they discovered other parts of Lucy's skeleton, but they were never able to find her skull. That was a disappointment, because the skull is the most important part of the skeleton. The skull is necessary to determine many important facts about the species that is being studied.

Based on the structure of Lucy's leg and pelvic bones, the scientists believed that she walked upright on two legs, making her a biped like us, instead of a quadruped that walked on all fours. But scientists still needed a skull to validate their theory that Lucy was the mother of all mankind.

Further archeological expeditions to Hadar were delayed for twelve years because the Ethiopian government closed the country to archeological exploration in the 80s. In January 1992, scientists returned to the volcanic ash of Hadar to search for Lucy's skull and other missing bones. They also hoped to find bones of her male counterparts. Their search proved fruitful. They collected 250 additional hominid specimens, all of which they believed were members of the same biological genus as humans, the Homo genus. They believed that Lucy was the common ancestor of all later hominids, and, in their words, "the mother of all humankind."

A number of skull fragments were found among the specimens they collected. The scientists were able to assemble these fragments into skulls. A man named Yoel Rak took a plaster cast of one of these skulls to the University of Zurich in Switzerland. He worked with two other scientists, Christopher Zollikofer and Marcia Ponce de Leon.

Using a computerized mirror imaging process and stereolithography, they created a three-dimensional model of Lucy's skull. [10]

The next step was for artist John Gurche, an expert in primate facial anatomy, to add plastic muscles to the skull. Bone markings indicated that the male had massive chewing jaws and neck muscles and a flat, wide nose. In addition, there were flaring cheeks, a muzzle-like mouth and ears set far back on the head. The final touches were added by an educated guess as to skin color and hair pattern. After 700 hours, the model of the apelike creature was completed. Gurche exclaimed, *"I wanted to get a human soul into the apelike face to indicate something about where he was headed."* [11]

These final touches were mainly guesswork. No drawings or other form of pictorial records were found in conjunction with the skeletal remains. There is no way to establish either skin color or hair pattern on the basis of bone markings or structure. Hair and skin are both soft tissues and would not have been preserved after that many years. [12]

The magazine exhibits the finished skull model along with an artist's rendering of what they believe Lucy's family may have looked like. They were apelike creatures that walked upright, but they were far from being human. In fact, Lucy is described as being 3.5 feet tall, with her arms dragging on the ground very much like today's apes and chimpanzees. She had less than one-third the brain capacity of a human being and weighed about 60 pounds. In fact, *Lucy*, this supposed *First Mother* that came from African soil, was nothing more than a monkey at best. [13]

It should be noted that not all scientists agree with the theories Johanson's team developed about *Lucy*. A German scientist named Ludwig says that *Lucy* is not a female at all. The pelvic opening is too narrow for birthing, so he believes that *Lucy* is indeed a male and suggests that _he_ be called _Lucifer_ instead. [14] This, of course, would be apropos. The Devil would have us believe that we descended from apes instead of being created by the Divine creator Himself, Jehovah.

THE MOTHER OF ALL HUMANS:
Lucy's discovery has thrilled the evolutionists and many African-American political activists and spokespersons, who have proclaimed,

"The White man does not want the world to know that the Mother of all the living humans remains have been discovered in African soil and indeed she was a Black woman!" One of those who seemed excited about this discovery is Minister Louis Farrakhan, of the Nation of Islam.

When Minister Farrakhan was on a Ted Koppel television interview, he proclaimed that there is a huge spaceship a half a mile in diameter, hovering over the United States. He went on to say that soon there will be similar spaceships hovering over every major nation of the world. He further stated that the aliens from this spaceship have been in contact with the U.S. government and have promised to destroy the White race and give control of the earth to the Black race. Minister Farrakhan also made the statement that the movie, *Independence Day*, which was about the attempted takeover of the earth by extraterrestrials, was indeed true.

I am sure that he received such mythical ideas from his mentor Khallid Muhammad, who said that the Black race actually came from the tribe of Shabazz. According to Khallid Muhammad, this tribe landed here from outer space some sixty-six trillion years ago. He said that Whites were *"...Frankensteins created by mad scientist named Yakub through a six hundred year hybridization experiment. This experiment produced devils who have ruled for 6,045 years by tricknology."* This is quoted from the April issue 1992 of *Emerge*, a Black magazine publication. I personally witnessed the interview between Minister Farrakhan and NBC's Ted Koppel.

A basic misconception that underlies these Black leader's attempts to prove that the mother of all mankind was Black is the assumption that scientific evidence <u>establishes</u> truth. In reality, scientific evidence is the basis for theory—*a system of assumptions, accepted principles, and rules of procedure devised to analyze, predict or otherwise explain the nature or behavior of a specified set of phenomena.* [15] You might also call it man's best guess, based on what is presently known. Scientists themselves do not always agree on which "guess" is right, as is evidenced in the conflicting theories regarding Lucy. People, however, have a tendency to take everything that scientists say as absolute truth. It's easy to take what you want to be truth and use it to support your own personal agenda.

Given free reign, the bias of racism will pervade every aspect of life, even scientific research. Conducting scientific research or interpreting the results of it under a cloud of racial prejudice makes it impossible to discover the truth. Instead of an unbiased examination of the facts available, we enter a courtroom in which we sit as judge, jury, and defendant. Everything becomes an exhibit for "our defense", all evidence supposedly establishing the superiority of our race and the inferiority of all other races. In this case, the truth which science is supposedly proving is not God's truth, but man's truth. As a result, it accomplishes man's purposes, not God's.

EVE OR LUCY?

Well, I challenge you, the reader, and those people who ascribe to any of the many theories of evolution—including even some Christian writers—to acquire the March 1996 issue of *The National Geographic* and come face to face with *Lucy*. If after seeing this monkey staring back at them, anyone insists on identifying with *Lucy* as their ancestor and the maternal progenitor of their race, that is definitely their right. But as for me and my house, we choose <u>*EVE*</u>.

As was said earlier, it is important that, as Christians, we do not compromise the word of God when faced with scientific issues. <u>We are indeed</u> Creationists and must maintain that position in light of all supposedly scientific evidence the secular scholars may produce.

End Notes:

[1-2] *The American Heritage Dictionary, Second College Edition,* Houghton Mifflin Company, Boston, 1985, pg. 1172.

[3-14] *The National Geographic Magazine,* March 1996.

[15] *The American Heritage Dictionary,* Ibid, pg.1260.

Chapter 13: Dinosaurs & Cavemen in the Garden?

The apparent conflict between science's view of creation and the biblical account of creation has stirred up no small amount of controversy over the years. It is important to address this issue in this text because of the division it brings within the Church and between believers and nonbelievers. In fact, some have never accepted Jesus over this issue, while others have abandoned any ties with the Church because of it.

Unquestionably, man's search for the origins of life and specifically for the origins of man himself has created its share of hoaxes over the centuries. But we have to ask ourselves, *"Is any of the evidence that scientists have uncovered valid?"* The answer is, *"Yes, it is."*

I come from a place called Bone Valley. It's the phosphate capital of the world, and it's very common to find dinosaur bones there. It's like the dinosaurs were just gathered there by the thousands when they died. They dig up huge dinosaur bones continuously every day—huge sharks' teeth, big leg bones. In fact, they have a very large museum there called the "Bone Valley Fossil Museum." It would be both difficult and unnecessary to say that dinosaurs never existed when there is so much evidence that they did.

When I was a kid, we would go out and look for fossils. I used to have vertebrae that were 10 or 12 inches thick from the back-bones of those huge creatures. They were so large I could sit on them. I gave them to a science professor.

We find so many fossils of dinosaurs in the Western Hemisphere. I have seen the fossils that have been dug up in New Mexico. We know that those things existed, don't we? But they didn't exist in the Garden where God created those who look like you and I.

We say, *"Well, there's such a conflict between the biblical account of Creation and what science tells us about it."* Indeed, Creationists are always having a conflict with Evolutionists. But there is no conflict for you and I. God created the ones that we came from—our first mother and father—in the Garden, and they looked just like we do today. I believe that if Adam walked into one of our churches today and he was dressed like you and I, we would welcome him like any other visitor. Why? Because God created him as he was. Adam didn't evolve from a lower life form. God created him out of the clay, and he was complete. God breathed life into him, and Adam walked upright. He wasn't swinging by his tail in the Garden for a few million years. God created him in His image!

Did the T-Rex ever walk the earth? You bet! With a head almost as big as a Volkswagen. But we find all of these things outside of the Garden! Remember, God said, *"I've created man in My image, and I'm giving him dominion over what he can subdue."* Now, no matter what authority and dominion we may have, it would be very difficult to hook a T-Rex up to a plow and make him plow a field. In fact, he would pull the roof off your house and have you for lunch.

Personally, I believe that when the flood came, God destroyed everything on the earth that man could not dominate. The creatures that went into the ark were those that man would be able to dominate. Man was never going to be able to tame the dinosaurs. Can you imagine having a cookout in your backyard with a T-Rex looking over your fence? You're waiting for the ribs to cook, and he's waiting on you.

So, what was going on outside the Garden has a lot of scientific validity. I'm not really sure what was happening outside the Garden, but I know what happened inside the Garden; and when Adam was created, he wasn't a lower form of primate in some early stage of the evolutionary process.

HEY, HARRY!

But some people will say, *"Wait a minute, we've got all of these different series in the development of the human race, going from a quadruped, walking on all fours and to a biped, walking on two feet."* I heard Walter Cronkite on television one night, talking about the stages in the development of man. There were two men dressed up like monkeys, sitting in a tree behind him, and he was talking about how man may have learned to walk.

This is a paraphrase of the scenario that followed: These two monkeys were sitting in a tree talking to each other, and one of them said, *"Hey, we're in trouble here. The forest is diminishing every year. If we don't do something, we're gonna starve. The desert is growing, and our habitat is getting smaller. If we are going to survive, we have to get across the desert to new feeding grounds!"*

The other monkey said, *"Hey, Hairy that's a long way. How we gonna get there?"*

"We're gonna have to learn to walk."

The other monkey said, *"Well, how are we going to do that, Hairy?"*

So Hairy jumps down out of the tree and demonstrates how some scientists think that this creature learned to walk. Remember, monkeys basically walk on all fours. Well, motivated by the knowledge that their food supply was soon going to be in short supply, Hairy got up and began to practice walking on just two legs—all so that he could walk over there to where the food was.

I think that's stretching it just a little bit. That didn't happen in my family tree! It's likely that if the monkeys could see all the evil man is doing today, they wouldn't want to claim us in their family tree either!

I personally believe that what happened in the Garden was **a distinct act of creation by God**. When God created Adam and Eve, He was beginning to make for Himself a people, created in His image and intended to rule over and populate the earth. God desired to have many, many sons and daughters!

God's distinct creation of man does not mean that He didn't create a lot of these other things as well in the parts of the earth that lay outside of the Garden. But whatever was happening outside of the Garden has nothing to do with what was happening inside of it. **A unique creation took place in the Garden.** God didn't place His spirit, His breath, His life in any of the other creatures He created. He didn't look at the monkeys and say, *"These are My sons and daughters."* So, as Creationists, we believe that we came from Adam, not from some lower form of life.

THE BIBLICAL ACCOUNT OF CREATION:

If we look at Genesis 1:1, we will see that there are five essential elements in Creation:

¹In the beginning God created the heaven and the earth.

The first of these elements was time: *In the beginning...* Time, as we know it, began at this point. God knows no time. He is the Alpha and the Omega. He always was, He is now, and He always will be. The second of these elements was force: *...God created the heaven and the earth.* God was the force, the power behind all of creation! The third of these elements was motion: *And the Spirit of God moved upon the face of the waters.* (Gen. 1:2) The force—God—created the motion, and the motion created all that there is. The fourth of these elements was space: *...God created the heaven...*Gen. 1:2). Heaven itself in which God was going to place His creation. The fifth was matter: *And the earth was without form, and void; and darkness was upon the face of the deep* Gen. 1:2). The earth, the matter, was certainly a part of God's creation.

These elements speak to what was happening within the Garden of Eden. It was there that God began creating a people, a holy nation, a royal priesthood, a peculiar people on the face of the earth. There might be a lot of controversy over what was happening outside the Garden at this time, but the events in the Garden are clearly recorded in the book of Genesis. It is upon these events that we want to concentrate as believers.

A GARDEN TERRARIUM:

There were no seasons in the Garden of Eden, because at least this portion of the world was in a sort of terrarium—a protective bubble, if you will. Genesis 2:5 tells us that *...God had not yet caused it to rain upon the earth.* Some people find this difficult to believe, because we all know how essential rain is to the growth of all plants and trees. But if we read on in verse 6, we see that the dew watered the earth: *But there went up a mist from the earth, and watered the whole face of the ground.* So moisture from the plant life supplied the moisture that both the plants and the animals needed. The rain wasn't necessary, or God would have sent it.

The Garden of Eden was a plush, perfectly climatically controlled environment. It had an even temperature and a natural moisture. There were no germs. Germs couldn't breed in that perfect environment. There were no ultraviolet rays from the sun. The protective bubble and the waters "stored" above it filtered the UV rays out. This is why they lived to be seven, eight, and nine hundred years old.

Things must have been very different then. Can you see it? A guy would be 200 years old, and they wouldn't even let him in on the conversation. They'd say, *"What's he know? That guy's not dry behind the ears! Only two hundred, and he's telling me? These kids!"*

But when the flood came, this bubble, this canopy, burst. That's what caused the forty days of rain that Noah and his family witnessed. The people didn't know what rain was before that time. When the canopy burst, the waters flooded the earth. But God preserved a remnant in the Ark. From this remnant, He would repopulate the earth.

A PRE-ADAMIC SOCIETY:

Some have offered the "Gap Theory" to reconcile differences between Evolutionists and Creationists. This theory says that after God initially created heaven and earth, some cataclysmic event occurred, and catastrophic change took place on the earth over a period of time, perhaps millions of years. Supporters of this theory say that it was during this time, that the earth was without form, void and full of darkness. These scientists believe that everything God created in the pre-Adamic society died or was destroyed in this cataclysmic event. They contend, therefore, that in Genesis God was actually recreating all that had been on the earth before in lower life forms.

Of course, this "Gap Theory" is one way for geologists to explain the "ice age", the dinosaurs, the cavemen, and all of the geological periods that they believe took place in the evolutionary process that supposedly brought man into existence. This "Gap Theory" also assumes that man existed in a somewhat lower form of life than we are. That would account for the cavemen.

But, if we are true Creationists, we cannot accept the "Gap Theory" as valid. The Gap Theory is, first of all, an attempt to resolve the conflicts between the biblical account of creation and science's assumptions about how this process took place. The "Gap Theory" also includes the concept of *uniformitarianism*. This aspect of the theory assumes that everything in creation has an order and that God does not intervene anywhere. This would put God in the position of stepping back from His creation once the initial work was completed and just letting things "play out"—a sort of "what will be will be" attitude.

This image of God bears little resemblance to our God. He is very much involved in our lives. He is a covenant-keeping God. He leads us and guides us. He teaches us to be like Him—to forgive and bless others. How can we believe God follows a "hands off" approach to His creation when He orchestrated the ultimate intervention in the history of Man? He gave His Son that whosoever should believe on Him could be rescued from the otherwise inevitable fate of spending eternity in Hell.

A third assumption of the "Gap Theory" is that the process of evolution—the random development of all living things—accounts for the great diversity we see around us. But there is an order in creation, and that order itself witnesses to the active involvement of the Creator.

> *For the invisible things of him from the creation of the world*
> *are clearly seen, being understood by the things that are made,*
> *even his eternal power and Godhead...* (Romans 1:20)

The "Gap Theory" then is an attempt really to accommodate science, to answer questions such as *"Where did this come from, where did that come from?"* There has to be some explanation of the origin of the dinosaurs, because we can dig up their bones. I'm not really sure where everything came from, but I know that my lineage started in the Garden with Adam and Eve, through **a distinct act of creation by God**.

THE ORIGIN OF LIFE:

Evolutionists often speak in sweeping terms of the creation of all things from a plasma cloud or from a great cosmic explosion. Who hasn't heard of the "Big Bang Theory"? These necessarily vague treatments of the origin of the Universe ignore a deeper question: What is the origin of the various chemicals and substances—the inanimate components—that make up the universe? Or if you take this question to the most basic level, *"How did the basic elements of the Universe come into existence?"*

Some educated people might believe an ape, first of all, would know that the forests were diminishing, endangering his food supply. A few might even believe that, on that basis, "Harry" decided they had to learn to walk so they could get across the desert to find better feeding grounds. But how many people do you think would believe that a bunch of electrons, protons, neutrons and the other assorted subatomic particles decided to rearrange themselves to form each of the 103+ elements that have been identified?

The characteristics of these 103+ elements define life itself. They combine in various ways to form all that we are and all that fills our world, both animate and inanimate. These elements are the "raw materials" from which God created all things. The genius of God's creation is reflected not only in the species He created, but also in the "raw materials" with which He created them.

The extraordinary nature of water alone makes all life possible. Water has a high specific heat, allowing it to absorb the tremendous amounts of heat that are generated in many of the chemical reactions that are essential to the basic physiological processes necessary to sustain life. If this heat was not carried away from the reaction site rapidly, it would "fry" the neighboring cellular proteins just as an egg fries in a hot skillet.

Likewise, water is known as the universal solvent. It forms a medium in which all of the chemicals necessary for life can interact freely. This characteristic of water makes it the prefect medium for getting essential nutrients through the cell walls. If these nutrients couldn't get into the cells, we would quickly starve to death.

It's interesting that God speaks of washing us with the water of the Word. Just as physical water is essential to life, spiritual water is essential to the formation of His life within us. His very life! Think of it! Sometimes He clothes His life in skin of brown; other times, in skin of Black, Red, Yellow, or White, but the life He places within each is the same. How much greater value is there in focusing on the origin of God's life within us—in understanding what causes people to desire to be saved—than in establishing the color of the skin which God selected for Adam and Eve?

Chapter 14: Was Jesus Black?

Today, there is a lot of controversy over Jesus' racial makeup. Those caught up in this controversy are anxious to prove that they are of the house and lineage of Jesus and that they share the same racial origin. There is a tendency to present and interpret the gospel within the context of individual races or cultures. Today, it is common in many ethnic churches to depict all Bible characters, including Jesus, as Blacks or Hamites. There is even an Afrocentric Bible available. If you took this to its logical extreme, you would have to develop an edition of the Bible for every group of people.

I do not believe, however, that the answer is in making everyone in the Bible suit our own racial preference. If that were the answer, we could just simply start producing bibles for everyone. We could print a bible depicting Jesus and Moses, Lot, Abraham, and everyone else with red hair and freckles and call it the Irish-centric bible. We could then print one with people having slanted eyes and yellow skin and call it the Oriental-centric bible. In a similar manner, we could make everyone Hispanic. That might make everyone somewhat happier, but would it produce the truth of the matter? I think not.

Presenting and interpreting the scriptures in terms of our particular racial preference is not a new phenomenon. This is exactly what the Anglo-Saxon versions of the Bible did for centuries, and we all know doing so was terribly wrong. For years, Europeans preached a White gospel. We made Jesus a White, an Anglo, a Caucasian, a Japhethite, a descendant of Noah's son Japheth. Hollywood often chooses someone with blonde hair and blue eyes to play Jesus. But, remember, Judas had to kiss Jesus when He was in the Garden with the other disciples so the soldiers would know which one He was. Trust me, if Jesus would have had blonde hair and blue eyes, Judas would not have had to kiss Him. He would have just said, *"Get the White guy in the Garden!"* On the other hand, if Jesus would have been extremely dark, guess what he would have said? *"Just get the Black guy in the Garden!"*

Just as the Japhethites tried to claim Jesus for so many years, now there is this push in the Afro-centric theology—the Cushite theology—for the Hamites (the descendants of Noah's son Ham) to claim Him as a member of their race. The Word of God does not say that Jesus came from Japheth or from Ham; it says that He came from Shem. His racial heritage, therefore, places Him somewhere in the middle of the skin tone spectrum. He would most likely look much like today's Palestinians.

We can't try to make Jesus anything other than what He was— Light, not White or Black. Hopefully, by the conclusion of this text you'll see why we don't even need to try to do so.

THE HISTORICAL RECORD:
Some years ago, I heard Mr. Khallid Muhammad, spokesperson for N.O.I.—the Nation of Islam—make this statement on the Donahue Show, (and I quote) *"I am tired of seeing the blonde-haired, blue-eyed Jesus that Hollywood portrays, when indeed Jesus was black and nappy-headed."* While in Houston, Texas a short while later, I heard a black Pastor on the television state, *"I can prove to you by the Bible that Jesus was indeed a Black man."* The first part of Khallid Muhammad,'s statement concerning Hollywood is certainly true. Of course, movie producers distort everything else as well. But I personally find the assumption that Jesus was Black quite doubtful. Why?

What do we know historically about Jesus? First of all, we know that He descended from Shem. Secondly, we know that very little is recorded about His physical appearance, except a few supposedly documented writings of those who saw Him. A Roman Officer, who was investigating a civil disturbance in Palestine, made this observation about Jesus in his official records: *"This man, Jesus—a Galilean—had shoulder length, dark, reddish-brown hair, and was fair complexioned."* The Historian, Josephus, also wrote about Jesus, but he said very little concerning His appearance.

Isaiah wrote in Isaiah 53:2 that the Messiah would have no special physical attraction, nor would He be very handsome. We can see this prophecy fulfilled in Jesus. The fact that Judas had to kiss Him so that the soldiers could recognize Him tells there was nothing about Jesus' appearance to set Him apart from His disciples.

The question is, does it really matter if indeed Jesus was dark or light? I do not think so. After all, shading Him darker or making Him lighter will not draw Him any closer to us than He already is. Neither will it help to exalt us as an individual or as a race.

JESUS' LINEAGE:

The Scripture clearly states the genealogy of Jesus in Luke 3:23-38:

So Jesus, when he began his ministry, was about thirty years of age.
He was the son (as was supposed) of Joseph,
 the son of Heli,
the son of Matthat,
the son of Levi,
the son of Melchi,
the son of Jannai,
the son of Joseph,
the son of Mattathias,
the son of Amos,
the son of Nahum,
the son of Esli,
the son of Naggai,
the son of Maath,
the son of Mattathias,
the son of Semein,
the son of Josech,
the son of Joda,
the son of Joanan
the son of Rhesa,
the son of Zerubbabel,
the son of Shealtiel,

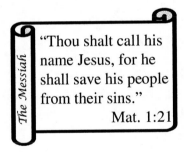

The Messiah

"Thou shalt call his name Jesus, for he shall save his people from their sins."
Mat. 1:21

The Messiah

For unto us a child is born, unto us a son is given...
Isaiah 9:6

the son of Neri,
the son of Melchi,
the son of Addi,
the son of Cosam,
the son of Elmadam,
the son of Er,
the son of Joshua,
the son of Eliezer,
the son of Jorim,
the son of Matthat,
the son of Levi,
the son of Simeon,
the son of Judah,
the son of Joseph,
the son of Jonam,
the son of Eliakim,
the son of Melea,
the son of Menna,
the son of Mattatha,
the son of Nathan,
the son of David,
the son of Jesse,
the son of Obed,
the son of Boaz,
the son of Salmon,
the son of Nahshon,
the son of Amminadab,
the son of Aram,
the son of Admin,
the son of Arni,
the son of Hezron,
the son of Perez,
the son of Judah,
the son of Jacob
the son of Isaac,
the son of Abraham,
the son of Terah,

The Messiah

"...in thee shall the families of the earth be blessed."
Gen. 12:2

The Messiah

His seed shall endure forever, and his throne as the sun before me.
Ps. 98:36

The Messiah

"...the Sun of righteousness shall arise with healing in his wings..."
Malachi 4:2

the son of Nahor,
the son of Serug,
the son of Reu,
the son of Peleg,
the son of Eber,
the son of Shelah,
the son of Cainan,
the son of Arphaxad,
the son of Shem,
the son of Noah,
the son of Lamech,
the son of Methuselah,
the son of Enoch,
the son of Jared,
the son of Mahalalel,
the son of Kenan,
the son of Enosh,
the son of Seth,
the son of Adam,
the son of God. (New English Translation[1])

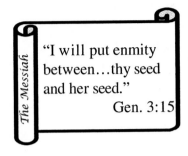

As much as the descendants of Ham or Japheth might want to include Jesus in their lineage, His lineage came down through Shem. You can't make Jesus anything other than what He was, a Shemite.

WAS MUHAMMAD BLACK?

A similar controversy arises in respect to Islam. Many Blacks are embracing Islam because they see Christianity as the "White man's religion." Interestingly enough, there are many passages in the Hadith that clearly state that Muhammad was White not Black. One writer comments, *"This is stated so many times in so many ways that it is quite obvious that the authors of the Hadith were deeply concerned less someone think Muhammad was a black man."* [2] Two examples of this are as follows:

In volume 1, Hadith no. 63, we read,

While we were sitting with the Prophet in the Mosque, a man came riding on a camel. He made his camel kneel down in the Mosque, tied its foreleg and then said, "Who amongst you is Muhammad?" At that time the Prophet was sitting amongst us [his companions] leaning on his arm. We replied, *"This white man reclining on his arm."* The man then addressed him, *"O Son of Abdul Muttalib."* [3]

The Hadith in volume 2, no.122, refers to Muhammad as a "white person." And in volume 2, no.141, we are told that when Muhammad raised his arms, *"the whiteness of his armpits became visible."* [4]

As much as ardent Black Muslims would be shocked if they read these passages, they would be even more taken back if they knew Muhammad's attitude toward Blacks. In volume 1, no.662, Muhammad refers to Blacks as *raisin heads* in volume 9, no.256 and in volume 9, no. 256. All throughout the Hadith, Blacks are referred to as slaves. In volume 9, numbers 162 and 163, Muhammad says that he believes that if somebody dreams about a black woman, he has seen an omen of a coming epidemic. [5]

Other entries in the Hadith indicate that Muhammad was a slave owner and that he held Black slaves. Hadith no.435, volume 6 tells us that when Umar bin Al-Khattab visited Muhammad's home, a Black slave belonging to Muhammad was sitting on the front step. In almost every instance that Black people are mentioned in the Hadith, they were, in fact, Muhammad's personal slaves. *"This was in stark contrast to Jesus of Nazarath who did not own slaves but came to set men free!"* [6]

(References 2-6 in this section were taken from The Islamic Invasion. Copyright © 1992 by Robert Morey. Published by Harvest House Publishers, Eugene, Oregon 97402. Used by Permission.)

Twelve Identical Loaves:

The debate over Jesus' racial makeup will likely continue until He returns, and we all see Him face to face. In the meantime, we can be sure of two things: Jesus is the Son of God, and those who accept Him as Savior and Lord are the children of God. Jesus told us many things about Himself. In John 6:51 Jesus said, *"I am the bread that came down out of heaven; if anyone eats of this bread, he shall live forever; and the bread also which I shall also give for the life of the world is My flesh."* We have to see this statement through the eyes of Jesus' listeners if we are to fully understand its meaning. For generations the Jews had followed the form of worship that God gave to Moses in the Wilderness. Under the Levitical priesthood, one of the first things that was to be done at the beginning of the Sabbath was the renewal of the "showbread"—the bread of His presence, which rested perpetually on a golden table along the north wall of the Tabernacle, the most sacred place in the Holy Place. On the table were twelve loaves, one for each of the twelve tribes.

The secret of making the "showbread" was given to the house of Garmu, a family of the Kohathites. This bread was baked with such care. Each loaf had to be identical. They baked it until they had twelve identical loaves. They had to have the same color, and all four sides had to be identical. They made it from the finest wheat after it had been passed through eleven sieves. The loaves were turned up on the end to resemble the ark of the covenant, the piece of furniture in the Holy of Holies upon which the presence of God rested when He manifested Himself to His people.

Every Sabbath the "showbread" was replaced. As the old bread was removed, the new bread was put in place, so that there was no interruption or lack of continuity of the twelve tribes' presence before God. The old bread was not discarded. Instead it was to be consumed by the High Priest and those who were in a "state of levitical purity."

This Sabbath ritual brought comfort and assurance to each generation of the Jewish people. Jesus came with a message that would bring comfort and assurance to all peoples. No longer was there any need to prepare fresh "showbread" for the Sabbath. Jesus, the Lord of the Sabbath, was the bread that came down from heaven, sent from the presence of God, prepared to provide eternal life for all who would "eat" of His flesh.

Jesus also said, *"I will never leave nor forsake you."* In another place, He said, *"The Father and I will come and abide with you and even dwell in you."* Just as Jesus came to dwell among the children of Israel 2000 years ago, He comes to us today, manifesting Himself to us, inviting us to come to Him—to enter His presence—through fellowship, worship, and prayer. This Jesus, this bread sent from heaven, is available for all to consume, not just the elect among the priesthood. Indeed, all who believe in Jesus are priests in the Kingdom of God.

In Jesus, the twelve loaves became one. The Old Covenant recognized twelve different tribes, so a loaf was provided for each tribe. Under the New Covenant, only one loaf was provided. That loaf was Jesus. In Him, all races, all peoples are made one. Our external differences remain, but on a spiritual level we are the same. We derive our life from one "Loaf", we are birthed into the family of the one living God, are conformed to His likeness, and we will be taken to be in His presence when we die or when Jesus returns to claim His own. We are His people. We are a supernatural race. Does it really matter if God chooses to wrap His likeness in flesh of differing colors?

If we will look past the external and look instead upon the internal, we will see that it is the same Jesus who indwells the heart of each believer. We may differ outwardly, but we are the same inwardly. We are made one, not by our natural heritage or by any works that we do, but by the work Jesus did when He allowed His body to be broken for us. As He came as one loaf, we are made one loaf when we partake of Him. Shall anyone divide those God has made one?

There are those who would like for all of us to resemble the "showbread"—all the loaves being the same, not one loaf lighter or darker than the others. But it is Jesus who kneads us into the "mixing bowl" of the Kingdom and then recreates us in His likeness.

End Notes:

[1] *New English Translation*, www.NetBible.org, 2000.

[2] Robert Morey, *The Islamic Invasion*, Harvest House Publishers, Eugene, Oregon, 1992, pg. 181.

[3-5] Ibid, pg. 182.

[6] Ibid, pp. 182, 183.

Chapter 15: The First Rainbow Coalition

It is often said that God is "colorblind." Not so! God created the racial diversity that is so evident in our world! His purpose for doing so was to bless and not to curse mankind.

Today there is this push among racial supremacists of whatever hue to claim Adam and Eve as members of their race. Why so much contention over the racial makeup of these first humans? It's a matter of dominion. God gave dominion over the whole earth to Adam and Eve. Their assumption is that this God-given dominion was passed to those who were of the same racial makeup as Adam and Eve.

There are a number of flaws in these theories. So many in fact that it would be almost humorous, if it weren't for the great harm these racist teachings have caused in the body of Christ and to the human race at large over the centuries.

The First Race:

In the beginning, there was no racial diversity. Adam and Eve and all of their descendants were of one color, they spoke one language, and they all lived in basically the same geographical region. Note that God does not tell us **what** color they were. Evidently that wasn't an issue with Him.

Genesis 1:26-28 tells us what God did consider to be "an issue"— to be important—in respect to Adam and Eve. First, God said, *"Let us make man in our image, after our likeness..."* (Genesis 1:26) As wonderfully diverse and complex as the rest of creation was, there was nothing in it that bore the image—the express likeness—of God Himself up to that point. God had reserved that gift for those who would rule over His creation. *So God created man in his own image, in the image of God created he him; male and female created he them.* (Genesis 1:27)

Second among the things that were important to God was the promise of His blessing: *And God blessed them...*(Genesis 1:28) Having blessed Adam and Eve, God came to point three in His agenda for them—fruitfulness and multiplicity: *...Be fruitful, and multiply, and replenish the earth, and subdue it: and have dominion over the fish of the sea, and over the fowl of the air, and over every living thing that moveth upon the earth.* (Genesis 1:28) This phrase, *"Be fruitful and multiply, replenish the earth..."*, usually speaks to us of a natural reproduction. But God is speaking of both a natural and a spiritual reproduction here. In other words, God did not just want Adam and Eve to be progenitors of the human race—to pass on their physical characteristics, their humanity—He wanted them to pass on His image, which He had placed within them. Adam and Eve were responsible for instilling godly character in the generations that followed them.

As believers, we need to remember that, like Adam and Eve, we are partakers of **a spiritual inheritance, as well as a physical inheritance**. Spiritual reproduction involves passing on our spiritual inheritance. It accomplishes God's highest goal—populating the earth with a race of beings who know God and who walk in His ways.

A lot of folks know God—that is to say, they know of Him—but they do not serve Him. Isn't this true? But that is not what God is looking for. He is looking for a race of people who will know Him and serve Him. Membership in this race is not based on physical characteristics, but upon spiritual characteristics. It is a supernatural race, one defined not by physical attributes, but by a spiritual inheritance that comes to us through the blood of Christ, not through the blood of our ancestors.

THE ORIGIN OF THE RACES:

If Adam and Eve and their descendants were all of one race, where did all the other races come from? We looked at this briefly in the chapter on old wives' tales and biblical misinterpretations. Because this issue causes so much division in the body of Christ, we need to look at it in more depth. Usually the point at issue in such discussions is which race God created first. As I said earlier, regardless of the racial makeup of Adam and Eve, they failed. Where? They did not fulfill God's will for His people. If we seek to be identified with them racially, we are seeking to be identified with those who failed.

I desire rather to be identified with Christ, who freely gives new life to all who come to Him. In Christ, we become one race, based not on our outward appearance, but upon the inward work of redemption, renewal and restoration that Jesus does in us by His Holy Spirit. We become a supernatural race, the people of God. Therefore, as we are one with Christ, we are one with each other.

But how did the different races come into being? I believe that racial diversity began with the family of Noah. What God did was He created three sons for Noah and Mrs. Noah: Ham, Shem, and Japheth; and He made each of these sons morphologically different. That is to say, they were different in form and structure, but the same in basic physiological functions. [1]

Why did God do this? Prior to the Flood, God had restricted man to the geographical area we know as the Middle East. After the Flood, He was going to commission man to spread out over the entire earth, and He intended for the descendants of sons of Noah to inhabit different parts of the world. The Japhethites were going to be the settlers of Europe. They would be the fathers of the Caucasians, the Anglos. Their descendants were going to settle where the cloud cover was the strongest in the world. They would have light skin, light hair, blonde hair, blue eyes, because the ultraviolet rays of the sun are not so strong there. Their nasal passages would be narrow to limit the amount of cold air they breathed in during the cold winter months.

On the other hand, the Hamites were going to inhabit the hottest place on earth— the Nile Delta and North Africa and eventually the entire African continent. It's interesting that in ancient Hebrew Ham means *dark, humid, or hot.* Ham's descendants were going to have a much darker skin to withstand the intense sunlight typical of that region of the world. They would have peppercorn hair to hold the perspiration in the scalp and help the body cool itself. They would have wide nasal passages to maximize airflow into and out of the lungs.

If you look up the Latin word for skin, you find that it means *peeling*. So we could say that the various races just have a different peeling. It's kind of like an apple. There are different colors of apples. Some are red, others are yellow. But, if you just take the peeling off of any of these apples, they all just look like an apple. People are the same. We have differing peelings, but underneath that peeling we are indistinguishable inside. Even our blood types are the same regardless of race.

Japhethites have one peeling that will burn very easily. That would be adequate for them, because the sunlight would be less intense in the lands they were going to populate. Hamites have five outer layers of skin that will tan, so they have a much darker skin, which will withstand the harmful ultraviolet rays in the sun much better, perfectly suiting them to Africa's intense sunlight.

What about the Shemites? The descendants of Shem were going to stay in Palestine. They would become the fathers of the Palestinians and the Asians. Their skin tone would be lighter than the Hamites, but darker than the Japhethites in accordance with the amount of sunlight that their region of the earth would receive. Remember the canopy surrounding the earth had burst, causing the great deluge, "The Flood", and now the UVs are piercing the earth's atmosphere.

You see, everything God does is perfect! Each of the sons of Noah and Mrs. Noah were racially different; each was suited to the region of the earth that their descendants were going to populate. But the point I want to make here is that they were full brothers! They were all the natural sons of one mother and one father. You might say, they constituted the first "rainbow coalition."

Now I can hear some people from a scientific background saying, *"How could one man and one woman produce three sons so racially diverse? That's impossible!"* Most people, including Christians, subscribe to the theory of environmental adaptation. In other words, they assume that each of the sons of Noah were of the same skin tone and that as the descendants of each son inhabited different areas of the globe, they grew darker over time, based on the amount of exposure to the sun or they got lighter as a result of little sun exposure. This seems much more plausible than assuming that Noah's sons were each racially different.

Are we talking about the same God who made Adam? This is the God who took a piece of clay, fashioned it into Adam, breathed life in him, and he walked upright on the earth. With our God, all things are possible.

ONE PURPOSE OF THE FLOOD:

So Noah's sons were created genetically different—one Black, one White, one Yellow. Each of them gave rise to one of the three mother races of the earth. Their descendants were going to populate the whole earth according to God's covenant promise to them:

> *And God blessed Noah and his sons, and said unto them, Be fruitful, and multiply, and replenish the earth.* (Genesis 9:1)

All of the other races came from these three mother races, whatever derivative they happen to be—light, dark, or in between. The important point for us is that their racial characteristics were part of God's plan to equip their descendants to populate the whole earth. We have centered so much on race that we easily miss God's intent for creating the races, which was simply to fill the earth with His children. We see this in Genesis 9:7—

> *7And you, be ye fruitful, and multiply; bring forth abundantly in the earth, and multiply therein.*

To *bring forth abundantly* comes from the Hebrew word, *shawrats,* which means to *swarm, or abound, to increase* Here we see a difference between *the covenant promise* God gave to Adam and Eve and that which He gave to Noah and his sons. Adam and Eve and their descendants were restricted to a limited geographical area. God placed no such restriction upon Noah and his sons. They were to swarm over, to fill, **the entire earth**.

Now, in order for them to populate the whole earth and have dominion over it, what does God have to do? He has to eliminate everything they can't take dominion over. We looked at this earlier in the chapter about dinosaurs. There was no way man was going to be able to take dominion over them or even coexist with them. You cannot coexist with something that weighs thirty-five thousand pounds and eats flesh. But an ox or an elephant is different. When I am in India or Africa, I see the people using elephants for bulldozers. They have them pushing down trees, pulling logs, doing all kind of things. They have dominion over them. Oxen can be put in a yoke and taught to pull a plow or grind wheat. Would you like to try that with a five-story Brontosaurs?

God used a universal flood to wipe out everything in the whole world except what He put on the ark with Noah. The animals that God put on the ark were the living creatures that man could rule over.

A Matter of Dominion:

So much of the racial controversy that is creating division in the Church concerns the dominion God gave to Adam and Eve. We considered this point in depth in a previous chapter, so it is only necessary to touch on it here briefly. But let me say only this: The dominion, which God gave to Adam and Eve would have been vested in Noah and his wife and subsequently to their children, because they were the only ones who survived the great Flood.

Because God does not distinguish between us when He fills us with His power under the New Covenant, I think it is reasonable to assume that all of Noah's sons inherited this God-given dominion to subdue the earth. It's a logical assumption. After all, God intended for their descendants to spread out and fill the earth. They would all need to be able to take dominion over the creatures they encountered in their sector of the world. Based on this assumption, one thing is clear: dominion passed to each of Noah and Mrs. Noah's sons.

There is sound biblical basis for accepting this assumption. When they emerged from the ark, God established an everlasting covenant, not only with Noah, but also with his three sons. We can see this in Genesis 9:8-11:

⁸And God spake unto Noah, and to his sons with him, saying, ⁹And I, behold, I establish my covenant with you, and with your seed after you; ¹⁰And with every living creature that is with you, of the fowl, of the cattle, and of every beast of the earth with you; from all that go out of the ark, to every beast of the earth. ¹¹And I will establish my covenant with you; neither shall all flesh be cut off any more by the waters of a flood; neither shall there any more be a flood to destroy the earth.

God extended this everlasting covenant to include not only Noah and all his sons, but also all their seed after them. So **all of the races** that would develop from this first rainbow coalition were included in God's covenant. As covenant people, they would be inheritors of the dominion needed to walk in that covenant.

THE TOWER OF BABEL:

Remember God's covenant promise to Noah and his sons—that they would replenish the whole earth? For that to happen, their descendants would have to be willing to be transplanted to the different regions of the earth. But we know they didn't go. Genesis, chapter 9 tells us of their plan to avoid <u>ever</u> having to go:

¹And the whole earth was of one language, and of one speech. ²And it came to pass, as they journeyed from the east, that they found a plain in the land of Shinar; and they dwelt there. ³And they said one to another, Go to, let us make brick, and burn them thoroughly. And they had brick for stone, and slime had they for morter. ⁴And they said, Go to, let us build us a city and a tower, whose top may reach unto heaven; and let us make us a name, lest we be scattered abroad upon the face of the whole earth. (Genesis 9:1-4)

They knew God's call on their lives, but they placed their will above God's will. God saw their rebellion and said, *Behold, the people is one, and they have all one language; and this they begin to do: and now nothing will be restrained from them, which they have imagined to do. (Genesis 9:6)*

God doesn't change His will for our lives just because we don't like it. This was no exception. God saw what they were doing, and His response was swift and decisive. God said,

> "...let us go down, and there confound their language, that they may not understand one another's speech. ^{8}So the LORD scattered them abroad from thence upon the face of all the earth: and they left off to build the city. ^{9}Therefore is the name of it called Babel; because the LORD did there confound the language of all the earth: and from thence did the LORD scatter them abroad upon the face of all the earth." (Genesis 9:7-9)

So the races were divided. God never intended for the bond of unity that He established in that first rainbow coalition to be broken, but man's rebellion left Him no choice.

Before we leave this point, I think it is important to stress that the morphological differences God created in Noah's sons are not a basis for assuming that the races are intended to be segregated from one another. God was simply giving them the best "equipment" possible to insure that they would flourish in the area of the world that they were to subdue and populate. That was in the short term. In the long term, we know that man has adapted to life on any continent regardless of racial makeup. Indeed, God often sends people to other nations with the gospel message.

A SUPERNATURAL RACE:

So much of our focus has been on the physical aspects of race that we have, for the most part, overlooked the spiritual aspects of race. What we need to understand today is that in the body of Christ there is only one race of people. It is a supernatural race, born of one Spirit, redeemed by the blood of one Lamb. When we are washed in the blood of Jesus—even though our racial consistency, our traditions, our culture, and our history are still very much a part of us—we become part of one supernatural race. We are God's children, and even as He is one, we are one! We are one!

Do you know that once we have been washed in His blood, our identity is in Jesus? When we know **who He is in us**, then we will know **who we are in Him**. When we know this, we no longer have to force Him into any particular mold. He is our Redeemer! He is our Savior! The racial makeup of the body in which God manifested Himself is really not important. What is important is the fact that He is our God and Father! Furthermore, we can rejoice that we are serving a God who ministers to us in our own cultural needs.

As I pointed out in chapter 10, Is God black? Yes, He is. Is God White? Yes, He is. Is God Asian or Oriental? Yes, He is. Is God Latino? Yes, He is. How can I say this? Because God is a spirit! We don't have to identify with Him according to our "peeling." We need to identify with Him as the One who has created us, as the One that has breathed His life into us and called us His own!

Let me tell you, the Jews are called God's chosen people, but do you know how they are going to get to heaven? The same way you and I are—by accepting Jesus Christ as their Lord and Savior as individuals. The Israelis have no ticket to ride except Jesus. I pray that God will remove the scales from their eyes and the stoniness of their hearts and take them from the Law of Moses and put them under the grace of Jesus Christ of Nazareth. Their Messiah has come, and He is coming again!

We all have to come to God in the same way—by the blood of the Lamb. When we do, we become a part of His glorious family—a supernatural family, purchased at a great price because of the God's great love for all mankind. What God separated at the Tower of Babel, He brought back together on the hill of Golgotha. People from any nation can ascend that hill today and be made one with God and their fellow-man through the blood of Jesus.

But I want to tell you something, Church. We talk about revival in America. I'm going to say this very plainly—**the God that I know and serve is not a racist!** Anywhere there is racism, my God is not there!

REVIVAL IN AMERICA:

We always think of racism in a Black/White context. It's not just Black and White. Rich people are not comfortable around poor people. Educated people sometimes are not comfortable around those who do not have as much education. I've ministered in many nations in Africa and India where there are such strong tribal differences that you can't get people under the same roof, the same tent, to worship the same God—and all of them professing to be Christians. Why? Because of all the bad blood that runs in their tribal history.

They're not much different than anyone else, are they? We divide up according to all kinds of silly notions as well.

But, you see, revival is going to come to America and to the world when we are willing to kick over all of the racial barriers that divide us. We need to understand that so much that has been taught from the European church was not true. Take for example, the prohibition against interracial marriages. Never do you find these things in the word of God, but they have been taught for years, adding to the walls of division.

When we destroy those walls and come to the realization that we're in the same family, that we're going to the same heaven, and that we're trying to stay out of the same hell, then revival is going to come! If we have trouble in these areas and still want to hold onto barriers that have separated what God made one in Christ, we need to let God do a work in us.

I am so glad when I see the Church moving in unity. Where there is unity, God is going to do some awesome things!

God is removing the barriers that separate us, He is removing all the stigmas and different things that keep us from worshipping as one, and we are going to flow together as one supernatural race. We are going to cover the face of the earth, forming a spiritual rainbow coalition that will truly transform nations and draw people together as one!

End Notes:

[1] *The American Heritage Dictionary, Second College Edition,* Houghton Mifflin Company, Boston, © 1985, *pg. 815.*

Section 3: A Closer Look at Slavery

Chapter 16: The Historical Roots of Slavery

There is value in taking a more in-depth look at the historical roots of slavery as it has been practiced worldwide. Few people would be surprised by the fact that slavery is recorded in the earliest annals of mankind. In ancient times, it was customary for conquering nations to enslave those they vanquished. The practice of slavery grew as the populations of nations increased and as the wars between them multiplied. The Roman Empire emerged as one of the dominant players as they conquered most of the known world. At the height of its power, a staggering 60 million people were enslaved. This represented over half of those subject to Rome's dominion.

The civilization process proceeded more slowly in the European nations. The slavery practices of these nations were even more cruel than the bondage Rome imposed on those it defeated.

THE CHURCH'S ROLE:

Even the Church contributed to the advancement of slavery in the 1400s. Dr. James Dana penned this commentary on the papal decrees, which gave the Portuguese authority to explore Africa, plant colonies there, and reduce the Africans to slavery:

*"The wholesome decrees of five successive Roman Pontiffs granted, conveyed and confirmed to the most faithful King a right to **appropriate** the kingdoms, goods, and possessions of all infidels, whatever to be found, to **reduce their persons to perpetual slavery, or destroy them** from the earth, for the declared purpose of bringing the Lord's sheep into one dominical fold, under one universal Pastor.*

"We suppose, then, that eight millions of slaves have been shipped from Africa for the West India Islands and the United States; ten millions for South America, and perhaps two millions have been taken and held in slavery in Africa. Great

*Britain and the United States have shipped about five mil-
lions, France two, Holland and other nations one; though
we undertake not to state the proportion with exactness. The
other twelve millions were sent to Portugal. Twenty million
slaves at £30 sterling each, amount to the commercial value
of £600,000,000.* **Six hundred times ten hundred thousand
pounds sterling traffic in the SOULS OF MEN.**

*"By whom hath this commerce been opened, and so long and
ardently pursued? The subjects of their* **most Faithful, most
Catholic, most Christian, most Protestant Majesties, defend-
ers of the faith;** *and by the citizens* **of the most republican
States,** *with the sanction of St. Peter's successor."* [1]

The fruit of the decrees these five Popes handed down are a so-
bering reminder of the awesome responsibility assumed by anyone who serves in leadership in the Church. The price these Popes'
decisions extracted in terms of human misery and death was enor-
mous. At the root of this incredible injustice lay a failure to see
these "infidels" as God sees them—simply as people in need of
salvation. Many others have made the same or similar errors.
The end result of this failure is a form of racism that justifies the
oppression of one people by another and, where the racism is
intense, the ethnic cleansing of the "inferior race."

Despite instances where the Church actually fostered the development of slavery, Christianity has historically been a major force
in abolition efforts. One early writer commented that, although
the New Testament did not forbid the holding of slaves, the moral
system put forth in the scriptures made the enslavement of others
inconsistent with the Christian faith. Many questioned how it was
possible to call a man your brother-in-Christ or a woman your
sister-in-Christ, yet hold them in bondage. That's a very good
question.

ETHNIC CLEANSING ON GRAND SCALE:

History often portrays the early explorers as great heroes. It took
great courage for these men to set out in fragile wooden boats to
discover new lands and new routes to the rich markets of Asia.
How could they know that two vast continents blocked their way?

We almost cheer as we read of their conquests in the New World. Many lost their lives in the process of opening up these vast wildernesses to those anxious to settle in new lands. America was birthed and the principles of freedom and democracy were advanced as the descendants of those first settlers fashioned a nation on this continent. Likewise other nations were established in Latin and South America and on the Caribbean Islands.

What is easy to miss in a brief overview is the reality that these lands were already occupied. Many of the civilizations that were already in place were very advanced; others were very primitive in comparison to what was typical in European cultures. Regardless of their stage of development, all were viewed as inferior— a people to be made subservient to the needs of the settlers.

Studies would later show that these seemingly simplistic people, in fact, had developed highly structured cultures with clearly defined laws regarding marriage, business dealings and interpersonal relationships. Their societies were anything but primitive— pagan, yes, but not primitive. Judging them as inferior greatly hampered the evangelistic outreach to these people. Although the gospel was spread, there was a failure to raise up indigenous leadership. We look at Africa today—and this "we" includes many Africans and African-Americans—and ask why the nations of this continent have not advanced like so many of the other nations. It would not be unreasonable to assume that the flawed missions outreach to these people played a role in the slowed growth process that is so evident there. The gospel brings new life in every aspect of our being, body, soul and spirit. Its effect extends far beyond booking our reservation in heaven.

Anywhere the gospel is preached and received, it brings a change, an upliftment of those who embrace its truths. This is one reason why there is so much persecution of Christians in India now. Many of those who are accepting Christ are those of the lowest classes. God is prospering these people, and jealousy, as much as religious fervor, is inspiring the "powers that be" to persecute them.

THE CONQUEST OF THE NEW WORLD:

Those who conquered and settled the New World were somewhat less than gracious toward the indigenous people they encountered. Sometimes they bought their lands for trinkets; other times they simply took their lands and enslaved or killed the people. The Taino Indians—natives of the Abaco Islands—were among the first to be eliminated. Today we would call it ethnic cleansing. The Spanish captured the Taino and exported them to other colonies to supply needed laborers. By 1550 all of the Taino had either been killed or deported and enslaved. The Abaco Island lay virtually uninhabited for almost 200 years. That says something about the devastation racism brings. [2]

In 1625, the French made a very short-lived attempt to colonize Abaco and her sister islands. After being abandoned by the French, they provided shelter for pirates and a few fishermen. In 1783 a new wave of settlers—a group of British Loyalists from the Southern colonies—came with their slaves to set up cotton plantations. The islands had met the needs of the Taino for centuries, but the frequent rock outcroppings and infertile soil were not suitable for growing cotton. As a result the plantations failed. By 1790, only 400 of the 2,000 original colonists remained. [3]

The island of Guanahani in the Bahamas is where Christopher Columbus is thought to have made landfall in the New World. The island had no gold or other significant mineral deposits, so Columbus and his crew continued their journey. There is no evidence that the Spanish ever established a colonial outpost there. [4]

The Spanish did return to the Bahamas when they needed more laborers on the island of Cuba. When they came, they didn't ask for volunteers. By 1520, nearly 20,000 native Lucayan Indians had been killed or captured and deported to serve as slaves on the plantations and in the mines and pearl fisheries in the Spanish colonies. Some of them chose to commit collective suicide rather than submit to slavery. [5]

Stripped of their inhabitants, the Bahamas became a haven for pirates and later for slave traders. By 1715 about 1,000 of these disreputable characters called the Bahamas home—among them, the notorious Blackbeard. When the British outlawed the slave trade, illegal slave traders began using the Bahamas as a base from which they continued to supply slaves to the Southern colonies of the United States.[6]

SLAVERY TRANSFORMS THE CARIBBEAN:

Slavery's imprint rests on the Caribbean. In nation after nation, existing cultures were overrun or absorbed by invading cultures. The Siboney—the Stone People—were the original inhabitants of this region. They are thought to have migrated from Florida or Mexico. Their settlements in Antigua date back to 2400 BC. The Siboney were absorbed as the peaceful Arawak migrated northward from the Guianas in South America.[7]

The Arawak had a highly developed society. They had made considerable technological advances in agriculture, arts and crafts. They were known for their superior boat-building techniques and their fishing skills. By 1492, the Arawak had settled in most of the larger islands in the region. It is estimated that 8 million Arawak lived on the island of Hispanola alone.[8]

The Arawak were no match for the inhabitants of the Lesser Antilles, the fierce Carib Indians. Like the Arawak, the Carib originated in South America. As they began their northward migration, they conquered the Arawak on island after island, killing or enslaving the men and capturing the women.[9]

The Carib were more formidable opponents against European colonizing forces. They withstood the Spanish, the English, and then the French in Grenada until 1650 when the French sent in an expedition from the island of Martinique. When "diplomacy" failed, the French sent in reinforcements and exterminated the Carib. A city on the northern coast of Grenada is named *Morne des Sauteurs*, because a number of the Caribs chose to jump to their death in the waters of the Caribbean rather than surrender to the French soldiers. *Morne des Sauteurs*, when translated into English, means *"The Mount of the Jumpers."*[10]

Over the next 100 years, Grenada's population and economy grew rapidly as colonists and slaves were brought in to set up sugar and tobacco plantations. Cotton, cocoa and coffee plantations soon followed. With this increase in production, came ever-increasing numbers of slaves from Africa. Greed, a lust of the flesh, is a well that cannot be filled. It constantly demands more regardless of the cost to others, and, in the eternal aspect of things, to ourselves as well. [11]

Where there is oppression, inevitably there will be those who will seek, and if need be, fight for freedom. Grenada was no exception. A major slave revolt took place there in 1795. It was lead by a freed Grenadian named Julian Fedon. Slavery was not abolished in Grenada until 1834, the year in which the slave trade was made illegal in the British Empire. [12]

What happened in Grenada was repeated in island after island. The indigenous people were killed or deported to other colonies to serve as slaves. When the islands were colonized, African slaves were imported to fill the growing need for laborers on the plantations. [13]

The emancipation of the slaves did not resolve all of the problems these forced African immigrants faced. In Antigua there were limited opportunities for the freed slaves. Most of the farming land was still in the hands of the plantation owners. The freedmen had no access to credit, and there were few jobs available in manufacturing. In most cases, their only option was to work for their former masters, many of whom treated them worse than they did when they were slaves. This sounds all too similar to the conditions Blacks faced in the post-Civil War South, doesn't it? [14]

It is not enough to free a people from slavery. Those who enslaved them also have to be freed from the beliefs, attitudes, and traditions that they believed justified holding slaves in the first place.

500 Years After Columbus:

If we judge the fruit of the conquest and colonization of the Caribbean, we will see the impact of totally stripping a region of its original inhabitants and repopulating that area with settlers and slaves. The mixture of cultures created by this process of conquest and colonization has generated tremendous cultural and political struggles in this region for generations. [15]

There is a basic struggle to establish a Caribbean identity today. This is most strongly reflected in the works of Caribbean writers and artists. A growing Black consciousness movement adds further complexities to these societies. Like their African American brothers and sisters, these African descendants are searching not only for their roots, but also for their unique identity as citizens of their individual nations. [16]

That is the natural aspect of things. The mission of the Church in each of these island nations is to present Christ in such a way that the people of the Caribbean hunger for an identity in the kingdom of God.

SLAVERY COMES TO AMERICA

The first Black Africans arrived in Virginia in 1619. Some came as indentured servants, while many others were brought as slaves. Those who came as indentured servants had the same rights as White indentured servants. After a period of service, they were promised freedom and the right to settle in the New World. These Blacks came with the same sense of adventure and hope of establishing a new life as their White counterparts did.

In the initial phases of the immigration of Black Africans, the promises made to the indentured servants were kept. When they completed the designated time of service, they were freed and allowed to purchase a portion of the New World for themselves. In fact, these freedmen began to own land in very significant amounts. Some of them even began to purchase slaves of their own. This was particularly true in the Louisiana Territory. The descendents of these Freedmen would be among the first to field a regiment of soldiers to fight for the Confederacy. [17]

This growing class of freed Blacks created inordinate fears in the hearts of the White majority. Fear is a typical response when different cultures begin to interact. We fear what is unknown unless

God frees us to peacefully coexist with and then to love those who seem to be "so different" from us. The Word says, *"There is no fear in love; but perfect love casteth out fear..."* (I John 4:18a) Having freed us from fear, God can open our hearts and show us that the "new folks on the block" really aren't so different from us after all. [18]

Unfortunately, the majority of Whites did not react to the freed Blacks in this way. Questions arose concerning granting them the right to vote. Were they to be treated as full citizens just like their White counterparts? In some areas, this did happen, but this was unusual.

Other questions arose concerning the intermarriage of Whites and Blacks. Many—likely both White and Black—believed such marriages should not take place. Others wrestled with the status of the offspring of such marriages. [19] As was stated previously, God has no objection to interracial marriages nor with the children that issue from them.

FEAR CONTINUED TO ERODE BLACKS' FREEDOM:

White majority resolved its fears by enacting laws that slowly stripped freed Blacks of their rights. Early in the history of the colonies, Blacks, who had been baptized, had the right to testify in court even when their testimony was against a White person. This right was stripped. Next, intermarriage between Blacks and Whites was made illegal. In 1668, the right to vote was limited to freeholders (those who had never been slaves or indentured servants) alone, eliminating the right of universal suffrage for all men. In doing so, they denied "freedmen" full citizenship in the nation they had helped to build. Freedom dies quickly when fear is allowed to guide the decisions of governments. [20]

Later in our nation's history, laws were passed which made it illegal to free a slave unless he or she was given passage out of the country. This added expense caused many slaveholders to renege on their promises to free their indentured servants after the agreed time period. Stripped of any hope for freedom, the slaves began to look for opportunities to run away. So many chose this option that fugitive slave laws were enacted which allowed owners to reclaim their "property" once they were located. [21]

Property! This is perhaps the greatest outrage of slavery—that one person should regard another person as mere property.

BRITAIN OPPOSED ABOLITION:

The practice of slavery in the colonies was undergirded by the British government. Parliament passed several laws, which regulated the rights and treatment of the slaves in the colonies. The attitude of the British legislators who drafted these laws could hardly be called charitable. They believed that the Blacks were *"...of a wild, barbarous and savage nature, to be controlled only with strict severity."* [22] These British directives were first put into effect in Virginia—the colony that had the most slaves.

Not all Americans favored slavery, however. In 1688, a group of Mennonite Quakers led the first recorded protest against slavery. They officially denounced all of their members who owned slaves, and they lobbied the Pennsylvania legislature to ban the slave trade. The law was passed, but the British Crown overruled it, opening the way for a massive influx of slaves. [23]

Colonel Byrd II, then governor of Virginia, succeeded in getting thirty-three laws passed that were directed at halting the importation of slaves. Once again the British government overruled this attempt to abolish slavery. [24]

In 1727 Benjamin Franklin became active in the abolition movement. He published antislavery articles and books and founded an abolition group called "Junto." [25] In his later years, he was the president of the "Pennsylvania Society for Promoting the Abolition of Slavery and the Relief of Free Negroes Unlawfully Held in Bondage." This group worked to get Congress to pass an antislavery amendment to the Constitution. On November 8, 1789, Franklin wrote a statement entitled "Address to the Public" and sent it to Congress. In this address, he once again urged Congress to pass the antislavery amendment, saying, *"Slavery is such an atrocious debasement of human nature, that its very extirpa-*

tion, if not performed with solicitous care, may sometimes open a source of serious evils." [26]

Opposition to emancipating the slaves was very strong. Prejudice against Blacks was deepening, often fed by calamities that were attributed to them even when there was little or no evidence to establish their guilt. For example, in 1741, eighteen Blacks were hanged and eleven were burned at the stake in New York City just because they had been found near where a series of fires had been set. [27]

Sadly, this shows that when the truth we believe is not God's truth, it will not set us free. We become subject to the lies we have accepted, and some truly horrible things can happen.

THE EFFECT OF SLAVERY:

In his *Address to the Public*, Franklin also considered the effect slavery has on the enslaved. He said, *"The unhappy man, who has long been treated as a brute animal, too frequently sinks beneath the common standard for the human species. The galling chains that bind his body do also bind his intellectual faculties, and impair the social affections of his heart. Accustomed to move like a mere machine, by the will of a master, reflection is suspended; he has not the power of choice; and reason and conscience have but little influence over his conduct, because he is chiefly governed by the passion of fear. He is poor and friendless; perhaps worn out by extreme labor, age, and disease."* [28]

Franklin understood that they could not keep a man, woman, or child in absolute bondage and not have it have an effect on them. Likewise, they could not set an enslaved person free and expect them to act like someone who had lived free all their lives. Franklin argued, therefore, that just as society had permitted slavery, it had an obligation to teach the slaves how to live as free people. Pointing out that it was not enough to work only for the emancipation of the slaves, Franklin said that society was obliged to *"...instruct, to advise, to qualify those who have been restored to freedom, for the exercised and enjoyment of civil liberty; to promote in them habits of industry; to furnish them with employ-*

*ments suited to their age, sex, talents, and other circumstances;
and to procure their children an education calculated for their
future situation in life...*" [29]

Had more people had Franklin's enlightened attitude toward the
freed slaves, the healing of the divisions between the races in this
nation would have progressed much more rapidly. Of course, had
more people shared his desire to abolish slavery, there would not
have been additional generations of slaves to integrate into society or additional years of abuse and degradation to be healed. But
his counsel went unheeded, as did that of the many other abolitionists of his generation. As a result, slavery continued to de-
base both the slaves and the slaveholders for another seven and a
half decades. It took the anguish of war to end what could have
been ended in the counsel chambers of the governing bodies to
this nation.

THE DECLARATION OF INDEPENDENCE:

Even as pro-slavery sentiments grew stronger, abolitionists became more vocal in their efforts to free the slaves. In the original
draft of the Declaration of Independence, Thomas Jefferson included this indictment of King George III for Britain's role in
fostering slavery in the colonies:

*"He has waged cruel war against human nature itself, vio-
lating its most sacred rights of life and liberty in the persons
of a distant people who never offended him, captivating them
and carrying them into slavery in another hemisphere, or to
incur miserable death in their transportation thither.* **This
piratical warfare,** *the opprobrium of infidel powers,* **is the
warfare of the Christian King of Great Britain.** *Determined
to keep open a market where MEN should be bought and sold,
he has prostituted his negative for suppressing every legislative attempt to prohibit or to restrain this execrable commerce."* [30]

This quote didn't make it into the final draft of the Declaration of
Independence, but other key phrases did—phrases, which clearly
proclaimed that all men were created equal, that each had a right
to life, liberty and the pursuit of happiness.

This is a portion of what the First Continental Congress did resolve for the original colonies:

> *That the inhabitants of the English colonies in North America by the immutable laws of nature, the principles of the English constitution, and the several charters and compacts, have the following RIGHTS:*

> *Resolved, N.C.D. 1. That they are entitled to life, liberty and property: and they have never ceded to any foreign power whatever, a right to dispose of either without their consent.*

> *Resolved, N.C.D. 2. That our ancestors, who first settled these colonies, were at the time of their emigration from the mother country, entitled to all the rights, liberties, and immunities of free and natural-born subjects, within the realm of England.*

> *Resolved, N.C.D. 3. That by emigration they by no means forfeited, surrendered, or lost any of those rights, but that they were, and their descendants now are, entitled to the exercise and enjoyment of all such of them, as local and other circumstances enable them to exercise and enjoy.* [31]

Assuring justice for <u>all</u> was of paramount importance to these first legislators, but the ideals that were penned in the Declaration of Independence and in the Constitution of the United States were not equally applied to <u>all</u>. Indeed, they have not yet become a reality for many people who dwell in this nation today. Human beings are amazingly capable of seeing the good they should do, but getting sidetracked somewhere between the "seeing" and the "doing."

SCIENCE AND PHILOSOPHY PROMOTED RACISM:

Thomas Jefferson's denunciation of the British government's role in fostering slavery in the colonies is somewhat perplexing when you consider that Jefferson himself was a slaveholder and did not believe that Blacks were equal with Whites. This belief was heavily influenced by the anti-Black bias that pervaded the scientific and philosophical communities at that time. As you read through some of Jefferson's writings on the differences between

Whites and Blacks, you see the heart of a man who was truly attempting to assess all the information he had objectively. Our objectivity is easily blinded by our prejudices or our lack of discernment of a lie that is made to look like a truth.

Like so many other colonial Americans, Jefferson wrestled with the issues surrounding the incorporation of the freed Blacks into the rest of society. He seemed doubtful that a peaceful, blended-society would ever develop when he wrote the following:

"It will probably be asked, Why not retain and incorporate the blacks into the state, and thus save the expense of supplying, by importation of white settlers, the vacancies they will leave? Deep rooted prejudices entertained by the whites; ten thousand recollections, by the blacks, of the injuries they have sustained; new provocations; the real distinctions which nature has made; and many other circumstances, will divide us into parties, and produce convulsions, which will probably never end but in the extermination of the one or the other race." [32]

The prejudices, which shaped much of Jefferson's thinking on the issue of race, become evident as you continue reading his text. He begins with the obvious difference—that of color. He asks,

"...is this difference of no importance? Is it not the foundation of a greater or less share of beauty in the two races? Are not the fine mixtures of red and white, the expressions of every passion by greater or less suffusions of color in the one, preferable to that eternal monotony, which reigns in the countenances, that immovable veil of black which covers all the emotions of the other race?" [33]

What a sad commentary on the part of such a great statesman in exhibiting such ignorance (lack of knowledge) concerning the color of his fellow man.

Jefferson then elaborates on the physical differences between the two races and addresses what he believes to be the differences in intellect. On this latter point, Jefferson commented,

> *"Comparing them by their faculties of memory, reason, and imagination, it appears to me that in memory they are equal to the whites; in reason much inferior, as I think one could scarcely be found capable of tracing and comprehending the investigations of Euclid; and that in imagination they are dull, tasteless, and anomalous."* [34]

This comment illustrates the incredible inaccuracy upon which racism was based. The accomplishments of African-Americans and the very significant contributions they have made to the development of this nation speak for themselves. Yet many old theories continue to surface from time to time concerning the question of intellectual equality.

Harvard debates between Black and White students proved that many of these theories were wrong. The Black students often excelled above the White students. These debates showed that where there is truly equal opportunity, there is also an equality of intellectual ability between Blacks and Whites.

THE POWER OF BELIEF:

Jefferson was a brilliant man. We might well ask, *"How could he believe Blacks were less capable of learning than Whites?"* But he did believe it. What we believe, whether it is right or wrong, determines how we see our world and how we relate to the people in it. Jefferson so strongly believed that Blacks were inferior to whites that he considered their racial differences to be *"...a powerful obstacle to (their) emancipation..."* [35]

To his credit, Jefferson did recognize the negative influence slavery was having, not only on his generation, but also on the generation that was growing up where slavery was permitted. On this point, he said,

> *"There must doubtless be an unhappy influence on the manners of our people produced by the existence of slavery among us. The whole commerce between master and slave is a perpetual exercise of the most boisterous passions, the most unremitting despotism on the one part, and degrading submissions on the other. Our children see this, and learn to imitate it; for man is an imitative animal.*

This quality is the germ of all education in him. From his cradle to his grave he is learning to do what he sees others do. If a parent could find no motive either in his philanthropy or his self-love, for restraining the intemperance of passion towards his slave, it should always be a sufficient one that his child is present. But generally it is not sufficient. The parent storms, the child looks on, catches the lineaments of wrath, puts on the same airs in the circle of smaller slaves, gives a loose to the worst of passions, and thus nursed, educated, and daily exercised in tyranny, cannot but be stamped by it with odious peculiarities. The man must be a prodigy who can retain his manners and morals undepraved by such circumstances. And with what execration should the statesman be loaded, who, permitting one half the citizens thus to trample on the rights of the other, transforms those into despots, and these into enemies, destroys the morals of the one part, and the amor patriae of the other.[36]

The erroneous theories Jefferson and others developed went largely unchallenged. Thus, the scientific community—whose purpose is to search out truth—propagated a lie. This lie created a divisive wedge between Blacks and Whites. Likewise, the philosophical community—whose purpose is to promote understanding of human nature—endorsed concepts that denied the equality of the races and perpetuated the oppression of Blacks by Whites.

PSEUDOSCIENCE STILL PROMOTES RACISM:

The issue of the supposed intellectual inferiority of Blacks is far from dead. *The Bell Curve*, a book published in 1994 by Charles Murray (a member of the conservative American Enterprise Institute) and Richard Herrnstein (a late Harvard psychologist), is just one example of current efforts to prove that Blacks are intellectually inferior to the other races. The central thesis of *The Bell Curve* is that the IQs of Black average 15 points lower than Whites. Murray and Herrnstein present evidence which they believe proves that IQ is an inherited, not an environmental factor. They indicate that while programs such as "Head Start" produce a temporary rise in IQ, the effect is short-term and relatively insignificant. Thankfully, this isn't the case.

Murray and Herrnstein's book created so much controversy that the American Psychological Association (APA) set up a task force on intelligence and *The Bell Curve* to analyze the validity of the theories they presented. The task force was charged with considering what is currently known about intelligence and with assessing the scientific accuracy both of the conclusions Murray and Herrnstein presented and of the data upon which these conclusions were based. Finally, the task force was to assess the underlying political agenda of *The Bell Curve.* [37]

This final point was very significant because a large portion of the research funding for the writing of *The Bell Curve* came from The Pioneer Fund, a neo-Nazi group which advocates eugenics— *"...a philosophy that maintains that 'genetically unfit' individuals or races are a threat to society...."* [38] Harry Laughlin, The Pioneer Fund's first president, favored the sterilization of those he considered genetically unfit. Laughlin worked for the passage of laws which restricted immigration from Southern and Eastern Europe, and *"...testified before Congress that 83 percent of Jewish immigrants were innately feeble-minded."* [39] Additional references reveal the racist overtones of the Pioneer Fund's literature and public positions. It seems unlikely that such a group would be sponsoring unbiased research in any area relating to race.

Further compromising Murray and Herrnstein's conclusions is the fact that Richard Lynn (a professor of psychology at the University of Ulster), who did most of the research for "The Bell Curve", received a $325,000 grant from the Pioneer Fund to fund his research. Lynn co-edits and writes articles for *Mankind Quarterly*, a eugenics journal. He also writes for *Personality and Individual Differences*, a eugenics journal edited by Pioneer Fund grantee Hans Eysenck. These facts make his objectivity in gathering and assessing data relating to racial issues in an unbiased manner highly unlikely. [40]

The APA Task Force entitled *Knowns and Unknowns of Intelligence* concluded that scholastic achievement is *"...not determined solely or even primarily by intelligence or any other individual-difference variables."* [41] Their research indicated that, while *"differences in genetic endowment contribute substantially to individual differences in (psychometric) intelligence...the pathway by which genes produce their effects is still unknown."* [42] This comment was made without respect to race.

The Task Force found that environmental factors do substantially contribute to the development of intelligence but could not identify what factors were most influential or how they positively or negatively affected the development of intelligence. Their conclusion corresponds to statistical studies done between 1970 and 1990, which show that the gap between the average IQ levels of Blacks and Whites is closing. Researchers attributed this change to the desegregation of the schools and the consequent increase in equal educational opportunity for all students. An increase in the number of Black students completing college was also a significant factor in this change. Environment does make a difference! [43]

Additional findings of the APA Task Force strongly called the "race factor" into question. The Task Force's press release stated the following:

> *The differential between the mean intelligence test scores of Blacks and Whites does not result from any obvious biases in test construction and administration, nor does it simply reflect differences in socio-economic status. Explanations based on factors of caste and culture may be appropriate, but so far there is little direct empirical support for them. There is certainly no such support for a genetic interpretation. At this time, no one knows what is responsible for the differential.* [44]

One factor that needs to be considered as a cause for this differential is the fact that during the first 250 years that Blacks came to this nation it was against the law to teach them to read. Even after their emancipation, the quality of the education they received was not comparable to what Whites received, despite all the "separate but equal" jargon. The subsequent closing of this IQ gap after the desegregation of the schools speaks volumes concerning the effect that truly equal educational opportunities has on IQ levels.

We have seen a powerful example of the effect greater opportunity has on educational performance in the After School program that our church initiated in 1999. We invited the children of our church and our neighborhood to come to the church each afternoon to receive help with their homework. They are also given a snack—what else do you do with youngsters when they first get home from school—and lots of love and encouragement. We offer them a time of Bible study, and when their homework is completed, they can play in the gym. The results have been phenomenal. Some youngsters who were failing are now making "As" and "Bs." Environment does make a difference!

One final point in respect to the APA task force on intelligence: Their press release says,

> *The APA task force distinguishes sharply between scientific research and political rhetoric. 'The study of intelligence does not need politicized assertions and recriminations; it needs self-restraint, reflection, and a great deal more research.'* [45]

Science with a political agenda to prove—or a prejudice to justify—is not pure science, and it will not be able to discover pure fact. This kind of science will not work for the advancement of society, but will only serve to perpetuate the misconceptions, old wives' tales, and ignorance (the lack of knowledge of the truth) that gives people a basis for assuming that those of a different race, cultural, or nationality are inferior to them.

WIDE MEDIA COVERAGE:

One of the most disturbing things about *The Bell Curve* is the wide media coverage it received. It was featured on the cover of *Newsweek* (10/24/94) and the *New York Times Magazine* (10/9/94). It was discussed on the *MacNeil/Lehrer NewsHour* (10/28/

94), *PrimeTime Live* (10/27/94), and *Nightline* (10/21/94). While there was sharp criticism of the book, *"...media accounts showed a disturbing tendency to accept Murray and Herrnstein's premises and evidence even while debating their conclusions."* [46] This coverage, no doubt, is part of the reason that *The Bell Curve* sold over 500,000 copies.

Richard Cohen, columnist for *The Washington Post*, chided those who labeled Murray and Herrnstein racists, saying, *"Their findings...have been accepted by most others in their field, and it would be wrong—both intellectually and politically—to suppress them."* [47] "Newsweek" writer Geoffrey Cowley voiced a similar position when he wrote, *"As the shouting begins, it's worth noting that the science behind The Bell Curve is overwhelmingly mainstream."* [48] The APA study showed that this is not the case. It's little wonder they organized a task force to examine the supposed truths presented in Murray and Herrnstein's book.

In time, all false teachings are proven false, but it is easier to disprove a theory than it is root it out from the hearts of those who have endorsed it. You can still find a "Flat Earth Society" to join today if you look hard enough.

Even Thomas Jefferson had some misgivings about the "truths" he had found self-evident in regard to the races. These misgivings are poignantly stated in his concluding remarks on the enslavement of Blacks:

Can the liberties of a nation be thought secure when we have removed their only firm basis, a conviction in the minds of the people that these liberties are of the gift of God? That they are not to be violated but with his wrath? Indeed I tremble for my country when I reflect that God is just: that his justice cannot sleep forever: that considering numbers, nature and natural means only, a revolution of the wheel of fortune, an exchange of situation is among possible events: that it may become probable by supernatural interference! The almighty has no attribute which can take side with us in such a contest. But it is impossible to be temperate and to pursue this subject through the various considerations of policy, of morals, of history natural and civil. We must be contented to hope they will force their way into every one's mind. I think a change already perceptible, since the origin of the present revolution. **The spirit of the master is abating, that of the slave rising from the dust**, *his condition mollifying, the way **I hope preparing**, under the auspices of heaven, **for a total emancipation,** and that this is disposed, in the order of events, to be with the consent of the masters, **rather than by their extirpation.** "* [49]

Interesting. Here we have a slaveholder prophesying the end of slavery.

THE FRITTER TREE:

Some will use science to justify their racist beliefs and actions; others will use science to debunk racism. Likewise some will use the Word of God to support racism, while others use it to prove that no man should oppress or enslave another. The debate ceases when you listen to the testimony of those who have lived the life of a slave. Several years ago, I had the opportunity of listening to the story of a man who came to America as a slave before the beginning of the Civil War. His name was Charlie Smith. He was 136 years old—the oldest living American at the time I talked with him.

Walt Disney made a movie about Mr. Smith's life called "Charlie Smith and the Fritter Tree." Charlie came to America as a young boy on board a slave ship. Some slavers had these little fried fritters—corn cakes—and they told Charlie and his young friends that fritters grew on trees in America. They said they had a lot more fritters on their ship and asked the boys to come with them. Being young boys, "all-you-can-eat" fritters sounded pretty good. They believed the men, and followed them onto the big boat anchored in the harbor. The men took them below the decks. Instead of giving them more fritters, they pulled up the anchor and set sail for America.

Needless to say, the boys discovered that America was not a land where fritters grew on trees. It was a land where young boys worked as men, and the innocence of childhood was short-lived.

I bought cookies from Mr. Smith when I was a young boy. Huge cookies for a nickel. That day I had the privilege of sharing the gospel with him. He accepted Jesus Christ as his Lord and Savior that day—a decision that gave him full entrance into all that God promises to His children. There's no such thing as "separate but equal" in Heaven.

THE FOUNDATIONS OF AMERICA:

Reviewing these facts concerning slavery in colonial America can stir up some painful emotions. But a willingness to make this journey through the pages of history has an ample reward: You come away from it with a profound awareness of the tremendous contribution African-Americans have made to this nation from its very foundations. A recognition of their contributions is essential to the healing process that is so needed in our nation.

"Colonial Williamsburg"—a theme park in Williamsburg, Virginia—has recognized the importance of the largely unheralded role that both slaves and freedmen played in the establishment of America. Their program "Enslaving Virginia" graphically portrays what it meant to be a slave in America. The response to this program has been powerful. When some of the segments of this program drove young children to tears, the Park added debriefing sessions so the children could talk about what they had seen.

"The program is about the contradiction between freedom and slavery in Colonial America, but it's also about the contradictions of race in America today," Harvey Bakari, the Development Manager of Williamsburg's African American program commented. *"One minute, they'll be standing and cheering when Patrick Henry talks about liberty, but the next minute they have to confront the reality of racial discrimination.... When they react the way they do, people almost seem to be attempting to right the wrongs of the past, to step into history and say, 'Don't do this!'"* [50]

Colonial Williamsburg

"A Taste of Slavery" Exhibit

Carter Grove Plantation

Exterior view of slave quarters with a typical garden

Exterior view of slave quarters with corral.

Some interior views of slave quarters.

There were
few comforts
in these homes.

"Carter Grove" photographs by Emilio A. Mastrorocco

The pictures of the Carter Grove Plantation were taken by Emilio Mastrorocco, one of the deacons at our church, during a recent visit to Colonial Williamsburg. The photos depict what slave quarters typically looked like. Viewing these stark surroundings indeed gives you a taste of what the life of a slave was like, but only a very small taste.

Nothing can right the wrongs of the past, of course, but God, moving on the hearts of men, women, and children, can end the wrongs of the present. He uses different vehicles to accomplish this, but His goal is singular: What He divided at the Tower of Babel because of man's rebellion, He is drawing together by His Spirit. The basis for the unity He is creating in the Body of Christ is the ground that all believers share in common—the ground that lies before the cross upon which Jesus purchased freedom for all of us. Upon that ground, all idea of inequality simply falls away. We stand there, not on the basis of any merit of ours or any work that we have done, but upon the finished work of Christ.

End Notes:

[1] Dr. James Dana's *Discourse on the African Slave Trade, 1790*

[2-16] *Island Connoissuer,* Country Studies: Abaco, Antigua, Aruba, the Bahamas, Barbados, Bermuda, Cayman Islands, Cuba, Dominican Republic, Grenada, Haiti, Jamaica, Puerto Rico. Accessed from an Internet site, which unfortunately is no longer available.

[17] Earl Parvin, *Mission USA*, Moody Press, Chicago, 1985, pg. 80 and Christian A. Fleetwood, Sergeant-Major 4th U.S. Colored Troops, *The Negro as a Soldier In the War of the Revolution*, originally given at or the Negro Congress at the Cotton States and International Exposition, Atlanta, Georgia, November 11 to November 23, 1895. Afro-American Almanac web site. Available at http://www.toptags.com/aama/voices/speeches/public/htm. Accessed on Oct. 14, 2000.

[18-20] Parvin p.82.

[21] Ibid, pg 85.

[22] Charles C. Tansill, *Documents Illustrative of the Formation of the Union of the American States*, Government Printing Office, Washington, DC, 1927.

[23-25] Parvin, pg. 84.

[26] Benjamin Franklin, *Address to the Public, November 9, 1789 Philadelphia*, Afro-American Almanac, Available at http://www.toptags.com/aama/

voices/speeches/public/htm. Accessed on Oct. 14, 2000.

[27] Parvin, Ibid.

[28-30] Franklin, Ibid.

[31] George M. Welling, Coordinator of *Computing in the Humanities,* a project of developed by the Department of Alfa-informatica at the University of Groningen in the Netherlands, *Thomas Jefferson on Slavery.* Available at <http://odur.let.rug.nl/~usa/I/pages.htm>. Accessed on Dec. 14, 2000.

[32] Tansil, Ibid.

[33-35] Welling, Ibid.

[36] Tori DeAngelis, *Psychologists Question the Findings of Bell Curve,* American Psychologist Association web site: Available at <http://www.apa.org/monitor/oct95/bell.html> Accessed on 6/9/00.

[37] Randolph T. Holhut, *Challenging the Racist Science of the "The Bell Curve."* Available at: <http://www.mdle.com/Written Word/rholhut/holhut27.htm> Accessed April 29, 2000.

[38-39] Jim Naureckas, *Racism Resurgent: How Media Let "The Bell Curve's" Pseudo-Science Define the Agenda on Races.* Available at: <http://www.fair.org/extra/9501/bell.html> Accessed April 29, 2000.

[40-41] American Psychological Association 1996 Press Release, *APA Task Force Examines the Knowns and Unknowns of Intelligence*, American Psychological Association web site: Available at <http://www.apa.org/psychnet/> Accessed 6/10/00

[42] Tori DeAngelis, *Psychologists Question Findings of Bell Curve.* Available at: <http://www.apa.org/monitor/oct95/bell.html> Accessed April 29, 2000.

[43-44] APA Press Release, Ibid.

[45-47] Naureckas, Ibid.

[48-49] Welling, Ibid.

[50] Dan Eggen, Washington Post Staff Writer, *A Taste of Slavery Has Tourists Up in Arms: Williamsburg's New Skits Elicit Raw Emotions*, The Washington Post, Wednesday, July 7, 1999, pg. A01.

Chapter 17: Transforming Society

When you look upon the heartache, sorrow, strife, division, and bitterness slavery has produced in our nation, you have to wonder why the framers of the Constitution didn't outlaw it in the beginning. We have to remember, however, that we cannot apply today's wisdom to yesterday's problems. This is true of us as individuals and as a nation.

If we are to understand what motivated the founding fathers when they drafted the Constitution, we need to gain an even deeper insight into the social and political climate within which they lived. First, we have to remember that the delegates, who gathered at the Constitutional Convention, were the spokesmen for 13 sovereign colonies. The Revolutionary War had drawn them together in a military alliance against a common enemy, but they were still separate political entities. When the war was over, thirteen individual colonies gathered to rejoice, not one sovereign nation. The colonists identified themselves as Virginians, Pennsylvanians, Georgians, etc., not as Americans.

Nothing obligated these "partners in war" to form a political union and become "partners in peace," but any student of history could tell you it was expedient for them to do so. Creating a new nation, of course, required drafting a constitution that was mutually acceptable to all the colonies, not just the majority of them. Not an easy process by any standard.

Rev. Ralph Randolph Gurley, writing in the early 1800s about this period of our nation's history, commented that the Federal Constitution was the result of a compromise between the North and the South. He said that *"...the Southern States would not have entered into the union of America without the temporary permission of the slave trade. When the Constitution was submitted, the great question to be decided was whether a union on such terms were as satisfactory to the several States con-*

cerned, as would produce a preponderating good. " [1] The delegates to the Constitutional Convention knew that finding a common ground for unity would greatly increase the colonies' chances of maintaining their independence from Great Britain. They believed that the good that would come from forming this alliance would outweigh the evil of permitting slavery to continue for a time. It is impossible to see what would have happened had they chosen otherwise. We will never know if Great Britain or some other world power would have been able to take over the fledgling colonies at some point in history or not. What we do know is their failure to abolish slavery caused untold suffering and sorrow.

We will judge the delegates less harshly when we remember that at the time the Constitution was being drafted slavery had been an established institution in the colonies for well over 200 years. Rather than condemn them, we can learn from them. Racism, slavery's close cousin, is still alive and well in America. Sadly, this is true even within the Church. Will we continue to tolerate racism in our own thoughts and actions toward others? Will we, like the delegates to the Constitutional Convention, choose to compromise with our racist brothers and sisters just to maintain unity in the family? If we do, the unity that we achieve will be an outward unity only, not the God-kind of unity that releases His Spirit to transform us as individuals and society as a whole.

THIRTEEN SOVEREIGN COLONIES:

When the debate over slavery intensified at the Constitutional Convention, some of the delegates wanted to exclude any colonies that refused to ban slavery. This is a natural response when an impasse is reached. We just walk away, break fellowship, let them do their own thing—whatever you want to call it. But, if "their thing" isn't "God's thing", we have an obligation to speak the truth in love to them. (Ephesians 4:15) How will they hear if there is no messenger?

One of the Constitutional Convention delegates argued against ostracizing the pro-slavery colonies. He himself was against slavery, but he "...*thought it more in favor of humanity, from a view of all circumstances, to let [the states] in than to exclude them from the Union."* [2]

Commenting on this point, Rev. Gurley said, *"The States being all free and independent, no one could, in any sense, be answerable for any injustice in the legal code of another; nor can we perceive that the law of conscience could, independent of circumstances, impose an obligation upon a State, in which **there was no legalized injustice....**"* [3] In other words, before the formal organization of the colonies into a new nation, there was no legal basis for one colony or a group of colonies to require any other colony to change its legal structures—in this case, to abolish slavery. The "law of the land" had not yet been framed, so there was no way to demand compliance with it.

Rev. Gurley further says, *"At the time the Constitution of the United States was established, the necessities of our country urgently demanded a new form of Government. **Unanimity in the adoption of it was justly considered a matter of first importance.** Many of those who gave their support to the Constitution, while they... recognized the moral wrong in the laws of some States, felt that circumstances were imperious, and did it with the hope and belief, that the National Union would favor the cause of general liberty; and that the system of slavery would be abolished at no distant period, in all the States, either by the sense of duty, the influence of example, in inducement of interest, or by all combined. **They could not believe that the eyes of any free and Christian community,** especially in this country, **could long be closed to that light of truth** beginning even then to be widely diffused, **which revealed the utter condemnation of slavery as a permanent institution.** But they felt, that the main responsibility touching this subject, was with those States who reserved to themselves the sovereign and exclusive right to regulate and control it within their respective limits."* [4]

There were some rights and laws that all of the colonies were willing to make subject to the control of the Federal Government, but there were others that the colonies adamantly retained for themselves. Slavery was one such matter. Those who opposed slavery decided to place the immediate goal of establishing the Union above the goal of emancipating the slaves. They did this in the confident hope that the slaveholders would soon see the evil of slavery and set the captives free.

Jesus did say, *"Blessed are the peacemakers...,"* but we need to consider carefully the things that we permit in order to keep the peace. If the peace that we keep is not God's peace—if it is not in conformity with His will and purpose but merely advantageous to our circumstances—it will not be lasting.

BLINDNESS TO ERROR:

Blindness to obvious error seems to trip all of us up at times. The scripture gives us many examples of man's capacity to believe a lie. One of them is found in Isaiah 44:19-20.

> [19] *"And none considereth in his heart, neither is there knowledge nor understanding to say, I have burned part of it in the fire; yea, also I have baked bread upon the coals thereof; I have roasted flesh, and eaten it: and shall I make the residue thereof an abomination? shall I fall down to the stock of a tree?* [20] *He feedeth on ashes:* **a deceived heart hath turned him aside**, *that he cannot deliver his soul, nor say, Is there not a lie in my right hand?"*

Amazing! The people were using part of the tree to make an idol and the rest of it to make a fire and cook their dinner! To us the contradiction is obvious. Who would want to worship a god made of wood? For that matter, who would want to worship a god he had to create, instead of the God who is the Creator of the entire Universe? But this idol creator/worshiper could not see his error. In the same way, the slaveholders couldn't see their error. Their blindness cost them and their fellow Americans dearly, not to mention the incredible price it cost those who suffered and died as slaves.

God's response to these idol worshippers is a powerful testimony to His grace, mercy and forgiveness. These people were not pagans; they were His people. They knew Him. They had experienced His miracle working power—or had at least heard accounts of it—from their childhood. Still they were turning to a block of wood for protection, provision, and guidance.

God didn't give up on them though. Instead He said, *"...thou art my servant: I have formed thee; thou art my servant: O Israel, thou shalt not be forgotten of me. ²²I have blotted out, as a thick cloud, thy transgressions, and, as a cloud, thy sins: return unto me; for I have redeemed thee."* (Isaiah 44:21-22) They had forgotten God, but He had not forgotten them. Instead, He forgave their transgressions and asked them to return to Him.

Looking forward to Calvary, Isaiah saw that God even had a plan for their redemption—and ours. On a rough wooden cross, the debt for the sins of all mankind would be paid, and the sting of death would be removed. In the same way, the sting of racism can be removed if we are willing to forgive those who have persecuted us. No, this is not easy to do, but neither is it optional.

NOT SO EASILY ACCOMPLISHED:

Our outrage over slavery makes it hard for us to understand why it was tolerated after the colonies won the war with Great Britain. We wonder why our nation had to go through four years of bitter civil warfare to end this vile institution. But, you see, we view slavery from a historical perspective. To us it is an evil that never should have been allowed in the first place. To Abraham Lincoln and his fellow citizens, however, slavery was a current reality—a legal institution which had been mandated by the British Crown and made legal by each successive Congress of the United States. These nineteenth century Americans could not discuss slavery from an uninvolved perspective. It was "in their face", as our young people say today. It evoked great passion in its opponents and its advocates alike. It brought division in the Halls of Congress; it brought division among friends and family. One of President Lincoln's brother-in-laws died fighting for the Confederacy.

Lincoln gives us a glimpse into the heart of 19th century Americans in his opening remarks in his first debate with Stephen Douglas:

"Before proceeding, let me say I think I have no prejudice against the Southern people. They are just what we would be in their situation. If slavery did not now exist amongst them, they would not introduce it. If it did now exist amongst us, we should not instantly give it up. This I believe of the masses north and south. Doubtless there are individuals, on both the sides, who would not hold slaves under any circumstances; and others who would gladly introduce slavery anew, if it were out of existence. We know that some southern men do free their slaves, go north, and become tip-top abolitionists; while some northern ones go south, and become most cruel slave-masters." [5]

Was Lincoln making an excuse for slavery when he said this? No, he was identifying the source of slavery—the social norm, the collective social morality that either permits or excludes the right of one person to enslave another. He was saying, *"Had I grown up in the South where slavery was an accepted practice, I, too might well be in favor of holding slaves."* Much in the same way, I grew up in the South when it was steeped in racial prejudice. It was their only known way of life, as it was also ours.

Lincoln's comments on this point merit consideration, for he directs our attention away from the slaveholders, who practiced slavery, and focuses it on the social order that made slavery legal. In doing so, Lincoln defuses our indignation against the slaveholders and gives us some understanding of why they believed in holding slaves. This understanding is essential, because, while slavery has ended in America, it is still widely practiced throughout our world today. If we, as Christians, do not take the time to understand what motivates these modern slaveholders, we will not be able to persuade them to allow Jesus to set them free of the desire to hold others in captivity.

A PLAN NEEDED FOR EMANCIPATION:

Lincoln recognized that moving from a slave-holding society to a totally free society was not going to be easy. There were many questions to be answered. Would the freed slaves have the right to vote? Would they be able to become a part of a society that had held them in bondage for generations? Should the freed slaves be returned to Africa?

Addressing the practical questions regarding emancipation, Lincoln said, *"When it is said that the institution exists, and that it is very difficult to get rid of it, in any satisfactory way, I can understand and appreciate the saying. I surely will not blame them for not doing what I should not know how to do myself. If all earthly power were given me, I should not know what to do, as to the existing institution."* [6] Lincoln's passion to see the slaves freed is evident in his speeches and writings. His statement here does not reflect an unwillingness to free the slaves, just a lack of means or organized plan for accomplishing their emancipation and their integration into society as free people.

In the second chapter of this book, I spoke of the "growing pains" our nation has faced each time a new wave of immigrants has come seeking to make a home in America. Each of these groups has experienced its own time in the cauldron of prejudice as the "home folks" sought to preserve their turf from the newcomers. The freed slaves would face an even more difficult cauldron of prejudice, for they were longtime residents, not newcomers to the American scene. They weren't the "new kids on the block"; they were an existing culture. As such they already had a defined "place" in our society. Emancipation would, therefore, require redefining their "place".

Further complicating the matter was the issue of citizenship. Emancipating the slaves was a formidable task in itself. Gaining the full rights of citizenship for the freed slaves would prove even more formidable. They had not yet won this victory in all of the existing free states. It would be even more difficult to secure these rights in the slave states. It wasn't until the Civil Rights Movement of our generation that these rights would be fully realized for many African-American citizens.

While Lincoln opposed slavery, he understood why some favored it, and he knew they would not easily give it up. Lincoln also knew that emancipation of the slaves would not accomplish the full effect abolitionists desired if it was imposed by the force of law or by the ravages of war, because, even though either of these instruments would free the slaves from their chains, they would remain bound by the heart attitudes of those who still favored slavery.

THE COLONIZATION MOVEMENT:

Many favored the repatriation of the freed slaves to Africa. One of the earliest supporters of efforts to establish a African colony for free Blacks was Paul Cuffee, a prominent African-American/ Native American. Some consider Cuffee to be the father of Black Nationalism in America. His experiences with racial prejudice convinced him that Whites would never accept free African-Americans as their equals. [7]

In 1811, Cuffee visited the British colony of Sierra Leone, which had been established as a repatriation point for freed British slaves. His visit convinced him that emigration was a needed option for the freed slaves in America. In 1815, Cuffee used one of his own ships to take 38 freed Blacks to Sierra Leone. His intention was to fund annual trips, offering passage home to freed Blacks, who desired to emigrate. [8]

Cuffee's role in the colonization movement was cut short by his untimely death in 1817, but his efforts laid the groundwork for other colonization societies, the most prominent of which was

the American Colonization Society (ACS), founded in the 1816 by a group of Presbyterian ministers in Washington, DC. Some Blacks criticized the colonization movement, saying that its goal was to deport freed Blacks and perpetuate slavery in America. Cuffee and other Blacks supported the ACS's work, believing that

American Colonization Life Membership Certificate: a standard fund-raising method for benevolent societies in the early 1800s. (Image from the Library of Congress, Manuscript Division)

their efforts would hasten the establishment of a free Black nation on African soil. [9]

Abraham Lincoln, James Monroe, James Madison, and Henry Clay were among the many prominent Americans who supported the work of the American Colonization Society. Memberships in the society were sold to provide funds for freed Blacks desiring to emigrate to Africa. Henry Clay unsuccessfully campaigned for the U.S. Congress to appropriate funds for this purpose, but some of the state legislatures did contribute funds to the society. Virginia, the state holding the most slaves, pledged $30,000 for five consecutive years. The New Jersey, Maryland, Pennsylvania, and Missouri legislatures also supported the society's work. Through their combined efforts, the colony of Liberia was established in 1822. In 1847, this colony would become the first democratic nation on the continent of Africa. [10]

OPPOSITION TO COLONIZATION:

In the 1830s, William Lloyd Garrison and other abolitionists were outspoken in their opposition to the ACS. The ACS responded to their objections by producing a pamphlet, which described the life of the settlers in Liberia. In this pamphlet, they emphasized that their purposes in establishing the colony were two fold: (1. to provide a country where freed African-Americans would be truly free, where they could pursue a new life, free from the prejudice that they commonly experienced in America, both in the North and in the South, and (2. that the colonists might be agents of transformation in Africa, i.e., that they might *"...spread civilization, sound morals, and true religion throughout Africa."* [11] Put more simply, it was believed that the colonists would be a strong Christian influence in Africa, that by setting up schools and sharing the gospel, they could make a profound difference in the development of the neighboring nations.

One of my ancestors, Ralph Randolph Gurley, likely had a hand in writing this pamphlet. He served as the Secretary of the ACS and as the editor of its quarterly journal, *The African Repository and Colonial Journal*. So again, our family has had a long history of working to advance the gospel and to open up opportunities for all races to walk in the fullness God has planned for all of His children.

THE CONSTITUTION OF THE ACS AND THE NATION OF LIBERIA:

The constitution of the ACS provided for the oversight of the groups' colonization efforts and for a system of membership, which would allow them to raise funds. It is noteworthy that many Southerners as well as Northerners were members of the ACS—a fact which did much to promote unity at a time when our nation was very much divided over the issue of slavery.

Congressional support of the colony of Liberia never came through to the degree that ACS's leadership had hoped. When it became evident that the fledgling colony was vulnerable to military take-over in the era of European colonial expansion, ACS leaders believed it was expedient to make Liberia a sovereign nation.

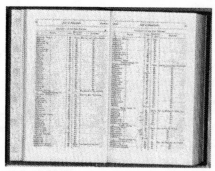

"Table of Emigrants," in *The African Repository and Colonial Journal.* (Image from the Library of Congress, General Collections)

The constitution, which was drawn up for the nation of Liberia, reflects the Constitution of our own nation in many ways. One key difference is evident however: Liberia's constitution expressly forbids the enslavement of any individual or any dealings in the slave trade. Many aspects of commerce would be developed, but not slavery. (Copies of the constitutions the American Colonization Society and of the nation of Liberia when it was established in 1847 follow this chapter.)

PILGRIMAGE TO LIBERIA:

So often we read of African-Americans journeying to Africa in search of their roots. In 1989, I traveled to the nation of Liberia, in part, in search of my roots. While I cannot identify with my African-American brothers and sisters in respect to my racial heritage, I can identify with them in their struggle to live free. As I said earlier, my family knew the sting of racial prejudice first hand. Some of my ancestors were among the Blackfoot Indians who were forced to migrate westward when President Andrew

Jackson claimed over 25 million acres of tribal lands in order to make them available for the cultivation of cotton. Others of my ancestors were among the Jewish people who lost their lives and their fortunes when Hitler's racist polices were reigning unchallenged in Germany.

When I walked the streets of Monrovia, it was like touching a portion of my personal history. Rev. Ralph Randolph Gurley had named that city after his friend and fellow member of the American Colonization Society, James Monroe. When the people found out that I was a descendant of Rev. Gurley's, they treated me like a hero. Many today might debate the motivations of those who founded the American Colonization Society, but if the people of Liberia regard them as heroes, that is a fair testimony of how the ACS was regarded by those who worked with them firsthand.

Gen. Robert E. Lee was among the southern supporters of the colonization movement. Prior to the beginning of the Civil War, Lee freed most of his slaves and offered to pay expenses for passage to Liberia for those who wanted to emigrate. Two of Lee's former slaves, William and Rosabella Burke, and their four children were among those who chose to go to Liberia. William Burke attended a newly established seminary there and became a Presbyterian minister. He also helped to educate many of the other members of his community and adopted several of the native children. The account of the Burkes' emigration is recorded in *The African Repository and Colonial Journal.* [12]

Some Considered America Home:

In reality, not all of the Freedmen wanted to return to Africa. Some of their families had lived here for over 200 years. They considered America their home. If the newly freed slaves were to be truly free, repatriation had to be an option, not a requirement. This meant that legislators still had to define the status of those who stayed in America, and they had to make those decisions within the context of their social moorings, not ours. The uncomfortable truth is that the basic rights that we regard as "givens" for every race were primarily restricted to Whites at that point in our nation's history.

The process of moving from "their way of thinking" to "our way of thinking" has not come easily. This transformation has exacted a high cost in terms of human suffering and pain. Even a brief review of the landmark events in the Civil Rights Movement vividly illustrates just how high the cost has been.

This transformation process is not yet complete—not from God's perspective anyway. It is human nature to hold onto the familiar. It requires God's nature, God's way of thinking in a matter, being instilled in us by the work of the Holy Spirit to move us out of our "comfort zone" into the perfect "comfort zone" God has purposed for His people—a "comfort zone" where every individual stands equal before God on the basis of the blood of Jesus Christ, not on the color of his or her skin. True peace is the result when we reach this level in our walk with the Lord.

What a contrast with the way man establishes peace! Often a "battle zone" ensues until we have conquered our foes. Then, in victory, we enter a comfort zone we have secured by our power. Unfortunately, where there is a victor, there is also a vanquished. What brings comfort to the victors, almost always brings oppression in one form or another to the vanquished.

NEITHER FRONT WAS UNIFIED:

When we read accounts of the Civil War, we tend to see two unified fronts, locked in mortal combat—the North determined to preserve the Union and free the slaves and the South determined to seceded and establish a new nation in which slavery was legal. In reality there were strongly dissenting voices in both camps. So deep was the division in Virginia on the secession issue, that its northern forty-two counties eventually broke off and formed the state of West Virginia. They did not, however, immediately ban slavery. In all, there were four slave states that remained loyal to the Union—Delaware, Kentucky, Maryland, and Missouri. In addition, there were significant numbers of Union supporters in the upper Confederate states, i.e., Tennessee, Arkansas, North Carolina, and even Virginia. [13] They desired to preserve the Union, while maintaining their right to hold slaves.

Lincoln took the reigns of government in perilous times indeed. He had an abundance of critics regardless of what position he took on issues related to the war. Frequently, he sought God for the course of action he should take. As I said earlier, another of my ancestors, the Rev. Phineas Gurley, was Lincoln's pastor and friend during the tumultuous Civil War years. Often these two friends spent the entire night praying about difficult decisions Lincoln had to make. These decisions and those made by Congress, guided our nation through one of the most difficult portions of our nation's history. During those four years, the foundation for emancipation of the slaves was laid, and we took our first faltering steps toward eliminating the racist attitudes and beliefs that had justified the enslavement.

PREJUDICE DIES HARD:
The war came because slaveholders were simply not ready for change. As the campaign for the abolition of slavery became more intense, some of the Southern slaveholders were angered by the constant criticism that was coming against them. Determined to silence the abolitionists, some of the Southerners urged Stephen Douglas to submit a sedition law to the Senate, **prohibiting any statement or inference that slavery was wrong**. The slaveholders believed that the abolitionists were attempting to incite an insurrection among the slaves and encourage the federal government to exercise more control at the state level.

When Douglas submitted this proposed "gag order", Lincoln made this comment:

"...what will convince them? This, and this only: cease to call slavery wrong, and join them in calling it right. And this must be done thoroughly—done in acts as well as in words. Silence will not be tolerated—we must place ourselves avowedly with them. Senator Douglas' new sedition law must be enacted and enforced, suppressing all

declarations that slavery is wrong, whether made in poli-
tics, in presses, in pulpits, or in private. We must arrest
and return their fugitive slaves with greedy pleasure. We
must pull down our Free State constitutions. The whole
atmosphere must be disinfected from all taint of opposi-
tion to slavery, before they will cease to believe that all
their troubles proceed from us." [14]

It's so easy to blame others when we're in the wrong. These Southerners were willing to violate abolitionists' right to freedom of
speech just to preserve their right to hold slaves. Thankfully,
Douglas' bill never became law.

INEFFECTIVE COMPROMISES:

Compromise on the issue of slavery had been necessary to establish the Union. Repeated compromises were needed in the decades that followed just to hold that fragile Union together.

Compromise, in and of itself, has a valid place in the dynamics of
human relationships. It is essential to preserve peace and unity
within the family and the church, as well as within a nation.
Compromise is often essential in matters, which involve our will
or desire, but there can be no compromise with evil; and slavery
is one of the greatest evils man has ever devised.

As we can see from Douglas' sedition bill, none of the legislative compromises that were passed were able to resolve the bitter
conflict between the abolitionists and the pro-slavery factions in
our nation. Lincoln made this comment on the temporary nature
of these compromises:

"These repeated settlements must have some fault about
them. There must be some inadequacy in their very nature
to the purpose for which they were designed. ...I think that
*one of the causes of these repeated failures is that **our***
best and greatest men have greatly underestimated the
size of this question. They have constantly brought for-
ward small cures for great sores—plasters too small to
***cover the wound.** That is one reason that all settlements*
have proved so temporary—so evanescent.

An illustration of the horrors of slavery that appeared in the American Anti-Slavery Society's 1840 almanac. (Image from the Library of Congress, Rare Book & Special Collections Division.)

❧❧❧❧❧❧❧❧

*"Look at the magnitude of this subject! ...about one sixth of the whole population of the United States are slaves! The owners of these slaves consider them property. The effect upon the minds of the owners is that of property, and nothing else—it induces them to insist upon all that will favorably affect its value as property, **to demand laws***

*and institutions and a public policy that shall increase
and secure its value, and make it durable, lasting and
universal."* [15]

A sixth of our nation, enslaved! A sixth of our nation, considered mere property! How could there be peace in our nation when a large portion of our citizens demanded laws that would secure their right to treat others as mere property?

Before we condemn these nineteenth century slaveholders, we need to ask ourselves if this kind of thinking still finds a place in our hearts and minds even in a very small way. If we, as Christians, embrace any doctrine or ideology, which places our race, culture, or nation above all others, we are denying their equality with us before God. No, that is not the same thing as regarding them as mere property, but it does demean them and assign them a lesser place in the kingdom of God. I see no such caste system when I study the Word of God. I see only one family, the family of God, made up of blood-bought sons and daughters.

The challenge then is to forgive as we have been forgiven. But remember that while forgiveness does not require us to deny that a transgression occurred, it does require us to look beyond the transgression and see what can happen in an individual's life when the Holy Spirit is released to work in them.

If we will forgive them, love them, and pray for them, God will work in their lives. Who knows? Perhaps they will be set free! Even if they aren't, we will be.

THE TREATMENT OF FUGITIVE SLAVES:

Where you have slavery, there you will inevitably have fugitive slaves and angry slaveholders who want to get their "property" back again. Slavery in America was no different. There actually was a provision for the return of fugitive slaves and runaway indentured servants in the Constitution. Article IV, Section 2 of the Constitution says that *"...persons 'held to Service or Labour' in one state who escape into another state 'shall be delivered up on Claim of the Party to whom such Service or Labour may be due.'"* [16] The Constitution contained no provision for enforcing this Section, however. The lack of such enforcement became a sore point between the states when slavery was abolished in most of the northern states.

Tensions between the North and the South further increased when Congress passed a more definitive fugitive slave law in 1793. Under this law, slaveholders were only required to present a statement of ownership before a magistrate in order to recover a runaway slave. An order was then issued for the arrest and return of the escaped slave. These recaptured slaves were forbidden a jury trial and denied the right to give evidence in their own behalf. This law angered the abolitionists, because it denied the slaves the right of due process.

This failure to grant the slaves due process gave rise to practices that even further enraged the abolitionists. In some instances, freed Blacks were kidnapped and taken before a magistrate. On the basis of false documents, these freed Blacks were then taken back to the South as slaves! No one could testify on their behalf, and their own testimony was not admissible in court. [17]

Some Northern states reacted to this harsh law by giving local authorities orders not to help recover any of the fugitive slaves. Some states made it illegal to house recaptured slaves in local jails to await trial and extradition. This law greatly escalated tensions between the North and the South and redoubled the activity of the Underground Railroad.

An even harsher fugitive slave law was included in the Compromise of 1850. This law imposed heavy penalties on anyone who helped a slave escape or interfered with their return to their master. Some Northern states were so angered by this law that they passed personal liberty laws, which in some instances prohibited state and local officers from obeying national fugitive slave laws. [18]

My wife and I were watching a movie recently about the Underground Railroad. One incident in the movie dealt with a fugitive slave who escaped to Canada with the assistance of a northern White man. In one scene, the fugitive slave was instructing his newfound friend in the proper way to treat a slave. The "fugi-tive" knew that if this White man kept treating him like an equal, they were never going to make it to Canada!

One thing this man said really struck me. He said, *"Never look into your slave's eyes. A slaveholder never does that."*

"Why not?" his friend asked.

"Because if you look into his eyes," the fugitive answered, *"you might see that he is a man just like you."*

This denial that slaves were equals with Whites was a founda-tional principle for justifying slavery. The majority of slaveholders refused to abandon this principle even when doing so could have meant victory against the North. Some of the Confederate military leadership began to consider using the slaves as combat soldiers when the North began to win some major battles. General Patrick R. Cleburne said, *"I recommended...that we immediately commence training a large reserve of the most courageous of our slaves and further that we guarantee free-dom within a reasonable time to every slave in the South who shall remain true to the Confederacy in this war."* [19]

General Howell Cobb strongly disagreed with Cleburne, how-ever. He said, *"You cannot make soldiers of slaves, or slaves of soldiers. The day you make a soldier of them, then our whole theory of slavery is wrong."* [20]

It is both man's strength and man's weakness that once people have fully embraced a theory, it is very difficult to get them to repudiate that theory, especially if they have gone to war to de-fend it.

Had the South followed General Cleburne's advice, the outcome of the war might have been very different not only from the stand-point of increasing the ranks of their armed forces, but also in the aid that would have come to them through other nations who had already freed their slaves. Slavery was a key obstacle to their com-ing to the assistance of the South, but the slaveholders were ada-mant. Slavery was an essential part of their way of life, and they were not willing to give it up voluntarily. [21]

AN END TO COMPROMISE:

The harsh treatment of fugitive slaves strained the compromises that had been holding the Union together to the breaking point. Lincoln's outrage over the Dred Scott decision compelled him to re-enter politics. In his famous "House Divided" speech, Lincoln considered the ramifications of the Supreme Court's decision in this landmark case. Believing that compromise had not and would not resolve the controversy over slavery, Lincoln said, *"'A house divided against itself cannot stand.' I believe this government cannot endure permanently half slave and half free. I do not expect the Union to be dissolved—I do not expect the house to fall—but I do expect it will cease to be divided. It will become all one thing, or all the other. Either the opponents of slavery will arrest the further spread of it, and place it where the public mind shall rest in the belief that it is in the course of ultimate extinction; or its advocates will push it forward, till it shall become alike lawful in all the States, old as well as new—North as well as South."* [22]

Lincoln was anticipating a political resolution of the slavery issue. There was no clear consensus at that point in our nation's history as to which group would be the victor, but one thing was clear: Slavery would either be abolished completely or it would become lawful in every state and territory. Praise God, it was abolished. I pray that one day we will also be able to say that racism has been abolished as well.

NO RETURN TO THE STATUS QUO:

The simply truth is, the preservation of the Union, not the emancipation of the slaves, was the key issue of the Civil War for many nineteenth century Americans. Many would have been content to resolve the "secession issue" and allow things to return to normal. Gradual changes in society were taking place, however, that made a return to a pre-Civil War status quo impossible. God has a way of burning bridges behind us when He has determined that it is time to move on.

One of these changes came about because of the active involvement of the American Missionary Association and some liberal Northern aid societies in the education of the children of slaves who escaped to the North. The American Missionary Association opened the first of schools for these children at Fortress Monroe, which lies opposite of Norfolk, Virginia. Mary Peake, a freed Black woman, was the instructor. In her classroom, fifty former slave children took the first steps to living free—they began to learn to read and write. [23]

The education of slave children was strictly forbidden in all of the Southern states with the exception of Tennessee. These states had even placed strict controls on the education of the children of freedmen. Opening the doors of learning to all Blacks threatened the Southern social order. Education stirs a greater hunger for freedom, for personal fulfillment, or for Christians, a pursuit of God's individual calling on their life. I said "a greater hunger" because, if you read some of the literature the slaves and ex-slaves wrote, you know that these hungers were already well developed in their hearts and minds. Slavery advocates might claim that the slaves were mere beasts, but the songs, poetry, speeches, and writings of the slaves and ex-slaves discredits this theory if nothing else does—and much else does! Returning these newly educated Black children to slavery would have been difficult, if not impossible, had the South won the war.

We see a similar effect in the spiritual realm. Once we know the freedom that is ours in Christ, we are not easily ensnared by the things of the world and the flesh again. This is why Jesus commanded His disciples to go and make disciples. He knew that teaching the new converts kingdom principles was essential to their growth in the Kingdom of God. The same was true for the freed slaves. Education was the key to their full integration into the American society. The slaveholders did not want Blacks to have access to that key.

Education is a powerful vehicle for shaping society. It is an essential tool for bringing healing between the races in our nation or any nation. Education's power lies in the fact that it reveals the misconceptions and old wives' tales that have defined our concepts of and attitudes toward people of different races or cultural backgrounds. Once the truth is presented to us, we must chose whether we will allow that truth to transform our relationships with others or whether we will continue to believe and act upon the "truths" that have been passed down through the generations.

Some will cling to what they have known and experienced since they were little children, rather than embrace a new way of life. Determined to preserve the Southern way of life, some of the slaveholders forcibly relocated their slaves far behind enemy lines. One transplanted Mississippi slave later commented, *"It looked like everybody in the world was going to Texas!"* [24] How hard we fight sometimes when God requires us to change.

PREJUDICE AMONG NORTHERNERS:
We shouldn't assume that it was only the Southerners that God had brought to this turning point in America's history. Not all Northerners exhibited the same measure of charity and grace toward the newly freed slaves that the American Missionary Association and the liberal aid societies did. Some of the Northerners actually exploited the ex-slaves.

One such case took place in Port Royal, South Carolina and in the islands that surround Beaufort, South Carolina. By the end of 1862, the AMA and the northern aid societies that were working there contracted several thousand "contrabands" (slaves who had escaped from their masters) to work on the abandoned plantations. Some people wanted to see the "contrabands" emancipated and these plantations parceled out to them, but most of the Union officers regarded the islands as a supply base. They came frequently and helped themselves to the islanders' provisions! [25]

Another case involved the South's primary crop, cotton. The Treasury Department had authority over any cotton that was confiscated in Confederate territory. The proceeds from the sale of this cotton were used to fund the war. The same was true of the cotton produced by the "contrabands." The Treasury Department encouraged them to produce as large a crop as possible to further the war effort. [26]

These and other events clearly indicated that there were Northerners, as well as Southerners, who were going to need some attitude adjustments when the slaves were freed. Lincoln recognized this as well as anyone. Prior to issuing the Emancipation Proclamation, he commented that *"...what prejudiced Northern whites feared most was for blacks to 'swarm northward' and 'intermingle,' competing for jobs...."* [27]

Isn't it interesting that where man sees problems, God sees opportunities? What one part is lacking, another part supplies. What a great loss a nation inflicts upon itself when it closes itself off to the gifts and talents resident in a particular group of people simply because they are of a different nationality, culture, or race—or because they might pose a threat to their livelihood!

FREEDOM WITHOUT LIBERTY:

There were two aspects to abolitionists' efforts to free the slaves, the first of which was freeing them from the bonds of slavery. The second was securing full citizenship for those former slaves who chose to make America their home. Without the right to vote, to hold a political office, to serve on a jury, to testify in court, to marry whoever they chose, to attend the school of their choice, etc. they would not be able to enjoy the full liberty that our Constitution promises to every American.

We associate the fight for voting rights with the Reconstruction Era in the South and with the Civil Rights Movement, but the right to vote had not been given to freed slaves in the majority of the free states of the North either. Stephen Douglas referred to this fact in the second Lincoln/Douglas debate. Defending the right of each state to determine whether it would be "slave" or "free," Douglas said,

"My answer is that ...each State must answer for itself. We in Illinois have decided it for ourselves. We tried slavery, kept it

*up for twelve years, and finding that it was not profitable we abolished it for that reason, and became a free State. We adopted in its stead the policy **that a negro in this State shall not be a slave and shall not be a citizen**. We have a right to adopt that policy. For my part I think it is a wise and sound policy for us. You in Missouri must judge for yourselves whether it is a wise policy for you. If you choose to follow our example, very good; if you reject it, still well, it is your business, not ours. If the people of all the States will act on that great principle, and each State mind its own business, attend to its own affairs, take care of its own negroes and not meddle with its neighbors, then there will be peace between the North and the South, the East and the West, throughout the whole Union. Why can we not thus have peace?"* [28]

Lincoln did not believe that the slaveholders were going to be content with this "live and let live" approach to slavery. He believed that they intended to make slavery lawful in every state and territory. Addressing this point, Lincoln said,

*"This declared indifference, but as I must think, covert real zeal for the spread of slavery, I can not but hate. **I hate it because of the monstrous injustice of slavery itself.** I hate it because it deprives our republican example of its just influence in the world—enables the enemies of free institutions, with plausibility, to taunt us as hypocrites—causes the real friends of freedom to doubt our sincerity, and especially because it forces so many really good men amongst ourselves into an open war with the very fundamental principles of civil liberty—criticizing the Declaration of Independence, and **insisting that there is no right principle of action but self-interest.**"* [29]

To Lincoln, slavery was a "monstrous injustice," one that brought shame to America and robbed her of her rightful influence in the world. How could we claim to be the land of the free, yet permit people to be held in bondage within our borders? How could we urge the world to move toward a democratic form of government when the shackles of over two million slaves were sounding out a cry for liberty in our own land? Not only was slavery keeping America from being a good influence in the world, Lincoln argued, but it was having a decidedly bad influence on our own citizens—it was leading them to question the intent of the Declaration of Independence and encouraging them to believe that self-interest should be the primary force guiding the policies of this nation.

Indeed, how can you justify enslaving another person or permitting their enslavement except on the basis of self-interest? "Self" shouts loudest when it has the most to lose, and the proponents of slavery had a lot to lose if slavery was abolished.

THE EMANCIPATION PROCLAMATION:

The emancipation of the slaves was a pivotal event that forever transformed the social development of this nation. Many of our great leaders prior to the Emancipation Proclamation had voiced a desire to see slavery come to an end. All of them envisioned a gradual emancipation but didn't have any idea how it was going to happen. Lincoln, himself, had favored a gradual emancipation when he first took office as president, but his efforts to move Congress to enact legislation that would define how it would take place failed.

Nevertheless, Lincoln believed that emancipation, regardless of the difficulties it presented, was the course God had chosen for America. Acting on that belief, he drew up a preliminary Emancipation Proclamation and presented it to his cabinet.

Rev. Phineas Gurley assisted Lincoln in the preparation of the Emancipation Proclamation. Lincoln retained some of Rev. Gurley's suggestions in the final version of the Proclamation. So the Gurley family has had a long history of involvement in the process of breaking down the barriers between the races in this nation.

Initially, Lincoln's proposal to free the slaves met with some opposition. One of his cabinet members suggested that he delay making his plans public until the Union Army began winning more battles against the Confederacy. *"Otherwise,"* this cabinet mem-

ber pointed out, *"it may be interpreted as a sign of defeat."* [30]
Reluctantly, Lincoln agreed, but he remained determined to free
the slaves at the first opportune moment. That moment came
with the Union victory at the battle of Antietam.

Following this victory, Lincoln called his Cabinet together to tell
them he was going to issue the Emancipation Proclamation on
January 1, 1863. Addressing them, Lincoln said resolutely,

> *"Gentlemen: I have as you are aware, thought a great deal
> about the relation of this war to Slavery...When the rebel
> army was at Frederick, I determined, as soon as it should be
> driven out of Maryland, to issue a Proclamation of Emanci-
> pation... I said nothing to any one; but I made the promise to
> myself, and...to my Maker. The rebel army is now driven
> out, and I am going to fulfill that promise. I have got you
> together to hear what I have written down. I do not wish
> your advice about the main matter—for that I have already
> determined for myself."* [31]

Lincoln had peace. It was time to act. Accordingly, he issued the
Emancipation Proclamation, which promised freedom to all slaves
in the states that were still in rebellion against the Union on
January 1, 1863. Lincoln's words sealed the death of the institution of slavery in America:

> *"That on the first day of January, in the year of our Lord one
> thousand eight hundred and sixty-three, all persons held as
> slaves within any state or designated part of a state, the people
> whereof shall then be in rebellion against the United States,
> shall be then, thenceforward, and forever free; and the Ex-
> ecutive Government of the United States, including the mili-
> tary and naval authority thereof, will recognize and maintain
> the freedom of such persons, and will do no act or acts to
> repress such persons, or any of them, in any efforts they may
> make for their actual freedom."* [32]

Support for Lincoln's Emancipation Proclamation was not universal even among those who were loyal to the Union. Some Union

soldiers threw down their weapons and went home. They were willing to fight to preserve the Union, but not to free the slaves.

Lincoln did not back down from the stand he had taken. He knew that it would require an amendment to the Constitution to make the slaves truly free, and he began campaigning for the passage of that amendment even before it was drafted. Writing to the public in Springfield, Lincoln said, *"You say you will not fight to free negroes... Some of them seem willing to fight for you. If they stake their lives for us, they must be prompted by the strongest motive—even the promise of freedom. And the promise being made, must be kept..."* [33]

In his annual message to Congress that December, Lincoln made this statement: *"In giving freedom to the slave, we assure freedom to the free."* [34] Fully aware of the potential greatness of the cost of taking such a stand, Lincoln was still determined to complete the task he had begun.

An Unexpected Result:

Subsequent to the issuing of the Emancipation Proclamation, Blacks became eligible for the first time to serve in the Union Army. Prior to that time, freed Blacks attempts to fight for the Union met stiff resistance. With the stroke of a pen, this resistance began to be broken down. Lincoln commented, *"They are '...the great available yet unavailed of, force for restoring the Union...'"* [35]

Many Blacks had been appealing for the right to enlist in the Union armed forces. Frederick Douglass had campaigned for Black recruitment from the beginning of the war. He said, *"The Negro is the key to the situation, the pivot upon which the whole rebellion turns....This war, disguise it as they may, is virtually nothing more or less than perpetual slavery against universal freedom."* [36]

In the months that followed Lincoln's Proclamation, recruiters actively sought to draw as many of these Blacks into the Union forces as they could. The ranks of Black soldiers grew rapidly. Vast numbers of former slaves joined the ranks of Grant's army in Mississippi and Tennessee. In all, over 180,000 Blacks fought on the side of the Union.

UNEQUAL TREATMENT:

While many of the newly recruited Blacks saw active combat, many others were restricted to menial tasks. Most of their officers were White, and none of the Black soldiers were ever promoted beyond captain. They were paid less than Whites, and they were not given a clothing allowance and were, therefore, less able to withstand severe weather conditions. White doctors were reluctant to serve with the all-Black companies. As a result, the death rate among the Blacks was double that of the rest of the Union forces.[37]

When Frederick Douglass took these grievances to President Lincoln, Lincoln's response was *"The employment of colored troops at all was a great gain to the colored people...their enlistment was a serious offense to popular prejudice... That they were not to receive the same pay as white soldiers seemed a necessary concession to smooth the way to their employment as soldiers."* [38] Lincoln's last comment, while offensive to many today, was ground-breaking in 1863.

Some of Lincoln's high-ranking officers opposed the recruitment of Blacks—William Sherman, among them. Sherman asked, *"Is not a negro as good as a white man to stop a bullet? Yes: and a sand-bag is better; but can a negro do our skirmishing and picket duty? Can they improvise bridges, sorties, flank movements, etc., like the white man? I say no."* [39] Had Sherman read some of the history of the Revolutionary War, he would have known that indeed the Black soldiers were equal with their White counterparts both in respect to courage and ability.

General Grant did not share Sherman's disparaging view of Blacks. He heartily supported enlisting Blacks, saying that doing so dealt a heavy blow against the Confederacy. *"By arming the Negro we have added a powerful ally,"* Grant contended. *"They will make good soldiers and taking them from the enemy weakens him in the same proportion they strengthen us."* [40] President Lincoln heartily agreed.

There were some bright spots in the treatment of Black soldiers. In addition to soldiering skills, civilian volunteers and some of the officers taught the new recruits in the Black regiments to read and write. In doing so, they not only armed them for battle; they prepared them for freedom after the war was over. [41]

MILLIKEN'S BEND:

The first major Civil War in which Black soldiers fought took place at Milliken's Bend, Louisiana. Fifteen hundred Texans were deployed against a smaller force of White and Black soldiers. The courage of the Blacks was noted in the journal of one of the White officers: *"The bravery of the blacks at Milliken's Bend completely revolutionized the sentiment of the army with regard to the employment of Negro troops. I heard prominent officers, who formerly had sneered...at the idea of the Negroes fighting, express themselves after that, heartily in favor of it."* [42]

The walls of prejudice were coming down, slowly perhaps, but it was impossible to witness the effectiveness of the Black troops and still maintain a belief that they should not be allowed to serve their country.

THE 54TH MASSACHUSETTS REGIMENT:

Other Black units also made great contributions to the war effort. The all-Black 54th Massachusetts Regiment distinguished itself in an important battle at Fort Wagner, South Carolina. They lead a heroic charge in which many of their ranks died. Frederick Douglass' two sons fought in this battle and survived. They and their fellow soldiers had proved themselves equal to the most courageous White soldiers.

The valor of the Black soldiers profoundly affected President Lincoln. One of his biographers commented that, *"Contemplating the heroism of these men, Lincoln was forever changed.* ***He spoke less and less (and finally not at all) about colonization, and more and more about the black man's earned*** *place in America.* " [43.] Any reservations Lincoln may have had about former slaves ability to integrate into American society were removed by the bravery of these Black soldiers. As Jesus said, knowing the truth will set us free.

BLACKS IN THE CONFEDERATE ARMY:

Unlike the Union Army, Blacks were involved in the Confederate Army from the beginning of the war. An all-Black regiment from Louisiana, made up of Freedmen—some of whom were themselves slaveholder—was among the first to answer the call to battle. They were just as determined as their White counterparts to keep slavery legal. [44]

This regiment was the exception though. Most of the Blacks who aided the Confederacy were slaves who were used as laborers to do menial tasks and to build fortifications, sometimes at gunpoint. Despite the suggestions of some Southern officers to use slaves as combat soldiers, the majority of the South's leadership insisted on maintaining the traditional roles of slaves and freemen.

Prejudice is a cruel thief. It keeps us from seeing the potential in others and robs them of a opportunity to give their best to a cause they might readily claim as their own. Christian Fleetwood, a Black Union officer, believed that had the slaves been set free, many would have fought for the Confederacy. *"But for slavery, the heart of the negro was with the South,"* Fleetwood said. [45]

ANOTHER EMANCIPATION PROCLAMATION:

Lincoln was in good company when he boldly declared liberty to those held in slavery behind enemy lines. Jesus made a similar declaration centuries earlier as He hung suspended between heaven and earth on a rough, wooden cross. With three simple words—*"Father, forgive them."*—He completed the work of setting the captives free. With those words, sin's power was broken and death's terror, removed. In Christ, the guilty were accounted innocent, and the wall dividing God from man was forever removed.

Sadly, the walls that divide man from man are, in many cases, still very much intact. Racism plays a powerful role in keeping these walls intact, and it will continue to do so unless we are willing to examine the false information we have been taught about other peoples, cultures, races, and nationalities and come to understand what God says about them. For in God's kingdom, *...there is neither Jew nor Greek, there is neither bond nor free, there is neither male nor female...* Truly, *we ...are all one in Christ Jesus.* (Gal. 3:28)

The simple truth is, we are all equal before God. We walk as equals in His kingdom. Proclaiming this ageless truth will not come without cost. It cost Lincoln and many other abolitionists their very lives to stand for the freedom and equality of their African-American brothers and sisters. Transforming society is not an easy task, but it is a task we cannot neglect if we want to be like Jesus.

End Notes:

[1] Ralph Randolph Gurley, *The Life of Jehudi Ashmun: Late Colonial Agent in Liberia*, Books for Libraries Press, Freeport, New York, first published in 1835; Reprinted in 1971, pg. 105.

[2] Charles C. Tansill, *Documents Illustrative of the Formation of the Union of the American States,* Government Printing Office, Washington, DC, 192, pp. 616-618.

[3-4] Gurley, Ibid.

[5] Abraham Lincoln, *"Speeches and Writings of Abraham Lincoln: Cooper Union Address"*, February. 27, 1860. Available at http://www.netins.net/showcase/creative/lincoln/speeches/greeley.htm. Accessed on Nov. 2, 1999.

[6] Abraham Lincoln and Stephen A. Douglas, *First Lincoln/Douglas Debate: Ottawa, Illinois August 21, 1858*, The Abraham Lincoln Association, http://www.alincolnassoc.com. Accessed on October 20, 1999.

[7-9] Microsoft Encarta Afriacan 2000, *Paul Cuffee*, <u>Microsoft Corporation</u>, 1999.

[10-12] Library of Congress, *African American Mosaic*, Accessed on Jan. 13, 2001

[13] Author unknown, *Timelines of Reconstruction*, page 4, Available at: http://www.ameritech.net/users/jklann/ABOUT.htm

[14] Roy P. Basler, Editor, et al., *The Collected Works of Abraham Lincoln:*

Volume 5 (of 9 Volumes), "*Lincoln's speech to Congress, July 12, 1862*, New Brunswick, N.J., 1953-55, pp. 317-319.

[15] Roy Basler, Editor, *The Collected Works of Abraham Lincoln, Vol. 4 (of 9 Volumes)*, pp. 13-30. Available at http://members.aol.com/jfepperson/ newhaven.html. Accessed on October 29, 1999.

[16] *Fugitive Slave Laws*, Encarta Encyclopedia Online. Available at: http:// encarta.msn. Accessed on Sept. 9, 1999)

[17-18] *African American Journey: Political Compromises: Fugitive Slave Laws*, World Book Online, http://www.worldbook.com/fun/aajourny. Accessed on Sept. 9, 1999

[19-20] Geoffrey C. Ward with Ric Burns and Ken Burns, *The Civil War: An Illustrated History,* Alfred A Knopf, New York, 1998, pg. 253.

[21] Christian A. Fleetwood, Sergeant-Major 4th U.S. Colored Troops, *The Negro as a Soldier In the War of the Revolution*, originally given at or the Negro Congress at the Cotton States and International Exposition, Atlanta, Ga., November 11 to November 23, 1895, Afro-American Almanac. Available at http://www.toptags.com/aama/bio/men/freddoug.htm. Accessed on July 27, 2000.

[22] Abraham Lincoln, *A House Divided*, Springfield, Illinois, June, 16, 1858.

[23-26] Author unknown, *Timelines of Reconstruction*, page 4. Available at http://www.ameritech.net/users/jklann/ABOUT.htm. Accessed on October 29, 1999.

[27] Philip B. Kunhardt, Jr., Philip B. Kunhardt, III, and Peter Kunhardt, *Lincoln: an Illustrated Biography*, Portland House, New York, NY, 1992, pp. 196

[28] Roy Basler, Editor, *The Collected Works of Abraham Lincoln*, Vol. 4, pp. 13-30. Available at http://members.aol.com/jfepperson/newhaven.html. Accessed on October 29, 1999.

[29] *First Lincoln/Douglas Debate*, Ibid.

[30] Kunhardt, Jr., pg. 227.

[31] Kunhardt, Jr., pg. 188.

[32] The Freedman and Southern Society Project, *The Chronology of Emancipation during the Civil War: "U.S., Statutes at Large, Treaties, and Proclamations of the United States of America"*, Vol. 12, Boston, 1863, pp. 1267-68. Available at http://www.inform.umd.edu/ARHU/Depts/History/ Freedman/prelep.htm. Accessed on October 29, 1999.

[33] Kunhardts, pg. 227.

[34] Ibid, pg. 197.

[35] Ibid, pg. 226.

[36-37] Ward, pg.253.

[38-39] Ward, pg.253.

[40] Ibid, pg.247.

[41] Ibid, pg.252.

[42] Ibid, pg.248.

[43] Kunhardts, pg.227.

[44-45] Fleetwood, Ibid.

Acknowledgments:

Life Membership Certificate for American Colonization Society, 1840.
Image from the Library of Congress, Manuscript Division. Available at
<http://lcweb.loc.gov/exhibits/african/lib.jpg> (3). Accessed on Dec. 10,
2000.

"Illustrations of the Anti-Slavery Almanac for 1840", New York: American
Anti-Slavery Society, 1840 edition. Library of Congress, Rare Book and
Special Collections Division . Available at <http://lcweb.loc.gov/exhibits/
african/lib.jpg> (48). Accessed on Dec. 10, 2000.

"Table of Emigrants," in *The African Repository and Colonial Journal,* vol.
30, no. 1, January 1854, p. 121. Library of Congress, General Collections
(17). Available at <http://lcweb.loc.gov/exhibits/african/lib.jpg> (48).
Accessed on Dec. 10, 2000.

The Constitution of the American Society, for Colonizing the Free People of Color of the United States

Article I.

This Society shall be called, "The American Society for colonizing the free people of color of the United States."

Article II.

The object to which attention is to be exclusively directed, is to promote and execute a plan for colonizing (with their consent) the free people of color, residing in our country, in Africa, or such other place as Congress shall deem most expedient. And the Society shall act, to effect this object in co-operation with the general government, and such of the states as may adopt regulations upon the subject.

Article III.

Every citizen of the United States, who shall subscribe these articles, and be an annual contributor of one dollar to the funds of the Society, shall be a member. On paying a sum not less than thirty dollars, at one subscription, shall be a member for life.

Article IV.

The officers of this Society shall be, a President, thirteen Vice Presidents, a Secretary, a Treasurer, a Recorder, and a Board of Managers, composed of the above named officers, and twelve other members of the Society. They shall be annually elected by the members of the Society, at their annual meeting on the last Saturday of December, and continue to discharge their respective duties till others are appointed.

Article V.

It shall be the duty of the President to preside at all meetings of the Society, and of the Board of Managers, and to call meetings of the Society, and of the Board, when he thinks necessary, or when required by any three members of the board.

Article VI.

The Vice Presidents, according to seniority, shall discharge these duties in the absence of the President.

Article VII.

The Secretary shall take minutes of the proceedings, prepare and publish notices, and discharge such other duties, as the Board, or the President, or in his absence the Vice President, according to the seniority, (when the Board is not sitting) shall direct. And the Recorder shall record the proceedings and the names of the members, and discharge such other duties as may be required of him.

Article VIII.

The Treasurer shall receive and take charge of the funds of the Society, under such security as may be prescribed by the Board of Managers: keep the accounts and exhibit a statement of receipts and expenditures at every annual meeting, and discharge such other duties as may be required of him.

Article IX.

The Board of managers shall meet on the first Monday in January, the first Monday in April, the first Monday in July, and the first Monday in October, every year, and at such other times as the President may direct. They shall conduct the business of the Society... They shall also fill up all vacancies occurring during the year, and make such by-laws for their government, as they may deem necessary, provided the same are not repugnant to this constitution.

Article X.

Every Society which shall be formed in the United States to aid in the object of this association, and which shall co-operate with its funds for the purposes thereof, agreeably to the rules and regulations of this Society, shall be considered auxiliary thereto, & its officers shall be entitled to attend and vote at all meetings of the Society, and of the Board of Managers.

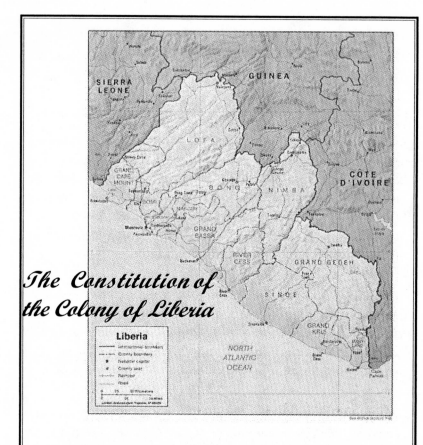

The Constitution of the Colony of Liberia

Adopted by the Board of Directors of the American Colonization Society, January 5, 1839.

The American Colonization Society hereby grants to the colonies or settlements in Liberia, on the western coast of Africa, under its care, the following Constitution:

Article I.

The colonies of settlements of Monrovia, New Georgia, Caldwell, Millsburg, Marshall, Bexley, Bassa Cove, and Edina, and such other Colonies hereafter established by this Society, or by Colonization Societies adopting the Constitution of the American Colonization Society, on the Western coast of Africa, are hereby united into one Government, under the name and style of the Commonwealth of Liberia.

Article II.

All Legislative powers herein granted, shall be vested in a Governor and Council of Liberia; but all laws by them enacted shall be subject to the revocation of the American Colonization Society.

Article III.

The Council shall consist of representatives to be elected by the people of the several colonies or settlements and shall be apportioned among them according to a just ratio of representation. Until otherwise provided, Monrovia New Georgia, Caldwell, and Millsburg, shall be entitled to six representatives; and Marshall, Bexley, Bassa Cove ,and Edina, to four representatives; to be appointed among them by the Governor.

Article IV.

The representatives shall, in all cases, except treason, felony, and breach of the peace, be privileged from arresting during their attendance at the session of the Council, and in going to or returning from the same; and for any speech or debate therein, they shall not be questioned in any other place.

Article V.

Until otherwise provided by law, the Governor shall appoint and publish the times, places, and manner, of holding elections, and making returns thereof, and the same for the meeting of the Council.

Article VI.

The Governor shall preside at the deliberations of the Council, and shall have a veto on all their acts.

Article VII.

A Colonial Secretary shall be appointed by the Governor; and it shall be the duty of such Colonial Secretary to record in a book or books, all the official acts and proceedings of the Governor, of the Council, and of the Governor and Council; to secure and preserve the same carefully; and to transmit a copy of each of such acts or proceedings to the American Colonization Society, from time to time. Provided, however, that such acts and proceedings be so transmitted at lease once a year.

Article VIII.

A great seal shall be provided for the Commonwealth of Liberia, whereby the official and public acts of the Governor shall be authenticated; and the custody of the said seal shall be committed to the Colonial Secretary.

Article IX.

The Governor and Council shall have power to provide a uniform system of military tactics and discipline: to provide for organizing, arming and disciplining the militia, and for governing such part of them as may be employed in the service of the Commonwealth:

To declare war in self-defence:

To make rules concerning captures on land and water:

To make treaties with the several African tribes, and to prescribe rules for regulating the commerce between the Commonwealth of Liberia and such tribes; except that all treaties for the acquisition of lands shall be subject to the approval of the American Colonization Society:

To prescribe uniform laws of naturalization for all persons of color. All persons now citizens of any part of the Commonwealth of Liberia shall continue to be so, and all colored persons emigrating from the United States of America, or any District or Territory thereof, which the approbation, or under the sanction of the American Colonization Society, or of any Society auxiliary to the same, or of any State Colonization Society of the United States, which shall have adopted the Constitution of the American Colonization Society, shall be entitled to all the privileges of citizens of Liberia; except the same shall have been lost or forfeited by conviction of some crime.

Article X.

The Executive power shall be vested in a Governor of Liberia, to be appointed by, and to hold his office during the pleasure of, the American Colonization Society.

Article XI.

The governor shall be Commander-in-Chief of the Army, of the Navy, and of the Militia of the Commonwealth; he shall have power to call the Militia or any portion thereof into actual service, whenever the public exigency shall require; and he shall have the appointment of all military and naval officers, except the captains and subalterns of militia companies, who may be elected by their respective companies.

Article XII.

The lands owned by the Society, and all other property belonging to the Society, and in the Commonwealth, shall be under the exclusive control of the Governor and such agents as he may appoint under the direction of the Society.

Article XIII.

The Governor, with the advice and consent of the Council, shall appoint all officers, whose appointment or election is not otherwise specially provided for in this Constitution.

Article XIV.

There shall be a Lieutenant Governor, who shall be elected by the people in such manner as shall be provided by law. He shall exercise the office of Governor, in case of a vacancy in that office, occasioned by the Governor's death or resignation, or in case the Governor shall delegate to him the temporary authority of Governor during the Governor's absence or sickness.

Article XV.

The judicial power of the Commonwealth of Liberia shall be vested in one Supreme Court, and in such inferior Courts as the Governor and Council may, from time to time, ordain and establish. The Governor shall be, ex officio, Chief Justice of Liberia, and as such shall preside in the Supreme Court, which shall have only appellate jurisdiction. The Judges, both of the Supreme and inferior Courts, except the Chief Justice, shall hold their offices during good behavior.

Article XVI.

A code or uniform system of civil and criminal law, shall be provided by the American Colonization Society for the Commonwealth of Liberia.

Article XVII.

The present criminal laws in force in the several colonies or settlements now forming the Commonwealth of Liberia, and such others as may, from time to time, be enacted, shall constitute the criminal code of the Commonwealth. Such parts of the common law as set forth in Blackstone's Commentaries, as may be applicable to the situation of the people, except as changed by the laws now in force, and such as may hereafter be enacted, shall be the civil code of law for the Commonwealth.

Article XVIII.

A great seal shall be provided for the Colonies, whereby the official and private acts of the Governor shall be authenticated, and the custody thereof shall be committed to the Colonial Secretary.

Article XIX.

Until otherwise provided by law, the Commonwealth of Liberia shall be divided into counties, as follows: Monrovia, New Georgia, Caldwell and Millsburg, shall constitute one county, under the name of the county of Montserado ; and Bassa Cove, Elina, Bexley, and Marshall, shall constitute the other county, under the name of the county of Grand Bassa

Article XX.

There shall be no slavery in the Commonwealth.

Article XXI.

There shall be no dealing in slaves by any citizen of the Commonwealth, either within or beyond the limits of the same.

Article XXII.

Emigration shall not be prohibited.

Article XXIII.

The right of trial by jury, and the right of petition, shall be inviolate.

Article XXIV.

No person shall be debarred from prosecuting or defending any civil cause for or against himself or herself, before any tribunal in the Commonwealth, by himself or herself or counsel.

Article XXV.

Every male citizen of the age of twenty-one years shall have the right of suffrage.

Article XXVI.

All elections shall be by ballot.

Article XXVII.

The military shall at all times, and in all cases, be in subjection to the civil power.

Article XXVIII.

Agriculture, the mechanic arts, and manufactures, shall be encouraged within the Commonwealth; and commerce shall be promoted by such methods as shall tend to develop the agricultural resources of the Commonwealth, advance the moral social and political interests of the people, increase their strength, and accelerate and firmly establish and secure their national independence.

Article XXIX.

The standards of weight, measure and money, used and approved by the Government of the United States of America, are hereby adopted as the standards of weight, measure and money within the Commonwealth of Liberia. But the Governor and Council shall have power to settle the value of the actual currency of the Commonwealth, according to the metallic currency of the United States of America.

Acknowledgments:

The map of Liberia is used with the permission of the General Library of The University of Texas at Austin. It is one of the exhibits in the Perry-Castaneda Library Map Collection." It is available at www.lib.utexas.edu/Libs'PCLMap_collection/liberia.html. The file was accessed on Oct. 15, 2000.

The Constitution of the American Society for Colonizing the Free People of Color of the United States and the Constitution of the Colony of Liberia are used with the permission of the Afro-American Almanac web site, which is available at http://www.toptags.com/aama/

Final comments from Lincoln's First Inaugural Address March 4, 1861

President elect Lincoln, 1861

Why should there not be a patient confidence in the ultimate justice of the people? Is there any better or equal hope in the world? In our present differences is either party without faith of being in the right? If the Almighty Ruler of Nations, with his eternal truth and justice, be on your side of the North, or on yours of the South, that truth and that justice will surely prevail, by the judgment of this great tribunal, the American people.

By the frame of the government under which we live, this same people have wisely given their public servants but little power for mischief; and have, with equal wisdom, provided for the return of that little to their own hands at very short intervals. While the people retain their virtue and vigilance, no administration, by any extreme of wickedness or folly, can very seriously injure the government in the short space of four years.

My countrymen, one and all, think calmly and well upon this whole subject. Nothing valuable can be lost by taking time. If there be an object to hurry any of you in hot haste to a step which you would never take deliberately, that object will be frustrated by taking time; but no good object can be frustrated by it. Such of you as are now dissatisfied, still have the old Constitution unimpaired, and, on the sensitive point, the laws of your own framing under it; while the new administration will have no immediate power, if it would, to change either. If it were admitted that you who are dissatisfied hold the right side in the dispute, there still is no single good reason for precipitate action. Intelligence, patriotism, Christianity, and a firm reliance on him who has never yet forsaken this favored land, are still competent to adjust in the best way all our present difficulty.

In your hands, my dissatisfied fellow-countrymen, and not in mine, is the momentous issue of civil war. The government will not assail you. You can have no conflict without being yourselves the aggressors. You have no oath registered in heaven to destroy the government, while, I shall have the most solemn one to "preserve, protect, and defend it."

I am loathe to close. We are not enemies, but friends. We must not be enemies. Though passion may have strained, it must not break our bonds of affection. The mystic chords of memory, stretching from every battle-field and patriot grave to every living heart and hearth-stone all over this broad land, will yet swell the chorus of the Union when again touched, as surely they will be, by the better angels of our nature.

Acknowledgement: This excerpt is provided courtsey of the Afro American Almanac, an Internet web site that is available at < http://toptags.com/ aama/docs/lincoln1.htm >.

Lincoln's Gettysburg Address
November 19, 1863

Four score and seven years ago our fathers brought forth on this continent, a new nation, conceived in Liberty, and dedicated to the proposition that all men are created equal.

Now we are engaged in a great civil war, testing whether that nation or any nation so conceived and so dedicated, can long endure. We are met on a great battlefield of that war. We have come to dedicate a portion of that field, as a final resting place for those who here gave their lives that that nation might live. It is altogether fitting and proper that we should do this.

But in a larger sense we cannot dedicate - we cannot consecrate - we cannot hallow this ground. The brave men, living and dead, who struggled here, have consecrated it, far above our poor power to add or detract. The world will little note, nor long remember what we say here, but it can never forget what they did here. It is for us the living, rather, to be dedicated here to the unfinished work which they who fought here have thus far so nobly advanced. It is rather for us to be here dedicated to the great task remaining before us - that from these honored dead we take increased devotion to that cause for which they gave the last full measure of devotion - that we here highly resolve that these dead shall not have died in vain that this nation, under God, shall have a new birth of freedom - and that government of the people, by the people, for the people, shall not perish from the earth.

Abraham Lincoln, Feb. 9, 1864

Lincoln's Second In- augural Address

"Fellow-countrymen: At this second appearing to take the oath of the presidential office, there is less occasion for an extended address than there was at the first. Then a statement, somewhat in detail, of a course to be pursued, seemed fitting and proper. Now, at the expiration of four years, during which the public declarations have been constantly called forth on every point and phase of the great contest which still absorbs the attention and engrosses the energies of the nation, little that is new could be presented. The progress of our arms, upon which all else chiefly depends, is as well known to the public as to myself; and it is, I trust, reasonably satisfactory and encouraging to all. With high hope for the future, no prediction in regard to it is ventured.

"On the occasion corresponding to this four years ago, all thoughts were anxiously directed to an impending civil war. All dreaded it — all sought to avert it. While the inaugural address was being delivered from this place, devoted altogether to saving the Union without war, insurgent agents were in the city seeking to destroy it without war — seeking to dissolve the Union, and divide effects, by negotiation. Both parties deprecated war; but one of them would rather make war than let the nation survive; and the other would accept war rather than let it perish. And the war came.

"One-eighth of the whole population were colored slaves, not distributed generally over the Union, but localized in the Southern part of it. These slaves constituted a peculiar and powerful interest. All knew that this interest was, somehow, the cause of the war. To strengthen, perpetuate, and extend this interest was the object for which the insurgents would rend the Union, even by war; while the government claimed no right to do more than restrict the territorial enlargement of it.

"Neither party expected for the war the magnitude or the duration which it has already attained. Neither anticipated that the cause of the conflict might cease with, or even before, the conflict itself should cease. Each looked for an easier triumph, and a result less fundamental and astounding. Both read the same Bible, and pray to the same God; and each invokes his aid against the other. It may seem strange that any men should dare to ask a just God's assistance in wringing their bread from the sweat of other men's faces; but let us judge not, that we be not judged. The prayers of both could not be answered — that of neither has been answered fully.

"The Almighty has his own purposes. 'Woe unto the world because of offenses! for it must needs be that offenses come; but woe to that man by whom the offense cometh.' If we shall suppose that American slavery is one of those offenses which, in the providence of God, must needs come, but which, having continued through his appointed time, he now wills to remove, and that he gives to both North and South this terrible war, as the woe due to those by whom the offense came, shall we discern therein any departure from those divine attributes which the believers in a living God always ascribe to him?

"Fondly do we hope — fervently do we pray — that this mighty scourge of war may speedily pass away. Yet, if God wills that it continue until all of the wealth piled by the bondman's two hundred and fifty years of unrequited toil shall be sunk, and until every drop of blood drawn with the lash shall be paid by another drawn by the sword, as was said three thousand years ago, so still it must be said, 'The judgments of the Lord are true and righteous altogether.'

"With malice toward none; with charity for all; with firmness in the right, as God gives us to see the right, let us strive on to finish the work we are in; to bind up the nation's wounds; to care for him who shall have borne the battle and for his widow, and his orphan — to do all which may achieve and cherish a just and a lasting peace among ourselves, and with all nations."

Acknowledgement: The photo of President Lincoln is from the Library of Congress "Presidents and Their Wives" Collection. It was taken on February 9, 1984 by Anthony Berger.

Chapter 18: The Heart of Lincoln

Lincoln's faith played a profound role in decisions he made as he guided the Union forces through the Civil War years. Following the Union victory at Gettysburg, Lincoln confided in a friend, *"...some precautions were taken, but for my part, I was sure of our success."* [1] When his friend asked how he could be so confident, Lincoln replied, *"...I felt a great crisis had come.... I went to my room and got down on my knees in prayer. Never before had I prayed with so much earnestness. I wish I could repeat my prayer. I felt I must put all my trust in Almighty God. He gave our people the best country ever given to man. He alone could save it from destruction. I had tried my best to do my duty and found myself unequal to the task. The burden was more than I could bear.... I asked him to help us and give us victory now. I was sure my prayer was answered. I had no misgivings about the result at Gettysburg."* [2]

Lincoln's confidence in God's ability to handle a task that he knew he was unequal to handle offers a word of encouragement for those of us who are praying for peace in our world today. So many nations are immersed in internal conflicts that threaten to destroy one group or another, if not the entire nation. Peace-making efforts sometimes secure a temporary cessation of hostilities, but the conflict soon erupts with unabated fury. Why? Because the root causes of these conflicts have not been removed. Indeed they cannot be removed except by the saving knowledge of the Lord Jesus Christ and the application of His blood to the roots of prejudice, hate, unforgiveness, and bitterness that divide race from race and nation from nation.

Lincoln's Speeches Reveal His Heart:
While Lincoln was confident of Union victory at Gettysburg, he never lost sight of the ultimate goal of the conflict that had occu-

pied so much of the time, energy, and resources of our nation for so many years. That goal not only involved the restoration of the Union, but also the perfection of that Union so that this nation might fulfill God's call upon it. For Lincoln, this meant not only that slavery would be abolished, but also that each State of the Confederacy would be restored to its former place in the Union. Lincoln's vision for Reconstruction bore little resemblance to the harsh practices that characterized that era. These practices only served to deepen the division between the North and the South. They did nothing to heal the differences that precipitated the war, let alone bring healing to the deep wounds the war caused.

Lincoln's charity toward members of the Confederacy was evident in the brief speech he gave at the dedication of the Gettysburg cemetery. Instead of reveling in the Union victory that took place there, he drew his listeners' attention to **all** of the men who had fought and died there:

> *"But in a larger sense, we cannot dedicate—we cannot consecrate—we cannot hallow—this ground. The brave men, living and dead, who struggled here, have consecrated it, far above our poor power to add or detract. The world will little note, nor long remember, what we say here, but it can never forget what they did here."*

Lincoln honored ally and enemy alike, for both had fought for a cause they believed to be just.

He exhorted his listeners to dedicate themselves to the completion of the task for which so many had given their lives:

> *"It is for us the living, rather, to be dedicated here to the unfinished work which they who fought here have thus far so nobly advanced. It is rather for us to be here dedicated to the great task remaining before us—that from these honored dead we may take increased devotion to that cause for which they gave the last full measure of devotion—that we here highly resolve that these dead shall not have died in vain—**that this nation, under God, shall have a new birth of freedom**—and*

that government of the people, by the people, for the people, shall not perish from the earth."

In many ways, this task is still incomplete. Surely great progress has been made on many fronts, but much remains to be done to secure true freedom for every citizen of this great nation. Progress has come at great cost. As I noted earlier, even a brief review of the Civil Rights Movement shows this time and again. But, no cost is too high when the cries of the oppressed stir our hearts to seek justice on their behalf.

EQUALITY FOR ALL:

Lincoln's declaration—*"Four score and seven years ago our fathers brought forth on this continent, a new nation, conceived in liberty, and dedicated to the proposition that all men are created equal"*—was not just a catchy phrase. It embodied one of the key issues that had fueled the war between the States. One side of this great conflict contended that the founding fathers never intended to include all the races in their proclamation of everyone's right to life, liberty and the pursuit of happiness. Lincoln fervently disagreed with them. While he was not certain how the process of emancipation could best be undertaken, he was definite about one thing: Every individual, regardless of race or cultural background, had the right to live free.

History shows us that the manner in which any group of people pursues freedom largely defines the character of the society they develop. Some pursue their freedom to oppress all who are different from them. The societies they found will stand until one stronger manages to subjugate them. Others pursue freedom for all, recognizing the inalienable rights God accords to all mankind. Lincoln was of the latter camp.

LINCOLN'S SECOND INAUGURAL ADDRESS:

The heart of Lincoln is perhaps nowhere more clearly revealed than in his second inaugural address. Shortly after the beginning of his first term in office, the nation was immersed in a war neither side wanted to fight. His second inaugural address contained this comment on the commencement of hostilities between the Union States and the Confederate States:

> *"On the occasion corresponding to this four years ago, all thoughts were anxiously directed to an impending civil war. All dreaded it—all sought to avert it. While the inaugural address was being delivered from this place, devoted altogether to saving the Union without war, insurgent agents were in the city seeking to destroy it without war—seeking to dissolve the Union, and divide effects, by negotiation. Both parties deprecated war; but* **one of them would rather make war than let the nation survive; and the other would accept war rather than let it perish.** *And the war came."*

From Lincoln's perspective, those who supported the Confederacy had chosen to make war, rather than remain a part of the Union. The Union States, on the other hand, had accepted war as the only way to preserve this nation as one nation under God.

We might well ask, *"Why couldn't the southern states break off from the Union? What bound them to an alliance that they felt did not reflect their best interests?"* As we said earlier, many nations around the world today are embroiled in similar conflicts. The availability of relatively inexpensive arms and an abundance of gun traders, who are more than willing to make their living selling to mutual enemies, has no doubt fueled many of these conflicts, but ethnic struggles are nothing new.

So why couldn't the Confederacy break off from the Union? The secessionists ignored one unchanging reality: America truly is one nation under God. For all our faults—and they have been many over the years—this nation reflects God's plan to call to Himself a people who will be His people. Our pledge of allegiance recognizes this—*"...one nation under God, indivisible, with liberty and justice for all."* Allowing these states to break away from the Union would have broken a covenant relationship, which God established among the original colonies.

Man had his purposes for the Union that emerged from the Revolutionary War. The seceding states judged that Union as counter-productive to their interests, but God's estimation of it had not changed. God had a plan for America, and He had not abandoned it.

God still has a plan for America. That plan will not be fulfilled through the efforts of those who wish to establish the superiority of their race, culture, or social class. It will be fulfilled by those who seek to know the will of God and then are faithful to do it.

LINCOLN'S HEART ACHED FOR THE OPPRESSED:

While the preservation of the Union was paramount, the necessity to free the slaves became increasingly clear. Lincoln drew attention to this issue in his second inaugural address:

"One-eighth of the whole population were colored slaves, [*] *not distributed generally over the Union, but localized in the Southern part of it. These slaves constituted a peculiar and powerful interest. All knew that this interest was, somehow, the cause of the war. To strengthen, perpetuate, and extend this interest was the object for which the insurgents would rend the Union, even by war; while the government claimed no right to do more than restrict the territorial enlargement of it.*

"Neither party expected... the magnitude or the duration which it has already attained. Neither anticipated that the cause of the conflict might cease with, or even before, the conflict itself should cease. Each looked for an easier triumph, and a result less fundamental and astounding."

* The figures given for the actual number of slaves being held in America at the time of the Civil war vary from one eighth to one fifth of the total population.

Even Lincoln was not anticipating an abrupt end to slavery when the Civil War began. He would have settled for a restriction of its expansion to the other states and territories.

Lincoln pondered the justice of the Union's cause, but he believed that its justice was established by the great injustice of slavery itself. Continuing on in his inaugural address, he observed,

"Both read the same Bible, and pray to the same God; and each invokes his aid against the other. It may seem strange

that any men should dare to ask a just God's assistance in wringing their bread from the sweat of other men's faces; but let us judge not, that we be not judged. The prayers of both could not be answered—that of neither has been answered fully.

"The Almighty has his own purposes. 'Woe unto the world because of offenses! for it must needs be that offenses come; but woe to that man by whom the offense cometh.' If we shall suppose that American slavery is one of those offenses which, in the providence of God, must needs come, but which, having continued through his appointed time, he now wills to remove, and that he gives to both North and South this terrible war, as the woe due to those by whom the offense came, shall we discern therein any departure from those divine attributes which the believers in a living God always ascribe to him?"

It is interesting that Lincoln did not blindly condemn those who practiced slavery. The practice of slavery was another matter however. The time for its end had come.

Lincoln's tender heart made him a reluctant executioner of judgment, but that same heart let him recognize the justice of that judgment. We see this blend of compassion and justice in the following passage from his second inaugral address:

"Fondly do we hope—fervently do we pray—that this mighty scourge of war may speedily pass away. Yet, if God wills that it continue until all of the wealth piled by the bondman's two hundred and fifty years of unrequited toil shall be sunk, and until every drop of blood drawn with the lash shall be paid by another drawn by the sword, as was said three thousand years ago, so still it must be said, 'The judgments of the Lord are true and righteous altogether.'"

WITH MALICE TOWARD NONE:

Lincoln's role as Commander and Chief of the Union forces earned him the love and admiration of many, but it also raised up scores who hated him with a hatred so deep that it ultimately lead to his assassination. Lincoln was very much aware that his enemies were at least as numerous as his friends. Even in Washington, DC there were those who were plotting his demise. Still Lincoln could say,

"With malice toward none; with charity for all; with firmness in the right, as God gives us to see the right, let us strive on to finish the work we are in; to bind up the nation's wounds; to care for him who shall have borne the battle and for his widow, and his orphan—to do all which may achieve and cherish a just and a lasting peace among ourselves, and with all nations."

You'll note that Lincoln did not differentiate between Northerner and Southerner, between Yankee or Rebel soldiers, in this speech. His intent was on healing the wounds of the nation—all the wounds. In his mind, everything that divided American from American needed to be eliminated.

Our objective for the Church today can be no less. Together, we need to bind up the wounds that have separated the body of Christ. We need to comfort those who have suffered because of the conflicts that have separated us. We must do all that is required to achieve a just and lasting peace among all of the races that call America home. This must not be a peace in which former enemies or antagonists merely tolerate one another. Jesus is calling us to love one another, even as He loves us.

This will not happen if our goal is to advance the interests of our race. Instead, our goal must be to see the kingdom of God expanded on the earth today. Together we can accomplish this goal, but if we continue to tolerate division among us, the expansion of His kingdom will be hindered. Perhaps this is one reason why such a great multitude of plans for World Evangelism have failed over the years.

LINCOLN'S PERSONAL FAITH:

Some Lincoln debunkers claim that he was not a Christian. Those who knew him best would disagree. His former law partner, William Herndon, made this comment about Lincoln's faith: *"He had his own religion...a religion based on exalted notions of right... He had no prejudice against any class... tolerating—as I never could—even the Irish."* [3] Herndon described Lincoln's faith as one of *"...broad sympathies and high moral passion."* We saw in an earlier chapter that his moral passion concerning the Dred Scott case was what compelled Lincoln to return to the political arena.

Herndon indicated that Lincoln's faith was inspired by the Bible. He tells us that Lincoln wrestled with issues that perplex us all— the process of Creation, the mystery of death, the passage of time. Lincoln's spiritual seeking lead him to the conclusion that *"...God had created all human beings fundamentally equal."* [4] This basic assumption fueled his active involvement in the anti-slavery movement in the late 1850s.

The death of their twelve-year-old son, Willie, deepened Lincoln's desire to know and understand God. Shortly before signing the Emancipation Proclamation, Lincoln commented, *"It is my earnest desire to know the will of Providence. And if I can learn what it is I will do it!"* [5] More than ever, Lincoln saw himself as one appointed by God for the express purpose of guiding our nation through one of the most difficult periods of its history.

Lincoln's remarks about why he never formerly became a church member bear sharp witness against the divisions that have plagued the Church from generation to generation. Always skeptical of denominational dogma, Lincoln commented, *"I have found difficulty in giving my assent... to the long, complicated statements of Christian doctrine... Where any church will inscribe over its altar, as its sole qualification for membership, the Savior's condensed statement of both Law and Gospel, 'Thou shalt love the Lord thy God with all thy heart, and with all thy soul, and with all thy mind, and thy neighbor as thyself,' that church I will join with all my heart and soul."* [6] For Lincoln, loving your neighbors as yourself precluded the possibility of enslaving them. *"As I would not desire to be a slave,"* Lincoln is quoted as having said, *"so I would not be a master."*

I wonder, would Lincoln be willing to join any of our churches today? His measure of "excellence" was unencumbered by the doctrines and practices that so easily divide us. He wanted to see a people who loved the Lord with all their heart, soul, and mind, and who loved their fellowman—all their fellowmen—even as they loved themselves.

Of course, Abraham Lincoln is not going to walk into any of our churches today, but today's Lincolns do every time our doors are open. Some of those Lincolns may be a little rough around the edges, some may be in deep bondage to drugs, some may be entangled in worldly pursuits, others may be living in blatant sin. When they come in our doors, will they find a people who love God? Even more important, will they find a people who will love them?

If the answer to both of these questions is yes, one question remains: Will they find a people who will love them without respect to their race, culture, or nationality? The Word says nothing about the "families of God." It speaks only of the family of God— one Father, one people, joined by the blood of one Lamb.

LINCOLN ON RECONSTRUCTION:

When it became evident that the Union forces were going to prevail, Lincoln turned his attention to the restoration of those states that had seceded. Lincoln addressed this subject in what proved to be his final speech. Lincoln noted the diversity of opinion as to how reconstruction should be carried out:

> *"By these recent successes the re-inauguration of the national authority — reconstruction — which has had a large share of thought from the first, is pressed much more closely upon our attention. It is fraught with great difficulty. Unlike the case of a war between independent nations, there is no authorized organ for us to treat with. No one man has authority to give up the rebellion for any other man. We simply must begin with, and mould from, disorganized and discordant elements. Nor is it a small additional embarrassment that we, the loyal people, differ among ourselves as to the mode, manner, and means of reconstruction."* [7]

For many, punishing the rebels was an essential objective for any plan of reconstruction. Lincoln favored a more forgiving approach. He said simply,

> *"We all agree that the seceded States, so called, are out of their proper practical relation with the Union; and that* **the sole object of the government, civil and military, in regard to those States is to again get them into that proper practical relation.** *I believe it is not only possible, but in fact, easier, to do this, without deciding, or even considering, whether these states have even been out of the Union, than with it. Finding themselves safely at home, it would be utterly immaterial whether they had ever been abroad.* **Let us all join in doing the acts necessary to restoring the proper practical relations between these states and the Union;** *and each forever after, innocently indulge his own opinion whether, in doing the acts, he brought the States from without, into the Union, or only gave them proper assistance, they never having been out of it."* [8]

That sounds very much like the attitude of the father toward the prodigal son, doesn't it? The father didn't call together a tribunal to judge his wayward son's actions. He ran to meet him, embraced him, robed him in clothes befitting his sonship, and ordered preparations for a celebration!

In this final speech, Lincoln was responding to criticisms of the government that citizens of Louisiana had formed in preparation for that state's restoration to full statehood. There were many objections to Louisiana's proposed government. To begin with, only twelve thousand Louisianans had approved it. In addition, it did not grant the right to vote to all Blacks. Lincoln himself wrestled with these shortcomings, but he commented, *"Still the question is not whether the Louisiana government, as it stands, is quite all that is desirable. The question is 'Will it be wiser to take it as it is, and help to improve it; or to reject, and disperse it?' 'Can Louisiana be brought into proper practical relation with the Union soon by sustaining, or by discarding her new State Government?'"* [9]

Lincoln pointed out the positive aspects of Louisiana's proposal: *"Some twelve thousand voters in the heretofore slave-state of Louisiana have sworn allegiance to the Union, assumed to be the rightful political power of the State, held elections, organized a State government, adopted a free-state constitution, giving the benefit of public schools equally to black and white, and empowering the Legislature to confer the elective franchise upon the colored man."* [10] In addition, the Legislature had already ratified the constitutional amendment which Congress had recently passed, abolishing slavery throughout the entire nation.

From Lincoln's perspective, these were very dramatic concessions and sufficient evidence that Louisiana should be, so to speak, "welcomed back into the fold." Lincoln's argument for doing so was strong:

> *These twelve thousand persons are thus fully committed to the Union, and to perpetual freedom in the state—**committed to the very things, and nearly all the things the nation wants**—and they ask the nation's recognition, and it's assistance to make good their committal. Now, if we reject, and spurn them, we do our utmost to disorganize and disperse them. We in effect say to the white men "You are worthless, or worse—we will neither help you, nor be helped by you." To the blacks we say "This cup of liberty which these, your old masters, hold to your lips, we will dash from you, and leave you to the chances of gathering the spilled and scattered contents in some vague and undefined when, where, and how." If this course, **discouraging and paralyzing both white and black**, has any tendency to bring Louisiana into proper practical relations with the Union, I have, so far, been unable to perceive it.* [11]

Lincoln recognized the shortcomings of Louisiana's proposal, but he also recognized that these twelve thousand former rebels had taken a drastic stand, advocating not only the end of hostilities but an abandonment of key issues that had caused the war. Acknowledging that these twelve thousand loyal citizens could do more to speed reconstruction than any government-devised and-enforced plan could hope to accomplish, Lincoln said,

> *If, on the contrary, we recognize, and sustain the new gov-ernment of Louisiana the converse of all this is made true. We encourage the hearts, and nerve the arms of the twelve thousand to adhere to their work, and argue for it, and pros-elyte for it, and fight for it, and feed it, and grow it, and ripen it to a complete success. The colored man too, in seeing all united for him, is inspired with vigilance, and energy, and daring, to the same end. Grant that he desires the elective franchise, will he not attain it sooner by saving the already advanced steps toward it, than by running backward over them?* [12]

Lincoln recognized the imperfections of Louisiana's plan, but he also saw the promise inherent in that plan. He conceded that, compared to what it should be, Louisiana's new government was only *"...as the egg is to the fowl...."* [13] But he pointed out that **"...we shall sooner have the fowl by hatching the egg than by smashing it."** [14]

Lincoln's advice was sound, but waiting has never been man's forte. The conclusion of the Civil War closed the door on over two and a half centuries of slavery in America. The laws that were being written in the statute books that govern this nation would have to be written in the hearts of men before their effect would be fully felt. It would take time for this to happen. The challenge to those serving in the various offices of government was to find ways to promote healing both between Blacks and Whites and between Northerners and Southerners.

In many ways this process is still going on. The bitterly disputed presidential election in 2000 showed us that.

End Notes:

[1-6] Philip B. Kunhardt, Jr., Philip B. Kunhardt, III, and Peter Kunhardt, *Lincoln: an Illustrated Biography*, Portland House, New York, NY, 1992, pg. 336

[7-14] Lincoln's final Speech, given on April 11, 1864, The History Place.

Available at http://www.historyplace.com/lincoln/reconst.htm. Accessed on Oct. 14, 2000.

Acknowledgment:
Anthony Berger, Lincoln photograph, Library of Congress, Prints and Photographs Division [reproduction number, LC-USP6-2415-A DLC], Feb. 9, 1864. Available at: Accessed on Oct. 16, 2000.

Chapter 19: The South Shall Rise Again

In many ways the Civil War continues to powerfully impact everyday life in America. The conflicts that brought the North and the South to the battlefield were not fully resolved when the peace accords were signed at Appomattox on April 9, 1865. The instruments of war were laid aside that day—guns were no longer aimed at enemy lines, cannons no longer pounded their fortifications, and prisoners of war no longer languished in enemy prison camps. Only the graves of the dead and the bandages of the wounded served as reminders of the struggle that almost divided this nation. Open conflict had ended, but the battle continued in the hearts of victor and vanquished alike; for peace accords, written by the hand of man, have no power to change the human heart. God alone can do that. Only the peace accords which are signed at His table remove the pride of victory or the sting of defeat and allow true healing to take place.

Not everyone will come to God's peace table, however. Nor will they always accept the peace accords signed by man. Five days after Lee surrendered at Appomattox, hate drove John Wilkes Booth to assassinate Abraham Lincoln. His act of violence didn't alter the outcome of the war, but it dramatically affected the nature of the peace that followed. As we discussed in the last chapter, Lincoln's intent was to bring the Confederate states back into the Union as quickly as possible. The Reconstruction Era would have progressed far differently under his guidance.

Hate is a destructive emotion. Nothing good comes from it, only evil in every form imaginable.

One of the downsides of the Internet is that is has facilitated the formation and growth of hate groups in America and around the world. Two years ago it was estimated that there were 450 hate groups on the Internet. Today there are thousands of these groups, filling cyberspace with their destructive philosophies, drawing more and more followers into their web of hate and prejudice.

Neo-Nazi groups in Germany cannot promote their propaganda on the Internet, but those same groups can come to America and freely post their White supremacist dogma without interference. As a result, there are over 1,000 such groups filling cyberspace with lies that did not die with Hitler.

The Council of Conservative Citizens is another of the hate groups that is utilizing the Internet to promote its racist views. The CCC was founded 14 years ago by Robert "Tut" Patterson and claims 15,000 members today. They describe themselves as the *"...active advocates for the no longer silent conservative majority."* [1] Many members of this group insist that they are not racists, but even a casual tour of the CCC's web site makes this claim hard to believe. Many of the books they offer for sale were written during the Civil War era. Book after book vilifies the North and glorifies the South. Abraham Lincoln's position as one of America's most revered presidents is vehemently refuted, and Martin Luther King, Jr.'s prominent place in American history is categorically denied. Clearly, the war is not over for CCC members.

Rev. Joseph Lowery, who helped Martin Luther King, Jr. found the Southern Leadership Conference, commented, *"The group is like the Ku Klux Klan with a coat and tie."* [2] Mark Potok, a researcher for the Southern Poverty Law Center in Montgomery, Alabama, said that the Council of Conservative Citizens is more dangerous than the KKK or the neo-Nazis because it has succeeded in masquerading as a mainstream conservative organization. He believes members of the CCC are *"...much more interested in genuine political power than in any kind of violence or terrorism."* Potok took little comfort in the CCC's non-violent strategies. He pointed out that a terrorist like *"...Timothy McVeigh can kill 168 people, but he's never going to be elected your senator or president."* [3] The CCC, however, already has many elected officials among its members—some of them presiding on school boards or in state legislatures.

A RESOLUTION DENOUNCING THE CCC:

Rep. Robert Wexler (D-FL) and Rep. James Clyburn (D-SC and Chairman of the Congressional Black Caucus), have called upon Congress to denounce the CCC. *"This so-called 'conservative' group is nothing more than a wolf in sheep's clothing and Congress must act quickly to expose them for the bigots that they are,"* [4] Wexler said. Citing the recent rise in racially motivated hate-crimes, Wexler said, *"It is more important than ever that Congress goes on record condemning groups with this type of dangerous agenda."* [5]

The Wexler/Clyburn Resolution reads as follows:

"Condemning the racism and bigotry espoused by the Council of Conservative Citizens: Whereas the population of the United States contains a spectrum of many diverse and rich cultures, races, and religious beliefs that contribute to the vitality and stability of the Nation; Whereas the House of Representatives strongly opposes racism, bigotry, and all forms of ethnic and religious intolerance; Whereas the Council of Conservative Citizens is an outgrowth of the segregationalist "White Citizens Council", commonly known as the White-Collar Klan, which helped to enforce segregation in the 1950s and 1960s; Whereas the Council of Conservative Citizens promotes racism, divisiveness, and intolerance through its newsletter, World Wide Web site, and public discourse; Whereas the Council of Conservative Citizens promulgates dogma that supports white supremacy and anti-Semitism and maliciously denigrates great American leaders including Abraham Lincoln and Dr. Martin Luther King, Jr.; and Whereas the Council of Conservative Citizens provides access to, and opportunities for the promotion of, extremist neo-Nazi ideology and propaganda that incites hate crimes and violence: Now, therefore, be it Resolved, That the House of Representatives (1) condemns the racism and bigotry espoused by the Council of Conservative Citizens; (2) condemns all manifestations and expressions of racism, bigotry, and religious intolerance wherever

they occur; and (3) urges all Members of the House of Representatives not to support or endorse the Council of Conservative Citizens and its views." [6]

Is the CCC a group we really need to be concerned about? Consider the following statement from the fall 1999 CCC Newsletter, the "Citizen Informer":

"Western civilization with all its might and glory would never have achieved its greatness without the directing hand of God and the creative genius of the white race. Any effort to destroy the race by a mixture of black blood is an effort to destroy western civilization itself." [12]

These words were not written by a radical member of the CCC, but by its founder, Robert "Tut" Patterson.

Does the CCC have a racist agenda? One of the links on their web site is entitled, "I Love White Folks." There's not much question where the writers of that site stand on the racial issue. Other links on the CCC's web site lead you to sites with similar racist material. That sounds like racism to me.

COUNTER RESOLUTION:
One hundred and forty-eight representatives have signed to co-sponsor the Wexler/Clyburn Resolution, so there is considerable support for its passage. It also has the support of a broad spectrum of civil rights leaders and organizations—the NAACP, the National Hispanic Leadership Agenda, the Leadership Conference on Civil Rights, the Anti Defamation League, the Religious Action Center, the National Council of Negro Women, the Black Leadership Forum Inc., the Southern Poverty Law Center, the National Council of Churches, the Douglass Policy Institute, the Human Rights Campaign, the National Jewish Democratic Council, and the Urban League. [9]

The passage of the Wexler/Clyburn Resolution is presently on hold. A counter resolution was submitted by J. C. Watts, Jr., a representative from Oklahoma. The Watts Resolution (H.R. 121) generically condemns racism but failed to cite the CCC specifically. Leading the opposition to the Watts Resolution, Representative Wexler made this comment:

> *"Revealing the true identity of the Council of Conservative Citizens is the right thing to do. The CCC attempts to mask its hateful ideology by posing as a mainstream conservative organization, but the racist agenda of this group is undeniable. An empty resolution that only gives lip service to condemning racism, but does not specifically cite the CCC does not strengthen our civil rights laws. It does nothing real. It offers cover, not content."* [10]

One hundred and fifty-two other members of the House of Representatives agreed, and the Watts Resolution was defeated. The Wexler/Clyburn Resolution is currently in committee.

PRECEDENCE FOR THE WEXLER/CLYBURN RESOLUTION:
Representative Wexler said that their Resolution had been modeled on a 1994 Resolution which condemned a speech made by Khalid Muhammad—a senior official in the Nation of Islam—because he had made a speech which many considered racist, anti-Semtic, and anti-Catholic. This 1994 Resolution passed overwhelmingly both in the House and the Senate. Reflecting on Watts' attempt to water down any condemnation of the CCC, Wexler questioned why there had been no objection about singling out one individual or group when the motion to condemn Khalid Muhammad came before Congress. No one tried to substitute a statement about the general evils of racism. *"What it all comes down to,"* Wexler concluded, *"is that when it's a black person who is racist, it's OK for Congress to condemn that individual and single him out, but when it is a white person or a white group, it is not OK to single them out."* [11]

That would be a dangerous precedence to set. It would be equally dangerous to say, *"It's okay to be racist, as long as you are not abrasive about it."*

A CAUSE FOR CONCERN:
Why should the Church be concerned about groups like the CCC? Because they keep fresh the wounds the Civil War inflicted on

our nation. The threat is not so much that they will succeed in inciting another civil war, but that they will attempt to win their war for racial supremacy on a different battleground—the political arena. Indeed the foundation for this "war" is already being laid in the CCC's secretive meetings.

Recently, in one such meeting, Dennis Wheeler, head of the Georgia Chapter of the CCC, told his listeners that they must look to their duty. *"The war for the hearts and minds of the people must be won before the political war can be won,"* [16] Wheeler said.

It would be a mistake to believe that the 15,000 members of the CCC speak for all Southerners. As I said earlier, many White Southerners risked their lives to aid slaves in their flight to freedom in the North. But for the vocal minority, which the CCC represents, the war clearly is not over. The desire of their hearts is indeed for the South to rise again!

To understand how these people could feel this way, we have to go back and look at the basic attitudes of those who supported the Confederacy. For a moment, let's look at how these people might have felt when the war was over and their world had been totally destroyed. Before reading this, remember that even the church had declared that their cause was just, that slavery was within God's will. Scientists of that day had wrongly assumed that Blacks were an inferior race. I say this not to justify their practice of slavery, but only to point out that two of the key guardians of social morality were saying that slavery was right and moral.

Reflections on a War, Lost

"The slaves very existence was by the hand of God as a result of a curse. So you see, it was not a matter of conscience. It was what was right. It was their lot in life to be slaves and the White man's responsibility to keep them that way. Having been destined to slavery, to consider any other situation in life for them was almost a sacrilege. Therefore, it was unlawful to teach them to read and write. If they thought they could rise above slavery, it would create an imbalance in God's plan for man and eventually

destroy the White man's way of life. After all, they were like children. They sang and danced and amused their owners. Believed by some to have evolved from a lower form of primate than humans, it was felt that they were not capable of being anything more than field hands and chambermaids at best.

"A Black man could be seriously beaten for staring at a White woman. The mixing of the races was a blasphemous thought. Yet admittedly many a White plantation owner visited the slave quarters at night to "claim his rights" as master. Young girls in their early teens were bathed and dressed and instructed by their mothers in their "duty" to please the master. Many mulatto children grew up on the plantation with the owner's blood running through their veins.

"Finally it had happened. The gracious Southern way of life had come to a tragic end. Most of the fine plantation houses lay in ashes. The fields lay fallow and the farms were sold for taxes to the Yankees, and the slaves were finally free.

"Depression and despair had replaced the joy and splendor of Anti-bellum life. Like the epic movie, it all seemed to have "gone with the wind." Those who had known only a life of riches and plenty were now in abject poverty and want. Virtually everyone had lost a loved one in the South's valent effort to form a separate nation.

"They blamed the Yankees. They blamed the Northern politicians and the Abolitionists, but most of all they blamed the Blacks. After all, the war had been fought primarily over their freedom.

"The flames that destroyed their way of life not only burned the mansions, but they would also ignite a flame of hatred in the Southerners' hearts that would burn against the freed slave—in the hearts of some even until this present day.

"The Black man was free—free to be educated, free to become anything he desired, from store clerk to professional *politician. He had kicked off the traces of slavery, apparently escaping his virtual caste, and he was now enjoying upward mobility on the social strata of society.*

"But he must be stopped. Thus in the hearts and minds of the defeated Southerners the creed was declared, "The South Shall Rise Again!"

In many ways, the South did rise again. Thankfully, armed conflict never broke out again, but the attitudes that are expressed in this short reflection weren't changed by the outcome of the war. The Reconstruction Era which followed the Civil War did little to improve relationships between Whites and the newly freed slaves. The "Carpetbaggers" who poured into the South after the war kept the antagonism between the "Yankees" and the "Rebs" alive. Jim Crow Laws were written to "keep the Black man in his place." Justice turned its back when Blacks were wronged and exacted harsh penalties when Blacks were accused of crimes. Lynchings were common place. Praise God, this is no longer the case, but there is still much to be done to bring healing between Blacks and Whites—and not only in the South. The Church can and should play a vital role in this healing process.

A VENDETTA AGAINST MULTICULTURALISM:

Not everyone wants to see healing take place between the races in our nation. There are growing numbers of people who believe that the central cause of the downward spiral in our society is America's devotion to multiculturalism—the concept that our society is enriched and strengthened by all the races that come to these shores. In one of the articles on the CCC's web site, the author says that the races should be kept separate. He takes sharp issue with the concept that all people are created equal. [13]

Before we discount this man as a relic from the past, we need to understand that he is not alone. Many others share his views, and some of them are radical enough to be dreaming and planning for a second Civil War. They are determined to complete what their forefathers began in the first one. The developer of a web site located at <www.civilwar.com> states that the purpose of his site is to examine "...*the coming civil war that will shatter imperial America into new, ethnically-based nations.*" [14] He has written a book which explains why this second Civil War will take place. That kind of thinking will do nothing to heal the wounds racism have produced in the fabric of our society.

Others share this scornful attitude toward multiculturalism. In an article entitled "Racial Partition of the United States", Dr. Michael Hart points out the problems reformists have encountered in their efforts to resolve racial tensions in America. Dr. Hart contends that these tensions will never be resolved, that the races were never intended to live together. He proposes splitting the United States into three separate countries—an independent Black country, an independent non-Black country, and an integrated country. He would give each individual the right to choose which nation he wants to live in. Those who still believe in multiculturalism could live in the integrated country. Those Blacks, who chose to do so, would live in the Black country. Those Whites (and perhaps some Asians and some others), who chose to do so, would live in the White country. There would, of course, have to be a division of the tangible wealth of the nation. Dr. Hart proposes that this redistribution should be based on the proportion of the population making up each new country. [15]

Can you imagine carrying out such a plan? One can hardly envision peace and harmony reigning if people were required to give up their property and businesses. People get upset enough when the government requires them to sell their property to make way for a new road or highway. Restructuring the entire nation would be a bureaucratic nightmare! Besides, South Africa tried a similar plan, and it certainly didn't bring peace there.

Even more than logistical considerations involved, such a plan would be a cultural nightmare. The majority of Americans—especially the younger generations—are multicultural in their outlook. To them, a monocultural society would be drab indeed.

Dr. Hart and his colleagues contend, however, that eliminating multiculturalism would produce the peace so many have sought for our nation over the years. Have you ever noticed that man's ways of attempting to create peace often get very complicated, while God's way is really very simple. He sent His Son to die for the sins of **all**, so that **all** might be alive in Him—one people, serving one God, **all** members of one kingdom.

One thing is certain, Heaven will be multicultural. Revelation 14:6-7 gives this picture of the ingathering of souls God is orchestrating in these last days:

> *⁶And I saw another angel fly in the midst of heaven, having the everlasting gospel to preach unto them that dwell on the earth, and to every nation, and kindred, and tongue, and people, ⁷Saying with a loud voice, Fear God, and give glory to him; for the hour of his judgment is come: and worship him that made heaven, and earth, and the sea, and the fountains of waters.*

From every nation, every people, God is gathering a family that will walk with Him for eternity. You can't get any more multicultural than that, can you?

A QUEST FOR RECONCILIATION:

It is both good and necessary to expose the racist character of organizations like the CCC, but we must be equally ardent about confronting racism within the Christian community. If there is one place where you would expect the races to walk as one, it is within the Christian community. Yet we know this is not always the case.

There has been much discussion about how to bring about racial reconciliation at least within the Church itself. Many leaders of the major denominations have made public apologies to Black Christians on behalf of White Christians. All of these attempts have been admirable. They have certainly helped to heal relationships between Blacks and Whites to some degree. But the truth of the matter is—and this must be made plain—that there has never been **conciliation** between the races in these United

States. It is, of course, impossible to **re-concile** something where there has never been **conciliation** in the first place.

The dictionary gives the following definitions for the word *reconcile*: *"1. To reestablish a close relationship between. 2. To settle or resolve. 3. To bring (oneself) to accept: He finally reconciled himself to the change in management. 4. To make compatible or consistent: reconcile my way of thinking with yours."* [17] The word *reconcile* comes from the Middle English word, *reconcilen*, from the Old French word, *reconcilier*, and from the Latin word, *reconcilire*. Reconcilre comes from *re-* + *concilire*, meaning **to conciliate again.**

So what does conciliate mean? The dictionary gives the following definition: *1. To overcome the distrust or animosity of; appease. 2. To regain or try to regain (friendship or goodwill) by pleasant behavior. 3. To make or attempt to make compatible; reconcile. intr. To gain or try to gain someone's friendship or goodwill.* [18] The word *conciliate* comes from the Latin word *concilire*, which is a derivative of *concilium*, meaning *meeting*. The inference is that there has been a meeting of the minds and hearts of those involved, that the hostility and distrust between them has been removed, that there has been a concerted effort to establish friendship and goodwill among or between those who are estranged for some reason. There will never be such a meeting of the minds until we eliminate the root sources of racism, i.e., ignorance (a lack of knowledge or a denial of readily demonstrated truth) and mis-information being two of the key sources.

Certainly there have been many instances in our history when conciliation took place between individuals of different races, but this was not the experience of the majority of Americans. The distrust, tradition, misinformation formed seemingly insurmountable barriers to true acceptance of the rightful place of all the races in this nation.

Conciliation is the process through which distrust is eliminated, tradition is challenged and altered, and mis-information is replaced by the truth. Until an axe is laid to these "roots", racism will continue to plague our nation. Even more tragically, it will continue to compromise the witness of the Christian community.

Conciliation is hard work, but its rewards are great. The reconciliation which it produces will bring true and lasting healing of the wounds caused by racism. Then we can begin to work on making the third definition of conciliation—*to gain or try to gain someone's friendship or goodwill*—a reality, first in the Church and then in the community at large.

"THEY HAD DARKER SKIN..."

Earlier we looked at how the defeated Confederates might have felt in the post war era. Now I would like to share with you a poem written for a "Language and Arts" class assignment by Daniel Knisley, a twelve-year-old young man whose grandparents I know very well. Daniel's insightful poem illustrates the experiences of all the generations of African-American—from those who came as slaves to those now walk in the freedom our Constitution guarantees to all citizens. Daniel is just five generations removed from slave-holding White Southerners. He gave me permission to share his poem in its entirety—

They were taken to a country where freedom reigned
all men were created equal they said
yet they were used as slaves
taken from Africa they had darker skin.

They worked hard and they slaved
no education at all
until one day they were freed
taken from slavery they had darker skin.

They were out in the world
no money at all
although they were free they had no rights at all
put into the world they had darker skin.

Some special people fought for their rights
after a long time of work
they were finally accepted
finally accepted they had darker skin.

Although discrimination still lives
they are free once again
people finally realized they are the same
free in the world they have darker skin.

by Daniel Knisley

The Civil War was a "defining moment" in our nation's history. It reset America on the path the founding fathers envisioned when they wrote about the equality of **all** men and their common right to be free. But, as Daniel observed, for many others the idea of racism is still valid, still an ever-present reality.

It's been said that the only way you can fight an idea is with a better idea. A better "idea" than racism was born in a lowly manger over two thousand years ago. His name is Jesus, Immanuel, God with us—the Word that was made flesh and dwelt among us. Through Him, **all** are offered equal access to the grace, giftings, and power of God without respect to race, nationality or culture. The truth of God's unconditional love for **all** people is the only idea that can set free those who are blinded by racial pride or by the oral traditions that have been handed down from generation to generation.

Condemnation will not open their ears, but the truth spoken in love may. It's certainly worth a try.

End Notes:

[1-4] Allen Breed, *Just who—and what—is the CCC?*, Prince George's Journal, Sunday, February 7, 1999, section A7, page 1.

[5-6] Robert Wexler, *Wexler/Clyburn Resolution Urges Congress to Condemn Racist "Council of Conservative Citizens"*, Available at: <http://www.house.gov/wexler/>. Accessed on July 29, 2000.

[7] Gordon Baum, *Conservative Group Denounces Resolution as Attack on Free Speech*, The Council of Conservative Citizens Press Release: February 4, 1999

[8-10] Robert Wexler, *House Defeats Meaningless Racism Resolution,* March 23, 1999. Available at <http://www.house.gov/wexler>. Accessed on July 29, 2000.

[11] Breed, Ibid.

[12] Michael Masters, *The Confederate Flag and the Struggle for Tomorrow.* Available at: <http://www.cofcc.org/rally0108.htm> Accessed on June 10, 2000.

[13] Thomas Chittum, *Civil War Two,* Available at: <www.civilwar.com> Accessed on April 15, 2000.

[14] Michael H. Hart, *Racial Partition of the United States,* a speech given at the 1996 American Renaissance Conference in Louisville, Kentucky. Available at <http://www.separatism.org>. Accessed on April 15, 2000.

[15] Breed, Ibid.

[16-17] The American Heritage Talking Dictionary, *Softkey.*

Chapter 20: A Current Issue

If in our quest for justice of the oppressed we focus only on the inequities experienced by past generations, we will forfeit the opportunity to play a significant role in liberating today's captives and securing the rights of those who are currently being oppressed. Even as you read these words, thousands upon thousands of people around the world are experiencing the same pain and degradation that so many generations of slaves experienced in America prior to their emancipation. From the rug weaving shops of Pakistan and India, to the prisons of China, to the embattled villages of Southern Sudan, the practice of slavery is not a historical event but a current reality for countless men, women and children—some of them only three years of age or even younger. A multitude of others experience persecution, in one form or another, daily.

Christians are often among those who are targeted for persecution, enslavement, or death. It is estimated that 365,000 of our brothers- and sisters-in-Christ lost their lives because of political- or religious-driven persecution during the year 2000 alone. That means that an average of 1,000 believers were martyred each day. In the March 1998 issue of *Jubilee Extra*, Charles Colson said that more Christians have been martyred for their faith in the twentieth century than in all of the previous 19 centuries. The list of the atrocities our fellow Christians are experiencing includes slavery, torture, imprisonment, murder, rape, flogging, crucifixion, amputation, bombing, deliberately engineered starvation, and forced displacement. *"Just as in the days of Daniel,"* Colson said, *"the presence of people who refuse to bow before state-sanctioned idols sends tyrants into genocidal rage."* [1]

Perhaps nowhere has the onslaught against Christians been more intense and long lasting than in Southern Sudan. Over two million southern Sudanese have died and another four million have been displaced from their homes in the fighting that began between the north and the south in 1983. Countless others have been kidnapped by government forces and enslaved. Four issues are involved in this protracted civil war: (1. The fundamental right of freedom of religion. (2. Disputes over the prized grazing lands of the South—a crucial issue in times of drought. (3. Rights to vast oil resources in Southern Sudan. (4. Racial bias against the Blacks of Southern Sudan.

Although the civil war began in 1983, the fighting intensified when the National Islamic Front, headed by Lieut. Gen. Omar Hassan al Bashir, overthrew Sudan's government in 1989. Since that time, Hassan and his followers have pursued what it believes is a divine commission to convert all of Sudan to Islam. Once the Sudan is converted, they are determined to take this holy war (jihad) to the rest of Africa. Their present targets are the Blacks of Southern Sudan—the Dinkas (a largely Christian tribe), the animists (a tribal religion), and those moderate Muslims in the south, who do not believe this jihad is just.

Spurred on by religious fervor, Hassan's government has waged a campaign of terror and destruction. Government-backed troops have raided the villages, burned the villagers' huts, killed the men and taken the women and children captive. These captives either become the personal possessions of the soldiers or are transported north and sold as slaves. The majority of the captives are children, some of whom watched as their fathers were shot or hacked to death. Others were torn out of their mothers' arms. Brothers and sisters were mercilessly separated from one another. Some of the children were so young when they were kidnapped that they have little memory of their family or friends when they do manage to escape captivity. Survivors of these raids say that Christians are often singled out and killed. Others, especially young boys, are forced to convert to Islam and fight in the war against their homeland. [2]

Denials of Slavery's Existence:
Sudan's government emphatically denies that any of these things are happening in their country. Rev. Farrakhan's newspaper, *The*

Final Call, labels reports on slavery in the Sudan a *"...big lie...(just) another manipulative device to divide the Black and Arab people in America."* [3] His accusation has a logical basis. Hassan's National Islamic Front is made up of lighter-skinned descendants of Arab ancestors, while the Southern Sudanese are Black Africans. This is not Whites enslaving Blacks as it was in America, but of Browns enslaving Blacks. Rather than divide Blacks and Arabs in America, however, the truth about what is happening in the Sudan can work to draw Blacks and Arabs— and all other racial groups in America—together in a focused effort to end this present-day holocaust.

Testimonies that are pouring out of Southern Sudan make it difficult to deny that racism is a factor in the slaughter of the innocents. Victoria Ajang, a mother of four, told Congress her narrow escapes from two villages that were raided by government troops. She was separated from her husband in the second raid and has never seen him again. *"There is a powerful ideology that drives these slave raids,"* Victoria said. *"In government's mentality, all blacks are 'abd'* (a word which means slaves). *Whether Christians, Moslem, or animist, we should be slaves forever. We are inferior beings who must submit or be killed."* [4] That sounds a lot like the kind of thinking that was used to justify slavery this nation, doesn't it?

When Rev. Farrakhan challenged the press to prove that Southern Sudanese were actually being enslaved, two reporters from the Baltimore Sun, Gilbert Lewthwaite and Gregory Kane, went to Sudan to get that proof. They were escorted by John Eibner, a member the board of the American Anti-Slavery Group. Also accompanying them was a crew from NBC's *Dateline* program and Baroness Caroline Cox, the deputy speaker of the House of Lords and a member of Christian Solidarity International—a Geneva-based abolitionist group that has orchestrated the purchase and release of thousands of southern Sudanese slaves. [5]

The *Dateline* crew photographed Lewthwaite, Kane, Eibner, and Cox as they talked with many southern Sudanese who had been freed from slavery. Through interpreters, each of these former slaves shared accounts of the horrors they experienced because of the North's jihad against the South. *Dateline* filmed Lewthwaite and Kane as they purchased the freedom of two brothers, one 10 and the other 12 years old. These boys had been taken as slaves when they were 4 and 6 years old. *Dateline* presented this compelling footage in an exposé on December 10, 1996. No longer could the world or Rev. Farrakhan question the reality of slavery in Sudan. [6]

Rev. Farrakhan cannot write off today's abolitionists as anti-Islamic. Moslems who have escaped from Sudan also testify about the enslavement and persecution of Blacks there. One of the earliest reports of the frequent, government sanctioned massacres and slave raids was compiled by two Sudanese intellectuals— Ushari Ahmad Mahmud and Suleyman Ali Baldo, both of whom are followers of Islam. These men were professors at the University of Khartoum. In 1987, they wrote a report, documenting the Al Dein Massacre—a "battle" in which the Sudanese government militia attacked "...*the villages of indigenous African tribes, murdering some blacks and kidnapping others.*" [7] The Al Dein Massacre was possible, Mahmud and Baldo believed, because the Rizerigat families in Dein viewed the Dinka tribe as subhuman; "...*all psychological barriers to the terminating the Dinka's had been broken down.*" There was no moral check that said, "*This is wrong.*" [8] The government used the Rizerigat families' prejudice against the Dinkas to accomplish their purposes.

THE LIBERALS ARE SILENT:
Charles Jacobs asks, "*Where are the liberals? In the fight against slavery in Africa they seem to have disappeared.*" [9] Rev. Jesse Jackson, the NAACP, and the Congressional Black Caucus have been largely silent about the atrocities occurring daily in Sudan. Even women's groups have not fought against slavery's progressively tightening grip on Sudan. When anti-slavery groups asked Rev. Jackson to help liberate enslaved Sudanese, he response was, "...*my plate is already full.*" Certainly there is much to be done to insure the rights of all races in the United States and other nations, but how can we ignore the cries of the oppressed in Sudan? [10]

When Rev. Jackson accompanied former President Clinton to Rwanda, *"...he witnessed Clinton's apology to the people of Rwanda for failing to do anything to stop the genocide there."* [11] Indeed an apology was needed. Over 800,000 Rwandase died in a few days time, in part because the United Nations failed to send in a peace keeping force in time. Former President Clinton was instrumental in blocking the deployment of those troops. But neither Rev. Jackson nor former President Clinton mentioned the holocaust that was taking place in Sudan even as they were speaking that day.

Rev. Jackson was one of the leaders in the Anti-Apartheid movement that helped to change the course of history in South Africa. One would expect that he would advocate similar divestment polices against Sudan's National Islamic Front. To date, that has not happened.

Dr. Charles Jacobs, Research Director of the American Anti-Slavery Group, believes that one reason why the situation in Southern Sudan has not raised the outcry that Apartheid did is that *"...the quarrels in...the Sudan are obscure. They do not occur against the backdrop of economic modernization, as in South Africa; nor do they mirror the Black-White tensions of the apartheid battle, which struck Americans so close to home."* [12] Dr. Jacobs pointed out that our deference to other peoples' culture may also be keeping America from coming to the aid Sudan's enslaved. Our reluctance to criticize other cultures sometimes blinds us or desensitizes us to the suffering people are experiencing, Jacobs said. In many respects, culture has become an untouchable line that outsiders cannot cross. This current "sacredness of culture" easily deafens our ears to truths we do not want to believe.

When Akban Muhammad, Rev. Farrakhan's spokesman, was on a PBS program, he dismissed the evidence of Sudan's slave trade as merely a Jewish conspiracy, saying, *"I know that the Jewish groups, the Zionists, have a problem with the Sudan."* When he was shown footage of young black captives being whipped by their Arab captors, Muhammad shrugged and commented, *"That's their culture. They'll beat 'em."* [13]

Indeed they will beat them. In a video put out by "Anti-Slavery International" a seventeen year old boy related his experiences at the hands of Sudanese government troops. When the soldiers raided his village, he and many other young people were kidnapped. He said that the soldiers tried to force them to convert to Islam. When they refused, they were beaten. When they still refused to deny Jesus, the soldiers tied their hands behind their backs and pressed their chests against burning coals. When asked how he endured this kind of torture, he replied, *"I passed out very quickly after my chest touched the coal."* His chest still bears deep scars from those searing coals.

The soldiers were so angry that the boys would not convert to Islam that they selected four of the younger boys—one only five years old—and beat them and tortured them until they died. Each of these youngsters accepted martyrdom rather than deny Christ. Hearing their screams, the other boys knew they were all going to be killed unless they converted to Islam. Escape was the only option if they wanted to remain Christians.

It's hard to imagine a five-year-old being so strong in his faith that he would suffer torture and death rather than deny Jesus. One would hope that the account of this young lad's martyrdom will compel liberal Christians—Rev. Jackson included—to take a stand against the Sudan's government-orchestrated holocaust against southern Sudanese Blacks.

THE ROLE OF ECONOMICS:

Abolitionists are advocating a divestment campaign against Sudan such as the one that was so effective against Apartheid. One of their key targets is Sudan's newly emerged oil industry. Canadian-based Talisman Energy—the world's third largest oil company—helped Sudan's government build a 1,000 mile pipeline from the interior of Southern Sudan. That pipeline is delivering 100,000 gallons of oil per day to Port Sudan. With the rightful owners killed or enslaved, Sudan's government and Talisman Energy are free to gather in the profits from Southern Sudan's rich oil fields. [14] It would seem that there is an economic aspect to the government's "holy war."

Dr. Charles Jacobs commented, *"The Sudanese Catholic Bishop Macram Gassis, whose dioceses are in the afflicted areas, has said, 'If the oil is pumped, we are finished. The Sudanese government will then be able to buy the weapons to wipe us out completely. Why are Western companies aiding in this pipeline project?'"* [15] That's a good question.

As more information filters out of Sudan, news of the gross human rights violations routinely being committed by the National Islamic Front is rallying opposition against the North's oppressive policies. Secretary of State Madeline Albright and Canadian Foreign Minister Lloyd Aixworthy have spoken out against Talisman Energy. Retirement fund managers and holders in the United States are reconsidering their holdings in this and other companies who, like Talisman Energy, are contributing to the Khartoum government's ability to kill or enslave the Southern Sudanese. Some Funds are divesting their holdings in companies, which are effectively aiding in the extermination of Christians and animists. Others, such as Fidelity, Vanguard, TIAA-CREF, and Prudential are not. [16]

Jacobs pointed out that *"...even those who may flinch at having human rights drive foreign policy should be concerned. On the realpolitik side, a wealthy Sudan can aggravate regional politics, diminish the hopes of moderate Muslims everywhere, and further fund Osama Bin Laden's anti-American terrorism."* [17] Overlooking or being reluctant to speak out against racial or economic tyranny can prove costly indeed.

A Worldwide Evil:

If slavery existed only in the Sudan today, it would be enough to outrage Christians and non-Christians alike; but slavery touches the lives of millions of men, women and children around the world today. Its form varies, but its effect is always the same: It debases people—all of whom have been created in God's image. Men, women and even small children are its victims. Their daily cries for relief from their suffering are a call to action for all who serve the living God; for He hears and is moved to compassion by the anguished petitions of the oppressed.

The *United Nations Supplementary Convention on the Abolition of Slavery, the Slave Trade and Institutions and Practices Similar to Slavery* has identified five basic forms of slavery present in the world today: Chattel slavery, bonded slavery, child slavery, the exploitation of women, and the forced resettlement of indigenous peoples. [18] **Chattel slavery** is the absolute ownership of one person by another. It is not only being practiced in Sudan, but it is also common in Mauritania, Ethiopia, the Gulf States of Africa, Senegal, Sierra Leone, and West Africa as well. Many of its victims are being transported along the same routes as African who were sold to Arab nations long before the development of the Atlantic Slave Trade.

Bonded slavery is common on the Indian subcontinent, in Thailand, and in a number of Latin American countries. Its victims typically face a financial need that forces them to take out a loan. Usually only a small amount of money is involved—sometimes for the wedding of a daughter or the funeral of a loved one. Because these people have no assets that can be mortgaged, the banks will not lend to them. The moneylenders and landowners will, however, at very high interest rates. These exorbitant rates mean that a loan of fifteen dollars may take from forty to sixty years to repay. During the repayment period, the borrower is in bonded slavery to the lender. To repay the loan, the borrower is sometimes required to work in the lender's garden for 3 to 6 months a year. In other instances, he must give half of the crops from his own land to the lender. His wife and children may also be included as bonded laborers in the contract. [19]

During the time he is bonded, he cannot change jobs without the permission of his lender. Sometimes his debt is bought by another landowner. In that case, he must follow his debt. Often the bonded laborer is never able to repay his debt. *"The life of those in bondage is nasty, brutal and short."* [20] Even death does not bring release from the debt. It is simply passed on to one of his children—usually a son. The child inherits the father's debt and with it the bondage.

Laws have been passed against bonded slavery, but these laws are difficult to enforce, because both tradition and racism underlie this practice. You see this particularly in India where people of lower castes are forced into bonded slavery to people of upper castes.

Child Slavery is becoming a global problem. It is estimated that in India alone there are over 55 million children under fourteen, some as young as four, who are enslaved in one way or another. Some work seven days a week, eighteen hours a day weaving carpets. Their pay for these long hours may be as little as 20 pence a week. The carpets they make sell for three or four thousand pounds in London. [21]

World opinion is being brought to bear on the carpet manufacturers. A consortium of European and Asian human rights groups initiated the RugMark Campaign in 1993. A manufacturer can affix the "RugMark" label on his carpets only if he is able to certify that children were not used to weave them. Amazingly, labor costs are so low in Asia that eliminating child labor will only increase the cost of the carpet by 1 to 2 percent. [22]

That's a small price to pay to keep other youngsters from going through what a young Indian boy named Santosh did. When Santosh was five-years-old, slavers kidnapped him and took him to a distant city. There he was locked in a room and given no food to eat until he agreed to weave on the looms. He made Oriental carpets for nine years, working from 4:00 in the morning until 11:00 at night every day without breaks. He was paid nothing for his labor. When he cut his finger on one of the sharp tools he had to work with, the loom master shaved match heads into the cut and set the shavings on fire to stop the bleeding. He didn't want the child's blood to stain the carpet he was making. [23]

The anguished mothers of Tungipara, Bangladesh know that slavery is a reality. These mothers, like thousands of other impoverished Bangladeshans, sent their children—over a thousand of them—to work in the Persian Gulf States to help support their families. Labor contractors came to their village, promising the children good wages. Their promises meant nothing, however, for these men were slave traders.

After months of investigation, *Women & Children International*—a human rights activist group—confirmed that the children of Tungipara were slaves. The girls had been sold to the brothels of India and Pakistan; the boys had been shipped to the Gulf States to be jockeys. [22] This kind of deceptive recruitment of young slave laborers is all too common.

Hundreds of thousands of Asian children have met a fate similar to that which befell the children of Tungipara. Many Asian children, some as young as six, have been forced into prostitution. Most of these child sex-slaves are used by Asian locals, but many also supply the demands of a thriving "sex tourism" industry which is supported largely by Western and Japanese men. Children are valued because they bring fees that are four to five times higher than "workers" over sixteen do. [25]

Some of these children have been rescued from their owners and placed in rehabilitation centers. But Amihan Abueva of the Salinlahi Foundation in Manila said, *"It's more difficult to reha-bilitate children who have been sexually exploited than even those who have been traumatized by war.* [26]

The exploitation of women continues to be a problem in many nations. In a report to the United Nations, the leaders of "Anti-Slavery International" noted that, for many reasons, women are among those who are most vulnerable to enslavement or slavery-like practices. Cultural traditions, which assign women a servile position in the family and in society in general, are among the most common reasons why this is true. Another reason, is that women generally have less physical strength than men, so male employers can use physical force against them as well as threatening them with sexual abuse. [27]

America has made significant progress in passing laws to protect women from exploitation, but this is not the case everywhere. For instances, In Afghanistan, women can be beaten or stoned to death if they fail to wear the traditional Islamic dress for women.

"One woman was beaten to death by an angry mob of fundamentalists for accidentally exposing her arm while she was driving." [28] In India, a man has the right to order his bride to be burned to death while still wearing her wedding dress if he is displeased with her in any way. The government is trying to bring a halt to the practice of "bride burning", but it still occurs. In Turkey alone over 100,000 women have been forced into prostitution. [29]

Islamic law is so oppressive toward women that I wonder why so many African-American women are embracing Islam today. Muhammad himself had a something less than gracious attitude toward women. In the Hadith, he is quoted as saying, *"Isn't the witness of a woman equal to half that of a man? This is because of the deficiency of a woman's mind"* (vol. 3, no.826). [30] *Believing that women were "deficient in intelligence",* Muhammad denied them equal rights under Islamic law and declared that a woman's testimony was only worth half that of a man. [31]

(References 30-31 in this section were taken from The Islamic Invasion. Copyright © 1992 by Robert Morey. Published by Harvest House Publishers, Eugene, Oregon 97402. Used by Permission.)

Forced resettlement robs indigenous peoples of their ancient tribal lands, reducing them to poverty, robbing them of dignity, and making them dependent upon government aid—all in the name of economic development. We have seen the devastating results this policy has had on the Native American tribes in America. Regrettably, it is happening to many of today's indigenous peoples. In his annual report to the London-based Anti-Slavery International group, Michael Harris included these observations about one such tribe in Brazil:

"...I visited an area inhabited by an Indian tribe which had lived there since the beginning of time. They were self-contained. They planted what they needed for their food; they had their own traditions, behavior, and ceremonies. They were a happy community. The next year I went and saw them again. Their land was wanted for cattle ranching, and they were being driven out. There was no compensation, no where to

go, no resettlement, nothing. If they didn't burn their house and go, it was burnt around them; and if they still protested, they were shot. ...I saw some of them who had been shot.

"Those poor people now live in some of the worst urban slums in the world. They have taken to prostitution, ...to drink, and goodness knows what. Most of the money for the cattle ranchers came from the World Bank and from some companies in various Western countries." [32]

The plight of indigenous peoples facing forced resettlement was the central theme of the Star Trek movie, *The Insurrection*. Many will see this movie solely as entertainment, not realizing that the struggle being portrayed is actually happening.

CHILD SOLDIERS:

On January 12, 1999 the BBC posted an Amnesty International report on the BurmaNet News. This report relates yet another present-day form of slavery: **the forced recruitment of child soldiers**. Uganda, Sri Lanka, Sudan, and Sierra Leone are just a few of the countries where armed militia compel children—some 10 and younger—to serve as soldiers. In Uganda, these child soldiers are often pitted against well-armed government troops. One girl, who had been forcibly recruited by Uganda's Lord's Resistance Army, said that she had been forced to kill another child who had attempted to run away. Then she was forced to watch as a boy was hacked to death because he didn't sound an alarm when he saw the child trying to escape.

The forced conscription of children has been fueled by the development of easy-to-use, lightweight weapons. With one of these miniaturized weapons, a child can kill as accurately and efficiently as an adult can. *"An AK-47 rifle, which in one West African country now costs no more than US$6, can be stripped and reassembled by a child of 10."* [33]

The frightening reality is that children not only can kill with these weapons, but it is easy to train them to do so. Human-rights lawyer Rachel Brett said, *"Once you indoctrinate the children—par-*

*ticularly if you supply them with drugs and alcohol—they be-
come very effective killers and torturers. Once you break that
inhibition, it tends to go on."* [34]

Breaking children's inhibition to kill is accomplished in different ways. Often the children are brutalized in some way to transform them into fierce warriors. There are reports that in 1995,
children in Sierra Leone were trained for battle by forcing them
*"...to take part in the torture and execution of their own rela-
tives. After this there is no going back."* [35]

"In some ways, children make better soldiers than adults," the
writer of a UNICEF press release observed. *"They are easier to
intimidate, and they do as they are told. They are less likely to
run away, and they do not demand pay."* [36]

It should be noted that not all of these child soldiers are forcibly
recruited; some actually volunteer. Why? Sometimes the conflicts
in which these children are fighting have lasted for a generation
or more. The children *"...become soldiers simply to survive. In
war-ravaged lands where schools have been closed, fields destroyed, and relatives arrested or killed, a gun is a meal ticket..."*
[37] Many are orphans of war. Joining a militia provides a home of
sorts for them. In the fighting in Rwanda in 1994 alone *"...an
estimated 114,000 Rwandese children were separated from their
families."* [38]

Some of the children who volunteer, like their adult counterparts,
have united their hearts to the cause of one side or the other. They
are fighting to change the status quo. One young girl, who had
served in the rebel forces in Honduras, shared her experiences:

*At the age of 13, I joined the student movement. I had a dream
to contribute to make things change, so that children would
not be hungry...later I joined the armed struggle. I had all
the inexperience and fears of a little girl. I found out that
girls were obliged to have sexual relations 'to alleviate the
sadness of the combatants.' And who alleviated our sadness
after going with someone we hardly knew? At my young age
I experienced abortion.... In spite of my commitment, they*

abused me, they trampled my human dignity. And above all, they did not understand that I was a child and that I had rights." [39]

What do you say when you read something like that?

The use of child soldiers has an addition negative effect; it increases the risks that civilian children face. *"Most of these contemporary wars are not between States (Nations) but within them. Battles are fought from street to street, and distinctions between combatant and non-combatant rapidly disappear. ...children and families are not just getting caught in the crossfire, they are also specific targets. As one political commentator expressed it in a 1994 radio broadcast before the violence erupted in Rwanda: 'To kill the big rats, you have to kill the little rats.'"* [40] Compassion has little place in the hearts of those who are controlled by racist attitudes. To them, killing an innocent child is no different than killing an armed combatant.

CASHING IN ON SLAVERY:

Slavery, it seems, is big business among organized crime groups. In a report issued on December 15, 2000, the United Nations Convention on Transnational Organized Crime indicates that *"...powerful criminal organizations such as the Yakuza, the Triads, and the Mafia..."* [41] are engaged in the trafficking of women and children for prostitution rings, as well as migrant workers for 21 st century sweatshops. The U.N. estimates that four million people become ensnared in some form of slavery each year through the efforts of organized crime.

Trafficking in women and children from Central and Eastern Europe has increased dramatically since the end of the cold war. Prior to that, most victims of prostitution rings came from Asia, Africa, and the Caribbean. The U.N. estimates that there are between 200,000 and 500,000 illegal "sex workers" in the European Union alone. Another 100,000 illegally immigrated prostitutes are working in the United States. Most of these prostitutes do not know what lies ahead when they agree to leave their home lands. When they arrive at their new "homes", they are at the mercy of the brothel owners. They must work to repay the debt they own their "job recruiter." The U.N. report notes that an Asian prostitute may sell for up to $20,000 dollars in the United States or Japan. A Russian prostitute working in Germany will earn up to $7,500 a month. The brothel owner typically takes $7,000 of this, leaving little for the victim to repay her debt. [42]

Prostitutes often work up to 18 hours a day. They are both mentally and physically enslaved. As illegal immigrants, they fear deportation if they seek legal help, but even more they fear retaliation on family members back home if they try to escape. [43]

Organized crime is also exploiting migrant workers. The U.N. estimates that there currently are 200 million migrant workers who are enslaved by smugglers. Frequently, victims indenture themselves in return for illegal passage to North American or Western European countries. They must work as indentured servants until their debt is repaid. Illegal passage into the U.S. averages about $45,000. There is little hope of paying off this kind of debt working in the sweatshops or restaurants where these illegal migrants are typically employed. Again no legal recourse is available to them. [44]

Migrant workers *"...frequently suffer physical and mental torture by their employers."* [45] Some die in ill-fated efforts to smuggle them into other nations. In one instance, an Albanian smuggler threw his human cargo overboard in an effort to escape the Italian police, navy and coast guard who had tracked his boat down. Many of the victims were rescued, but many of them drowned. Italian officials indicate that at least one vessel carrying human cargo is intercepted every night, sometimes up to 20. [46]

Thus a new generation of slaves is growing up in brothels and sweatshops around the world. These slaves come from all races, if not from all nations. They live without hope in oppressive situations that wear on the human spirit. *"It's terrible,"* one friend said after a trip to New York City. *"They're putting them in the same sweatshops where they put the Jews. You can see the faces of the little children in the windows. What can you do?"*

The U.N. is attempting to draft uniform international codes of law that will expedite the extradition and trial of criminals who exploit fellow humans. That will take time, as all things requiring international agreement do. The question is, what can we as the Church do to alleviate the suffering of these millions of men, women, and children who are ensnared in slavery courtesy of organized crime?

Many years ago, Alan Paton, a White South African, wrote a book entitled, *Cry, the Beloved Country*. If you fill in the comma, his title reads, *Cry for the Beloved Country*. It recounts the devastation Apartheid was causing in that nation. Today he might well write a book entitled, *Cry, the Beloved Countries*. For in God's eyes, each country is beloved, each people, each race, treasured and desired—created with a purpose, which is designed to bring good and not evil in the lives of the people.

THE PERSECUTED CHURCH:

The Church has suffered persecution from its inception, yet it has continued to flourish and grow. Indeed, sometimes it seems to grow most rapidly where it is most oppressed. This is the case in Sudan and in China, nations where persecution has been the most intense. The reports that come out of these and so many other countries redefine the meaning of the word persecution. One mother in a so called peace camp in Sudan was confronted with the choice of denying Jesus or letting her children starve to death. *"If you convert to Islam, we will give you food for your children,"* a soldier said. Without hesitation she answered, *"If my children do die, they will go to a far better place."* The hope of their salvation sustained her. She chose the eternal, rather than enjoy the temporal for a short time.

Similar stories are pouring out of other nations. The fighting in the Middle East has heightened tensions between Christians and Moslems around the world. Radical Islamic groups in Indonesia have intensified their efforts to drive their Christians neighbors out of their country. One seventeen year old told of watching as the militants executed a man. They tied him to a pole and cut off his head.

Stories of similar executions abound, yet accounts of miracles of deliverance are also emerging from the intense persecution Christians are enduring in Indonesia. There is the story of a young man who survived an attack in which a machete almost severed his spinal column. He was left for dead, but when relatives prepared him for burial, life suddenly returned to his body. He said that someone told him he must come back. His work was not yet done. Women told of climbing a steep cliff, holding onto very thin roots and branches that should have easily broken under their weight.

Militant Islamic forces in Niger are also increasing their opposition to the Church. The church I pastor has sponsored a missionary couple to Niger for four years. Shortly after the missionaries' return to Niger after a seven-month furlough, we received a fax from them. Moslem extremists had barricaded them in their home, saying, *"This Christian thing has to stop!"* They proceeded to set fire to the church and the bible school missionaries oversee. Thankfully, the students and their families were able to escape without harm, but the church and bible school were both a total loss. This report came in the day that our church was joining with hundreds of other churches around the world for the International Day of Prayer for the Persecuted Church.

Our congregation was stunned when I shared this report with them. The cost of carrying the gospel to other lands became very real as we all prayed for the family in Niger that night. It will be difficult for this missionary family to forget the Moslems' parting words: *"...we won't harm you this time."* But they are staying in Niger. They believe that God will use what has happened to bring many people to Christ.

THOUSANDS DIE IN NIGERIA:
About 40% of the population of southern Nigeria is Christian. Relationships between Moslems and Christians had been cordial, but tensions between these two groups escalated when Islamic extremists gained power and tried to introduce Islamic law— Shariá—and made Nigeria a part of the Organization of the Islamic Conference. Thousands of people have died in periodic mass rioting since that time.

Christians make up a much smaller portion of the population in northern Nigeria. As a result they have experienced far harsher persecution than believers in the south. Building churches is forbidden. Sometimes existing churches cannot be used, and Christians routinely experience discrimination in the educational system. When my wife and I visited Nigeria in the fall of 2000, we learned that thousands of people were burned alive in a church where one of our Harvest International mentors pastors. Moslem extremists had barricaded the parishioners in the church, boarded up the windows and doors and set fire to the church. Soldiers stationed outside shot anyone who did manage to escape. They forced the pastor's wife and children to watch as they forced him into his car and then set it on fire, burning him alive.

Think of it, thousands of Christians, burned alive. And in this century! This happened in February 2000. Amazingly, this assault did not destroy this church. By the time of our visit in September to ordain a new pastor, the church had grown to 1,000 strong. You see it again and again—the Church grows despite persecution, often faster than where there is peace.

The experiences of believers in Sudan, Indonesia, Niger, and Nigeria are being repeated in many other nations around the world. The Communist Party's vendetta against the Church has claimed the lives of thousands of believers in the past few decades. This campaign to stamp out the Church has been intensified recently. Directives issued by the Communist Party were smuggled to the West recently. These directives confirmed what witnesses have been reporting: A special class struggle is being waged against unregistered Catholic and Protestant churches in China. Hundreds of Chinese Christians are being "re-educated" in labor camps. Many more have been arrested and never heard from again.

Chinese government leaders have declared their intent to eradicate Christianity from China. Their goal is to *"...strangle the baby in the manger."* [47] They forget that Jesus is not in the manger anymore. He's on the throne of heaven, and He's watching over His Church.

In Colombia, dozens of key church leaders have been brutally murdered, churches have been burned to the ground, women raped, and families forced from their land in Colombia's Uribia region. Yet the Church is growing at a faster pace there than in any other part of that country.

Columbia is one of the most violent nations on earth. Forty-five percent of all the kidnappings that occur in the world happen there. Someone is murdered there every 20 minutes. Almost half of Colombia's children are said to be victims of some form of abuse. Christians are often the targets of violence, because guerrilla forces know that they won't take an active role in the country's thriving drug trade and they can't be trusted to lie about rebel activities. [48]

In Egypt, terrorists attack churches, church properties, and Christian-owned businesses, and target Christians for execution. Christians are forced to pay extortionists to protect themselves, their families and their friends. There have been reports of Christian girls being abducted, raped, and forced to convert to Islam. Rumors of churches making repairs or constructing buildings without permits have sometimes resulted in anti-Christian riots. [49]

In Iran, Iranian Christians International (ICI) has reported that the persecution of Christians has escalated despite the election of Iran's more moderate president. Christians—both leaders and laity alike—have been arrested, threatened, imprisoned, and tortured for their faith. Others are kept under heavy surveillance. Their phones are tapped, and their mail is opened routinely. Some have lost their jobs. Others have been refused employment, housing and education. Iranian Christians sometimes disappear for days, weeks, months, or years. Many fear reporting the persecution they have experienced until years later when they flee the country. [50]

The European Union drew up a resolution, criticizing *"...the wide-scale practice of torture, extra-judicial killings and summary executions; restriction of freedom of speech and opinion; and discrimination against ethnic and religious minorities."* [51]

In North Korea, Christians are living under a brutal and oppressive regime. North Korea's capital, Pyongyang, was known as "The Second Jerusalem" prior to the Communist take-over, but now believers are suffering severe persecution. Special death squads kill many of them by pouring molten metal over them. Others are taken to electric treatment rooms where they are tortured and killed. Still others are sent to prison camps. There they are special targets for persecution. They are deprived of rest, beaten, and assigned the most difficult and dangerous jobs in the camp. Repeatedly, they are ordered to recant, but they refuse. Many sing hymns even as they are being beaten. [52]

In Pakistan, Christians are the victims of a "religious apartheid system" that is even more oppressive than the political apartheid system in South Africa was. Pakistani believers face discrimination in regard to their property right and opportunities for employment and education. Militant Islamic forces have been waging a war of hatred and violence against Christian believers for many years. Christian girls are sometimes kidnapped, raped and forced to convert to Islam. Christians, accused of blaspheming the prophet Mohammed or of desecrating the Koran, have been beaten and killed by mobs before they even go to trial. If they are convicted of either of these offenses, they are executed. [53]

The Pakistani government, the police, and the legal system offer Christians little or no protection from Islamic extremists because of fear of reprisals. Their fears are not without basis. One judge was murdered when he dared to acquit several Christians of blasphemy. [54]

In Saudi Arabia, the government absolutely prohibits any form of Christian worship within its borders, yet it actively presses its right to expand Islam into other nations, including the United States where it has been financing the building of Islamic academies. Saudi Christians are not permitted to worship in their own homes. Islamic police routinely raid private homes if they suspect that worship services are being held in them. The homes of foreign workers from less influential countries such as the Philippines, Korea, Egypt and India are especially targeted in these raids. Those captured in such raids are subject to lengthy imprisonment without trial. There they may be tortured or even killed. [55]

Foreign visitors are forbidden to share evangelistic materials of any faith other than Islam. Those who do so are subject to deportation or even more severe penalties. Citizens of Saudi Arabia, who accept Jesus, are automatically subject to death. Despite this threat, underground churches are thriving. These courageous believers are willing to forsake all, including life, for Jesus! [56]

In Vietnam, Christians are routinely harassed by government security forces. They levy heavy fines against Christians and often subject them to brutal interrogations, imprisonment, and hard labor. There are over 600,000 Protestants in Vietnam, but the government has not given official recognition to even one church or Christian agency since the end of the Vietnam War twenty-three years ago. The government also restricts the activities of Vietnam's 5 to 8 million Catholics, forbidding them to appoint bishops, limiting the number of those who can enter the seminaries, restricting the number who can be ordained each year, and sometimes imprisoning members of the clergy. [57]

The tribal minorities in Vietnam's Central Highlands, where the house church movement is expanding rapidly, are particularly subject to government persecution. Tribal converts also face persecution by members of their own tribes if they abandon spirit worship to follow Jesus. Evangelist Ha Seing's experienced this kind of persecution first hand—

"In October 1996, evangelist Ha Seing was arrested and brutally beaten with iron bars for sharing the gospel with his people, the Koho tribe. Although both his life and his sanity were feared for, he recovered completely. His recovery so deeply touched the tribe that upon his return home, 50 more Kohos gave their lives to Christ. Approximately one-third of the Koho people are Christians." [58]

This pattern of oppression and persecution is repeated in nation after nation. **In Cuba,** the Church is forbidden access to radio and television, and the government has denied official recognition to any church publication, making them subject to random closures. **In Albania,** the activities of Protestant and other minority religious communities are severely restricted. **In Uzbekistan**, the recently passed "Law on Freedom of Conscience and Religious Organizations" makes failing to register a religious organization a crime. Many Christian churches and organizations have less than 100 members, so it is very difficult for them to gain official recognition. Violating this law can land the organizer in prison for five years. Just conducting a home Bible study can get you 3 years in prison. [59]

Living in a nation where religious freedom is a given makes it difficult for most of us to comprehend this kind of persecution. True, even here believers are facing increasing persecution, but we don't risk imprisonment, enslavement, or death when we gather to worship God. Identifying ourselves as Christians does not cost us our jobs, separate us from family and friends, or limit our access to higher education, much less place our lives in jeopardy. This is not the case in other nations. There such suffering is the rule, not the exception, for those who dare to follow Jesus.

End Notes:

[1-2] Charles Colson, *Standing Up Against Slavery Today*, Jubilee Extra, March 1998.

[3] Charles Jacobs, President of the American Anti-Slavery Group, *Slavery: A Worldwide Evil*, The World & I, April 1996 http://www.anti-slavery.org/.

[4] Nat Hentoff, *Our People Were Turned to Ash*, The Village Voice, April 4, 2000. Available at <http://www.villagevoice.com>, accessed on Nov. 27, 2000.

[5-6] Gilbert Lewthwaite and Gregory Kane, *Witness to Slavery: Part 3*, The Baltimore Sun, June 18, 1996, Section 1A.

[7-8] Ushari Ahmad Mahmud and Suleyman Ali Baldo (University of Khartoum professors), *Human Rights Violations in the Sudan The Al Dein Massacre, 1987*. Available at http://www.anti-slavery.org/. Accessed on Sept. 24, 2000.

[9] Terry Mattingly, *What to Do About Religious Persecution*, The Prince George's County Journal: Religious Section, November 13, 1998, pg. A8.

[10-11] Nat Hentoff, *We Descendants of These Slaves*, The Village Voice, July 5-

11, 2000. Available at <http://www.villagevoice.com>, accessed on Nov. 27, 2000.

[12] Joseph R. Gregory, *African Slavery—1996,* © 1996, First Things, May 1996, pp. 37-39.

[13-17] Jacobs, Ibid.

[18-21] Michael Harris, *Slavery, a Recurring Evil,* Anti-Slavery International Annual Report, 1994-5. Anti-Slavery International. Available at <http://www.antislavery.org/nwstraf.htm> For more information, write The Stableyard, Broomgrove Road, London SW9 9TL, United Kingdom.

[22-24] Jacobs, Ibid

[25] HARRIS, IBID.

[26] Jacobs, Ibid.

[27] Anti-Slavery International paper prepared for the United Nations Working Group on Contemporary Forms of Slavery, *Contemporary Forms of Slavery Requiring Action by Governments: Examples of a Large-Scale and Persisting Problem in the 1990s,* Anti-Slavery International, June 1995. Available at <http://www.antislavery.org/nwstraf.htm>.

[28] Sara Band, *A Necessary Cause:Women in Afghanistan,* Available from <sarabande@brandeis.edu> Accessed on 4/15/00.

[29] Anti-Slavery International, Ibid.

[30-31] Robert Morey, *The Islamic Invasion,* Harvest House Publishers, Eugene, Oregon, 1992, pg. 202.

[32] Harris, Ibid.

[33] UNICEF Press Release, *Children at War.* Available at http://www.unicef.org. Accessd on Nov. 13. 2000.

[34] BurmaNet News, *Amnesty Declares War on Child Armies,* BBC Report, Available at http://www.soros.org/burma/ai1129.html, Jan. 12,1999.

[35-36] *Children at War,* Ibid.

[37] *Children at Both Ends of the Gun,* UNICEF, Available at http://www.unicef.org.

[38] *Children at War,* Ibid.

[39] *Children at Both Ends of the Gun,* Ibid.

[40] *Children at War,* Ibid.

[41-43] U.N. Convention Against Transnational Organized Crime: Palermo, Italy, December 12-15, 2000. *Trafficking in Persons: the New Protocol.* United Nations. Available at http://www.odcep.org/palermo/schedule99.html> Accessed on Jan. 1, 2001.

[44-46] U.N. Convention Against Transnational Organized Crime: Palermo,

Italy, December 12-15, 2000. *The Protocol against the Smuggling of Migrants*, United Nations. Available at http://www.odcep.org/palermo/schedule99.html>. Accessed on Jan. 1, 2001.

[47-59] Anti-Slavery International, *The Persecuted Church: the situation in countries around the world*. Available at <http://www.persecutedchurch.org>. *g>. Accessed on Mar. 2, 2000.*

Section 4: Racism, Past and Present

Chapter 21: Racism, a Deterrent to Effective Missions

We have addressed some of the societial changes that need to take place to insure equity for all races. We also need to address changes that are essential within the ministry of the Church itself in order to eliminate any vestiges of racism. I am addressing this need for change—for *metanoia*—in the context of our missions efforts, particularly in relationship to cross-cultural ministry.

Christian missions cannot avoid the question of *metanoia*—the change of attitude that is necessary for any mission effort to be carried out successfully. This change of attitude is necessary, not only in relation to the poor and the oppressed, but also in relation to the rich and powerful. I am not addressing the change of attitude that needs to take place in these groups, but rather of the change of attitude that has to take place in the minister or in the missionary who has been sent to minister to one of these groups. As God's representative, the minister or missionary must have God's attitude toward the people God directs him/her to serve. Truly coming into this godly attitude requires allowing God to strip us of our racial prejudices or preconceptions regarding these people. Allowing this *metanoia*, this change of attitude, to take place requires a deep work of the Holy Spirit. Without such a work, effective cross-cultural ministry simply cannot take place.

The prophet Jonah illustrates a failed cross-cultural ministry about as well as anybody. When God said, *"Arise, go to Nineveh, that great city and cry out against it, for their wickedness has come up before me." (Jonah 1:2)* Jonah allowed his prejudice against the Ninevites to keep him from obeying God. Jonah's thoughts may have run something like this: *"The Ninevites were cruel to my people, the Ninevites overran us, the Ninevites put hooks in* _our jaws and lead us through the street; the Ninevites were cruel butchers. I want God to blast them off the face of the earth. I'm not going to preach repentance to them. I want to see them get it!"_

It is important to note that Jonah was not wrong in what he said about the Ninevites. They had indeed done all of these things to the Israelites. Jonah was wrong because he refused to adopt God's heart attitude for them. _Metanoia_, a change of attitude toward his people's cruel oppressors was out of the question for Jonah. As a result he booked passage on a ship that was heading for Tarshish— the absolute opposite direction from where God had told him to go.

AND GOD PREPARED A GREAT WIND...
The great storm God sent effectively "arrested" Jonah. Everyone else on the ship cried out to their god for deliverance from this terrible storm, but Jonah was fast asleep in the hold. He was probably suffering from acute anxiety because he was out of God's will and he knew it. His sleep was interrupted when the shipmaster came to him and asked, _"What meanest thou, O sleeper? arise, call upon thy God, if so be that God will think upon us, that we perish not."_ (Jonah 1:6)

We know the story. When the crew cast lots to see who was the cause of the evil that had come upon them, Jonah's straw came up. Immediately, these guys wanted to know what Jonah's country was, what his occupation was, and who his people were. Jonah answered, _"I am a Hebrew; and I fear the Lord, the God of heaven, which hath made the sea and the dry land."_ (Jonah 1:9)

It's interesting that the crew was upset with Jonah for causing their problem, but they weren't ready to throw him overboard. Instead, they rowed hard, trying to bring the ship to safe harbor, but the storm opposed them. Really, the Lord opposed them.

Jonah, for his part, was ready to get it over with. He was out of God's will, and he knew it. He figured that if they threw him overboard that would be the end of it. He was going to die, but he was not going to Nineveh. He underestimated God.

AND GOD PREPARED A FISH...

Some people now believe that God sent a shark to rescue Jonah. Picture Jonah, sinking down under the waves. He's just drowning—just giving it up—and all of a sudden he sees the mouth of a Great White closing over him. Fortunately for Jonah, God had given this shark very specific instructions: *"I want you to swallow Jonah. Swallow, not eat! Don't bite! Don't swallow him a piece at a time! Just swallow him and hold him until I tell you to let him go."*

It's amazing what ending up in the belly of a shark will do for your prayer life. When "Jaws" has you for lunch, you'll break out the prayer rug in a hurry!

Jonah began to cry out to God and to praise Him from the belly of the shark. When God heard him say, *"...I will sacrifice unto thee with the voice of thanksgiving; I will pay that I have vowed. Salvation is of the Lord"* (Jonah 2:9), the Lord gave the shark permission to unload his passenger. I figure that shark just went out, got a good running start, headed full steam toward shore, hit a sand bar, opened his mouth, and boom! Jonah came out and landed on his feet.

As Jonah's feet hit dry land, the word of the Lord came to him again: *"Arise, go unto Nineveh, that great city, and preach unto it the preaching that I bid thee."* (Jonah 3:2), This time Jonah obeyed God.

Can you imagine what the people thought when they saw Jonah? The stomach acid of the shark would have bleached him white as paper. Even his hair was white. He probably had a little seaweed hanging on him yet; maybe a few crabs. When a guy looking like this walks into a city and says, "Repent!", revival is going to break out!

Ordinarily, if a Jew would have walked into Nineveh and started preaching to them, they would have just whacked off his head. But the Ninevites repented, and God relented of the disaster He had planned to bring on them. Now this displeased Jonah, and he became very angry. He prayed to the Lord and said, *"Ah, Lord is this not what I said when I was in my country? Therefore I fled previously to Tarshish, for I knew that you are a gracious and merciful God, slow to anger, abundant in lovingkindness, one who repents from doing harm. Therefore now, O Lord, take my life from me. It is better to die than to live."* (Jonah 4:2-3, KJV paraphrased)

Jonah was miserable. He wanted God to scorch the Ninevites. He went out on the east side of the city and made himself a shelter. Sitting in the shade under it, he waited to see what would become of Nineveh. He was hoping to the last moment that the Ninevites would blow it and God would rain down fire and brimstone on them. There had been no *metanoia*, no change of attitude in Jonah, toward the Ninevites.

AND GOD PREPARED A VINE...
God caused a vine to grow up over the shelter Jonah had pre-pared for himself. The King James translates the word for vine here as a gourd plant. In the Hebrew it actually translates as a castor bean plant. The castor bean produces castor oil—the most bitter thing in the world. It was fitting for this guy to be sitting under the most bitter thing the world has to offer, because he was so steeped in bitterness.

AND GOD PREPARED A WORM...
Jonah was very grateful for the vine, but God had intended for it to soften Jonah's heart as well as shade his head. When Jonah held onto his bitterness, God spoke to a worm: *"Yo, grub! In the morning, go and eat the roots of Jonah's vine!"* The worm obeyed God, and Jonah's vine withered. Now the sun was again beating down on Jonah's head.

AND GOD PREPARED A VEHEMENT EAST WIND...
God added a strong, easterly wind to the heat of the sun that was pouring down on Jonah's head. Jonah grew faint, but he did not repent of his attitude toward the Ninevites. Instead he said, *"It is better for me to die than to live."* Jonah was not going to give up

his hatred! There was absolutely no *metanoia*, no change in attitude in Jonah. He hated the Ninevites, and he wanted God to strike them dead.

But God asked Jonah, *"Is it right for you to be angry about this plant? I mean, a plant! Do you know, you have had pity on the plant, but you didn't labor to make it grow. It came up overnight and perished the same night. Should I not pity Nineveh, that great city in which are more than 120,000 persons who cannot discern between their right and their left and much livestock. There's children, women, young—120,000 inhabitants—and you don't even care."* (Jonah 4:9-11, KJV paraphrased) Jonah hadn't labored for the vine, but God had labored for the Ninevites. He wanted them to be *changed* not *charred.* He wanted to bring the joy of revival **to them,** rather than finality of judgment **upon them.**

Jonah's story ends here. He's still filled with bitterness and anger. There has been no change in attitude toward the Ninevites. He's still saying, *"They deserve God's judgment!"*

In reality, we all deserve God's judgment. Look around you! Think back on our lives. God made us worthy through the propitiation of His Son. That's the only reason we are spared His judgment. None of us deserved His grace, but He gave it anyway. We need to have that same attitude toward everyone else.

A MESSAGE FOR TODAY:

Jonah's experience speaks volumes to the Church today. We need to discern God's purpose in each missionary situation and, for the sake of obedience, go where God tells us to go. Before we go, however, we need to allow God to let us see these people as God sees them. For God sees them without reference to socioeconomic strata and without racial superiority or inferiority. He sees them as neither rich nor poor, but as lost souls—sheep without a shepherd.

In the midst of the suffering and struggling of the multitudes, we are to be a light, a city of refuge, bearing the message, *"God has something better for you. You can live through this and come out better on the other side."* Often, just as He sent Jonah to the

Ninevites—to the people he hated the most—sometimes God will send us to the people we have hated the most, bearing this message of hope and grace and salvation. God has something better for them, and He has something better for us—something better than holding onto the bigotry, hate, or prejudice that divides race from race.

Jesus, Crossing Cultural Barriers:

Jesus was teaching this same lesson in Missiology to His disciples when He stopped to talk to a young woman who had come in the middle of the day to draw water from a well in Samaria. The Samaritans had been ostracized by the Jews, because they had intermarried with their oppressors during the 70 years of captivity in Babylon. Because they were no longer purebred Jews, they were not allowed to touch the Temple proper, lest they defile it.

The Samaritans got upset, and said, *"Look, we'll build our own temple!"* So they went into Samaria and built their own temple and worshipped God there. The result was a gulf of prejudice that had separated the Jews and the Samaritans for generations. The depth of the division between them is reflected in the woman's answer when Jesus asked her for a drink of water. *"How is it that you, a Jew, ask me, a woman of Samaria, for a drink? Jews have no dealings with Samaritans."* (John 4:9, KJV paraphrased)

Jesus ignored the issue that divided Jew from Samaritan, and moved quickly to the issue that divided God from all men—spiritual death. His request for a drink of water from the well Jacob had dug was only a springboard for the gift He wanted to give her—living water from the well of salvation. *"Whoever drinks from the water of this well Jacob dug will thirst again,"* Jesus told her, *"but whoever drinks the water I give shall never thirst again. Indeed, it shall become a well of water springing up into everlasting life."* (John 4:13-14, KJV paraphrased)

Jesus concluded his ministry to this Samaritan woman by confronting her with the sin that lead her to come to the well alone, in the heat of the day, instead of earlier when all the other women came to draw water. This woman was not only a Samaritan; she was an adulteress. Neither her race nor her sin deterred Jesus. He offered her a drink from the well of salvation, and she accepted it. She was so excited that she left her water pot and headed back to town to tell everyone she'd found the Christ.

In the meantime, the disciples returned with food and urged Him, saying, *"Rabbi, eat."* Jesus said to them, *"I have food to eat you do not know."* (John 4:32, KJV paraphrased) The disciples were really puzzled. They didn't understand that He was speaking about something spiritual. So Jesus said, *"My food is to do the will of Him who sent me and to finish His work."* (John 4:34, paraphrased)

Then Jesus began to speak to them about the great harvest of souls that He was going to be sending them out to reap. *"Lift up your eyes, and look on the fields; for they are white to harvest. And he who reaps gathers wages and gathers fruit for eternal life."* (John 4:35-36, paraphrased)

Do you know what Jesus was doing here? He was striking at the very roots of racism, in this case, the racism that divided the Jews and the Samaritans. *"Here's where you can start reaping,"* Jesus was saying, *"right here in Samaria."*

It's hard for us to appreciate what a traumatic statement that was to the disciples. It would be like going to Mississippi in the 40s or 50s and saying to a group of White preachers, *"Begin to preach the love of God and the gospel to the Black people here."* Even this does not allow us to understand the depth of the challenge Jesus placed before His disciples that day. The Jews hated the Samaritans. He was telling them to go to the people they hated the most and share the gospel. *"You have to have a change in attitude toward these Samaritans,"* Jesus was saying. *"You have to see them the way I see them and the way God the Father sees them."*

As Jesus was speaking with His disciples, a large group of Samaritans, lead by "the woman at the well", descended upon the "camp." They had heard her testimony and had come to see for themselves if Jesus was indeed the Messiah.

Jesus had set His disciples up with a perfect object lesson. They didn't even have to go into the fields to reap this harvest. The harvest had come to them. Jesus ignored centuries of Jewish prejudice and ministered the truth of the gospel to these thirsty souls. Many of them believed His message and asked Jesus to come and stay with them. He agreed, and for two days He taught them the basics of the gospel message. As He was teaching them, He was also teaching His disciples some basic lessons in Missiology:

- "When God sends you to any people, you need to obey Him."

- "If you have a prejudice against that people, you must first ask God for *metanoia*, for a change in your attitude toward them."

- "You must see them as God sees them."

- "You must ask, 'How do we make these people God's people?'"

Jesus didn't just tell them how to conduct a missions effort; He did it. As a result, many souls were gathered into the Kingdom of God that day.

The price of holding onto our prejudices is just too high. A harvest of eternal souls hangs in the balance.

Chapter 22: A Challenge to Love

Racial prejudice is not innate in man; it is taught. Jesus taught a different way. His teachings strike at the very roots of the carnal attitudes that perpetuate racism. He says, *"You have to change your attitude toward those who have persecuted you, who have spitefully used you, who have wounded you. You have to forgive them and demonstrate God's love toward them."* Why? *"They will know you are my disciples because you love one another."* Jesus very clearly included our enemies in the "others" we are to love.

The Church has to demonstrate this kind of love to the world. Is this difficult to do sometimes? Yes, it is, but Jesus did not make this kind of love an option for the believer. Where there is a failure of love, all manner of evil can be justified.

As of this writing, over 50 nations are currently engaged in war at some level! Fifty nations! Not only is there an ethnic cleansing with the Serbs and the Albanians in Kosovo; it is happening all over the world. Look at the tribal wars in Africa. Mass slaughter and genocide is commonplace there. Do you know what usually starts these wars and motivates the atrocities that so often accompany them? It is not an infringement by an aggressor in most cases; nor is it because one nation's border has been violated by another nation. People are killing those within their own nation in Rwanda, Burundi, Liberia, Sierra Leon, Guinea, Sudan, China, Palestine, Central America—all over the world.

The roots of these internal conflicts are found in tribal wars and differences that have been going on for millenniums—in some cases, two, three, or four thousand years. Most of the people don't even know what started it, nor do they know why they hate their enemy. Most have no inclination whatsoever to even want to know. If you ask them, *"Why do you hate these people?"*, they will answer, *"I don't know. It's always been that way."* There is no logic involved, no determination of present guilt or offenses. It simply comes down to saying, *"We are Hutus; they are Tutsies. We hate them. We kill them."*

The Hutus and Tutsie are both African, both have the same skin and the same, identical physical makeup. You cannot identify Hutu from Tutsie except by their tribal markings. Yet they hate one another, and they pass these grievances—these prejudices—from generation to generation.

Once I read an account where one of these groups had lined up children who were 6, 7 and 8 years old and had them kill children of the other group who were only 6, 7 and 8 years old with a machete. Another account spoke of soldiers taking little children and smashing their heads together to kill them. Thirty-eight thousand children in Central Africa were slaughtered in a tribal genocide just because somebody said, *"They did this to us."* They keep hating one another because it has always been that way.

We need to ask, *"Why has it always been that way?"* It has always been that way because someone in the flesh has told them, *"A eye for an eye; a tooth for a tooth."* Without grace's covering, this principle fosters a desire for revenge and retribution. Are they totally lacking in love? No, but the command to love your neighbor gets translated a little differently. If you ask, *"Who is your neighbor?"*, they will answer, *"Those who are like you."* If you ask, *"Who is your enemy?"*, they will answer, *"Those who are not."*

History sometimes reveals the roots of these conflicts. In the case of the Hutus and the Tutsies, it started with the methods the Europeans used to develop a loyal following in their new colony. They set the weaker tribe over the stronger tribe. This created a following that was fiercely loyal to the Europeans. Whereas they had been the lower class in the pre-colonial era, they were now the favored class.

This policy completely inverted the political and social structure among the tribes. It did help to keep peace while the Europeans were in power, but it also created racial tension between the tribes. When the Europeans relinquished governmental rule, this tension erupted into open warfare.

I am of the opinion that all the European nations—as well as the United States—that had a part in creating these tribal and ethnic struggles should also be a part of bringing healing as well. Thank God for missionaries who preach unity and God's love!

LOVE'S TRANSFORMING POWER:

Is there any way to eliminate these ancient walls of prejudice? For weeks NATO dropped bombs on the walls that separated the Serbians and the ethnic Albanians in Kosovo. Many lives were lost and much property was destroyed, but those walls of prejudice are still standing firm. Centuries of tradition do not fall easily.

NATO's efforts have secured a peace of sorts, but it will not be lasting. That's not a prophecy of doom; it's a simple statement of reality. Bombs may force compliance, but they cannot change hearts. Only God can do that, and He uses the most powerful weapon known to man—His agape love.

Agape love is ethical love moved to a higher dimension. Ethical love involves an adherence to a higher moral standard. Even before we were Christians, we knew that we should treat our fellow man in certain ways. In other words, we had an ethical persuasion based on the demands of our society. But when we speak of agape love, we're talking about a love that really exceeds what we can call love as far as humanity goes. Agape love originates with God. It is the love of God that flows in us and through us. It will allow us to do things that we could never do naturally, including forgiving old enemies.

Part of what we receive from God in our "package of grace" is His agape love. It is shed abroad in our heart, bringing change in us first. That's where change has to start—in each of us.

So often in our society we talk about love like it is not a necessity to everyone. How can we ask some macho man to say, *"I love you"?* Some marriages fail because husbands neglect to say those three simple words often enough. *"I told her I loved her the day we were married. Isn't that enough?"* one husband asked.

Love starts with God and is extended to us. This is not the *phileo*—the friendship kind of love—or the *storge*—the family kind of love. Nor is it the *eros*, the sensual—fleshy kind of love. It is the *agape* love of God, flowing into us and through us.

The word love appears as a noun—*agape*—120 times in the New Testament. But it appears as a verb—*agapao*—130 times. This tells us that love is love when you demonstrate it! It is not just a word; it is **a demonstration of the likeness of Christ in us!** This demonstration of God's love is what changes us.

Vines' *Expository Dictionary of New Testament Words* tells us that *agape* and *agapao* are used in three different senses:

- "to describe God's attitude toward Jesus (John 17:26) and toward the human race in general (John 3:16) and believers specifically (John 14:21)."

- "to teach us the attitude He wants us to have toward one another (John 13:34) and toward all men (I Thes. 3:12; I Cor. 16:14; II Peter 1:7)"

- "to express God's essential nature. (I John 4:8)"[1]

Some of Vines' comments on these two words for love are very relevant to our discussion of racism. He points out that *"Love can be known only from the actions it prompts"*[2] and reminds us that God's love comes to us because of His *"...deliberate choice, made without assignable cause save that which lies in the nature of God Himself."*[3] God's love for us, therefore, is based on His sovereign choice, not on our worth.

This God-kind of love is intended to flow not only between us and God, but also between others and ourselves. Vines wrote: *"Christian love, whether exercised toward the brethren, or toward men generally, is not an impulse from the feelings, it does not always run with the natural inclinations, nor does it spend itself only upon those for whom some affinity is discovered. Love seeks the welfare of all, Rom. 15:2, and works no ill to any, 13:8-10; love seeks opportunity to do good to 'all men and especially toward them that are of the household of the faith,' Gal. 6:10."* [4]

If we are to practice *agape* love toward all mankind, we cannot allow our natural inclinations—those things that we have been taught about others—to guide us if they are contrary to God's word. Likewise, we are not to direct our ministry exclusively toward those who are like us. Instead we should seek to do good to everyone, especially fellow believers.

Vines' comments on the verb *agapao* gives us insight into the effect God's love has in peoples' lives. In regard to God, Vines said, *"agapao ... expresses the deep and constant love and interest of a perfect Being towards entirely unworthy objects, producing and fostering a reverential love in them towards the Giver, and a practical love towards those who are partakers of the same, and a desire to help others to seek the Giver."* [5] God's love changes us. It causes us to love Him and to love others. It also inspires us to lead others to Christ.

As we are transformed by God's love, the barriers that separate us from our traditional enemies will be removed. We would never do this naturally.

End Notes:

[1-5] W. E. Vines, *An Expository Dictionary of New Testament Words: Vol. III,* Fleming H. Revell Company, Old Tappan, New Jersey, 1996, pp. 20, 21.

Chapter 23: Unity Fosters Revival

Today, just as in the early days of the Church, Christians need to be united. Unity is so important. A house divided cannot stand. We must be one! If we would see revival in our nation, our communities, our churches, our families, in our own lives, we must guard against anything that brings division in the body of Christ. Only then can our hearts truly beat in the same rhythm with Jesus' heart. Then we will begin to see God move in power to break down the strongholds that are threatening to destroy our nation and every other nation in the world.

Unity was very much on Jesus' heart when He prayed what we refer to as His high priestly prayer. In verse 20 of John 17, we see that His directed this prayer to us as well as the original disciples:

> *20Neither pray I for these alone, but for them also which shall believe on me through their word; 21That they all may be one; as thou, Father, art in me, and I in thee, that they also may be one in us: that the world may believe that thou hast sent me. (John 17:20-21)*

Clearly unity was a priority with Jesus. It needs to be a priority with us as well.

WHEN DIVISION COMES:

What do we do when division comes? God commanded the children of Israel to bring a peace offering when a dispute arose among them. This peace offering was very important to the people and to Israel because it brought them back into unity with themselves and with the God that they served. When unity is restored, God is going to do something great!

The word for *peace* in relation to this prescribed offering is *shalem*, which is a derivative of the word *shalahmim*. It is also connected with the word *shalom*, which we know stands for peace. *Shalem* speaks of **a specific kind of peace**—one that reflects *the harmonious relationship of the worshippers and the worshipped.* God was very concerned that there be no disruption in our relationships, whether on a vertical or a horizontal level.

Under the Old Covenant, if two families or two individuals were at odds, they would come together and bring their peace offering to the priest. The offering would be handled by the priest, lifted up unto the Lord, offered up in sacrifice, and then consumed by everybody involved and by the priest as well. This public act of bringing, offering, and consuming the sacrifice was God's instrument for restoring peace (harmonious relationships) among His people. Then and only then could they move together in unity with God and with one another.

We can easily see the concept of such a peace offering into the context of the Church today. Jesus is our high priest. When we have a dispute with another brother- or sister-in-Christ, we need to go to Jesus together. What sacrifice should we bring? A heart that is ready to forgive and allow restoration to take place. When the offense is great, as in the case of racism, this is a difficult thing to do. In such cases, we have Jesus' example to follow. From the cross of Calvary, He looked down upon His persecutors and said, *"Father, forgive them...."*

Is it difficult to do what Jesus did? Yes, sometimes it is **very difficult**, but forgiveness is not optional for the believer.

Forgiveness Is Not Enough:
Forgiveness is not enough to restore the chasms that separate the various segments in the body of Christ today. If unity is to be restored to the Body, we must follow the full prescription given in the Old Testament regarding the peace offering. No, we do not have to sacrifice an animal and share its flesh, but we do need to sit down and sup with one another.

To sup with one another means far more than sharing an occasional meal together—a brief encounter, requiring little long-range commitment. No, to sup with one another means to spend time with one another, to get to know one another, to share our burdens, to touch each others' hearts in a way that gives us understanding of the hopes and fears that shape our lives, our outlooks and our actions. A superficial encounter will not suffice.

Moving beyond the superficial will be costly. Superficiality allows us to hold onto the old wives tales and biblical misinterpretations that have been handed down to us from our fathers. Furthermore, superficiality perpetuates division. But if we will sup together with our Lord at the foot of His cross, He will pour His truth into our hearts. His truth will allow us to see one another as He sees us.

In his letter to the Galatians, Paul gives a clear picture of God's view of His followers:

> *26For ye are all the children of God by faith in Christ Jesus. 27For as many of you as have been baptized into Christ have put on Christ. 28There is neither Jew nor Greek, there is neither bond nor free, there is neither male nor female: for ye are all one in Christ Jesus. 29And if ye be Christ's, then are ye Abraham's seed, and heirs according to the promise.* (Galatians 3:26-29)

We are His children. We come into His family through our faith in Christ. Through baptism, we are clothed in Christ. The robe of His righteousness covers not only our sin, but all the differences— all the natural characteristics—we use to categorize ourselves. Finally, we are Abraham's seed and co-heirs with Christ according to the promise. In Christ, we are one!

Another thing about supping together—the invitation must be open to all who will come. God's invitation to salvation is extended to whosoever will accept it. Likewise we must be willing to sup with all who come, excluding none—not even *"them folk"*, who *"everybody knows will never amount to anything."* That's what the world tells us, doesn't it? Philip had a similar response when he learned that Jesus was from Nazareth. *"Has anything good come out of Nazareth?"* he asked. It only took a brief encounter with Jesus for Philip to recognize that something good had indeed come out of Nazareth! In the same way, if we will take the time to sup with one another, to really get to know one another, we will recognize Jesus in them, the only hope of glory.

UNITY, A KEY TO BLESSING:

Why is unity so vital to the body of Christ? Where there is no unity among the worshipers, the blessings from the One being worshipped are not going to flow. But when we are one with each other and we become one with Him, He will move heaven and earth for us! He will drive out our enemies, and we will see the glorious manifestation of God's presence like never before! Where there is peace between man and man and between God and man, things begin to happen! *We can then have access to that upper room experience.*

The unity that God is calling us into is not one that disregards our natural identity, for He created diversity. Rather, God is calling us into unity on a supernatural level. On this level, there is no diversity, for we are all birthed of one Father, empowered by one Spirit, cleansed by the blood of one Lamb. It is our God-given, God-purchased, God-sustained identity that joins our hearts with His and with our fellow Christians. As His work is perfected in us, we will be united in one purpose—to do the will of God even as Jesus did. Where this happens, the blessings and power of God will flow!

WHO'S KINGDOM ARE WE BUILDING?

For centuries, Whites have "painted" Jesus White. Doing so has hindered, rather than advanced the Kingdom of God. Will "painting" Jesus Black, as the followers of the Cushite Theology desire, advance the Kingdom of God? I don't think so. Doing so would just be error, clothed in a different color.

Regardless of what color Jesus was when He walked this earth, He was Immanuel, God with us, deity clothed in human flesh! We miss the purpose of His coming when we focus only on the color of His skin. He came to establish the Kingdom of God upon the earth and to provide a way of entrance into that kingdom. The only qualification God places on entrance into this kingdom is our redemption through the blood of Christ.

GUARD YOUR HEART:

We must guard our hearts when we are offended, when we're insulted, when we're accused falsely. Why? Because whatever overshadows our hearts puts a barrier between our spirit and God's Spirit. Furthermore, it puts a barrier between us and others. It doesn't matter what the source of the shadow is—whether bitterness, unforgiveness, sadness, discouragement, hatred, meanness, anger, unbelief, or pride—the effect is the same: it separates us from God and from each other. Where there is division, the army of God is vulnerable to defeat.

How do we guard our hearts? Psalm 108:1 speaks of our hearts being established in our faith in God:

O God, my heart is fixed; I will sing and give praise, even with my glory.

The psalmist is saying, *"Oh God, my heart is steadfast, my heart is sure, my heart is established, my heart is stable, therefore I can sing and give praise."* Surely, there's going to be some **glory** involved when God inhabits the praises of His people!

The New English Translation renders this verse is this way:

"I am determined, O God! I will sing and praise you with my whole heart." [1]

If we are going to be able to penetrate the barriers racism has erected in the body of Christ, we must fix our hearts on Him and determine to sing praises unto God with our whole heart regardless of our circumstances! But be warned; the cost will be high. For where our hearts are not right before God, where our hearts are not beating as one with His, where our will is not choosing what God says is good and right and desirable, He will require change in us.

HOW DID JESUS GUARD HIS HEART?

What enabled Jesus to guard His heart in the midst of the pain and suffering He experienced during His arrest, trial, and crucifixion? John gives us some insight into this in the thirteenth chapter of his gospel:

³ Jesus knowing that the Father had given all things into his hands, and that he was come from God, and went to God; ⁴ He riseth from supper, and laid aside his garments; and took a towel, and girded himself. ⁵ After that he poureth water into a bason, and began to wash the disciples' feet, and to wipe them with the towel wherewith he was girded. (John 13:3-5)

The peace that allowed Jesus to walk through "passion week" was rooted in His knowledge of and confidence in God. He knew that **He had come from God**, that **He was God's only Son**, the Lamb of God, given to take away the sins of the world. He knew that **He was going to return to God**, He knew that **the gates of Hell were not going to prevail against Him**, that, instead of being held captive in Paradise, **He was going to take the keys of death and Hades from Satan's hands and lead captivity captive.**

Likewise, we need to know our spiritual roots. We need to know that we are born of God, that we are His children, adopted into His family, co-heirs with Christ. We need to be assured that we have been grafted into the Vine. We need to remember that there is only one Vine, one source of the vibrant life that surges in our hearts. Our natural roots may vary according to our culture, nationality, or race; but our spiritual roots are the same. We are all grounded and rooted in Christ—in His life and in His love!

THE HEART-MENDER:
Political activism is an essential aspect of righting the wrongs of racism. But activism is not enough, for racism wounds the heart of man. If we are its victims, it assigns a lower worth to us as individuals and as a people. If we are its perpetrators, it cuts off fellowship with those whom we regard as inferiors and blinds us to God's view of those whom **He** regards as our equals. No legislation can heal the wounds concealed in the heart of a man, woman, or child, but Jesus can. The question is, will we allow Him to do so?

End Notes:
¹ *NET Bible, the New English Translation.* Available at www.netbible.org.

Chapter 24: The Power of the Mustard Seed

Great strides have been made by those in the Civil Rights Movement and in the various affirmative action groups in establishing equity for people of every race in this nation. There remains one battleground where racism cannot be legislated out of existence, one place where it cannot be silenced regardless of the size of the weapon brandished. That battleground is the human heart. New laws may bring an external compliance with prohibitions against racism, but no legislation has the power to change the internal root system from which racism grows—man's traditions, wrong thinking, and supremacist theologies. The Spirit of God alone can enter into the heart of man and bind together in love those who have long been separated by hate, scorn or indifference.

Some accept racism as inevitable. They say, *"It has always existed. It always will."* Change seems impossible, but we have to remember that *nothing is impossible for God.*

In Luke 17, Jesus is teaching the disciples about the offenses that so easily come in and threaten to separate the members of the body of Christ:

> *Then said he unto the disciples, It is impossible but that offences will come: but woe unto him, through whom they come! It were better for him that a millstone were hanged about his neck, and he cast into the sea, than that he should offend one of these little ones. Take heed to yourselves: If thy brother trespass against thee, rebuke him; and if he repent, forgive him. And if he trespass against thee seven times in a day, and seven times in a day turn again to thee, saying, I repent; thou shalt forgive him. And the apostles said unto the Lord, Increase our faith.* (Luke 17:1-5)

In regard to these offenses, Jesus says, *"woe unto those through whom they come!"* In other words, He is saying that whoever creates strife, stress, or disunity in the body will indeed be judged by God. In Titus 3:10, we are admonished to mark those who cause division. Titus was referring to those who make shipwreck of other's faith, those who come into the body and bring doubt, and those who, through some divisiveness of sin, separate brother from brother. The judgment of God will rest upon such as these.

Jesus said it would be better for such a person that a millstone be hung around his neck and he be cast into the sea, *"...than he should offend one of these little ones"* Jesus is talking about new believers, as well as young children in this passage.

Our Response to Offenses:

Jesus then taught His disciples how to respond to those who offended them—who have in some way shaken or challenged their faith in God. He said, *"Take heed to yourselves: If thy brother trespass against thee, rebuke him; and if he repent, forgive him."* In other passages of scripture, we are told to forgive others just as we have been freely forgiven. No indication is given that we should wait until our offenders repent. But that is not what Jesus said in this case. Instead, He said, *"Rebuke your offender, and then if he repents, forgive him."*

Why was Jesus so adamant? The offenses He's addressing here are those that have the potential of bringing division in the church by shipwrecking the faith of new believers. Rebuking those who bring offense in this manner guards the faith of new believers and preserves the unity of the body of Christ.

Now how do you rebuke them? Not with a Louisville Slugger baseball bat, not by refusing to talk to them from that point on, not by getting up and moving across the aisle when they sit down next to you; but in the same way you would want to be rebuked— with gentleness and meekness as we are instructed in Galatians 6:1. We need to open the lines of communication in a way that says, *"I love you and God loves you, but you have offended me!"* We are not to hold it in until it causes great harm.

Then Jesus added, *"And if he trespass against thee seven times in a day, and seven times in a day turn again to thee, saying, I repent; thou shalt forgive him."* (Luke 17:4, KJV) The disciples were astounded. Seven times in a day! But they didn't try to talk Jesus down to six, or five, or maybe three times a day. They simply said, *"Lord, increase our faith!"*

There was great wisdom in their request. Problems are going to arise in the body of Christ. We need to be people of faith, because faith is the key to resolving every situation in the Church. Faith is the key to communication. Why? Because, by faith, we should say, *"Lord, I believe you're going to send me to speak to him/her and you're going to prepare his/her heart. You're going to go before me to open his/her ears, so that there can be communication heart to heart, and healing is going to take place"*. In every situation, we need faith—faith in God.

Offenses even arose among the disciples. Consider the crew Jesus put together. He didn't go to the seminary to recruit them. He didn't choose them based on their theological degrees. Some of them were mending nets when He said, *"Come, follow Me."* One was a tax collector! Another was involved in guerrilla warfare, and he couldn't wait until they over threw the Romans. Jesus had to take all of these diverse personalities and different temperaments and mold and shape them into an apostolic body. Through them, He would birth the New Testament Church, using each of them as purveyors of the new covenant of the new testament of God. Like the Twelve, the church is made up of individuals with diverse personalities and temperaments. We need faith to get along!

INCREASING OUR FAITH:
Jesus didn't rebuke the disciples' request for more faith. Instead, He began to teach them how their faith could be increased.

And the Lord said, If ye had faith as a grain of mustard seed, ye might say unto this sycamine tree, Be thou plucked up by the root, and be thou planted in the sea; and it should obey you. (Luke 17:6)

Some translations say, *a black mulberry tree*, instead of *a sycamine tree*. The characteristics of the black mulberry tree give us some insight into what is needed to increase our faith. The black mulberry tree has one of the largest root systems of any tree in the world. It also has one of the fastest growing root systems of any tree in the world. Because it has such an intricate root system, it can live up to six hundred years. That's an old tree!

Mulberry trees will grow anywhere. Their roots will grow under sidewalks and driveways and into septic tanks. They'll break up everything in their way. It is this tremendous root system that allows the mulberry tree to grow so fast and become so strong.

Likewise, if you and I are to be successful as Christians, we have to develop a very strong root system. Often we are so excited about what can be seen above ground, but the most important thing in the beginning of our walk with Christ is what's happening below ground. After we have come to Jesus, we want to look like Christians, walk like Christians, talk like Christians, let our light shine before men, etc. But what's happening on the exterior is not as important as what is happening on the interior. That's why, when we start "clothesline preaching" and become so legalistic in our outward appearance that we don't take time to emphasize inward development, we can end up with people who look good on the outside, but who lack character on the inside.

ROOTED AND GROUNDED IN LOVE:
The first thing we must do after we accept Jesus is establish a sound root system. We must be rooted and grounded in love and in the Word of God. Once we are rooted and grounded in these things, nothing can come into our lives and take root—especially a root of bitterness—that cannot be plucked up by faith and cast into the sea far from us. When bitterness goes, unforgiveness and division can go with it.

Jesus is saying, *"Listen, no matter how strong something tries to take root in your life, if you are rooted and grounded in God and you learn how to process your faith, then you're going to be able to speak to it, and by faith, the power of God is going to pluck it up by the roots and remove it from you!"*

If we don't exercise our faith and pluck up the mulberry trees—the roots of bitterness, etc.—that come into our lives, they will occupy space that should be filled with faith in God and love for others. This is part of what perpetuates racism. We are offended by the racial slurs others hurl at us, by the injustices we experience, by the oppression we suffer. These offenses quickly grow into trees of bitterness that will defile our hearts if we do not, by faith, pluck them up and cast them into the sea. Note that Jesus was not ignoring the fact that offenses do occur. He was simply teaching us how to handle them when they do come.

Like the disciples, we might well say, *"Lord, increase our faith!"* We might even ask, *"Do you really expect me to forgive them?"* The Scriptures answer this question clearly: *"Yes, He does!"*

POISON TO THE SOUL:

Failing to handle offenses as Jesus has instructed us keeps past offenses active in our lives. What wounded us once is thereby given power to wound us again and again; and these offenses become like poison to our soul. They fester like an untended wound—never healing, always inflamed, always painful.

This is part of the problem with the reconciliation movement. Its supporters are saying, in effect, that the wounds they have experienced because of the oppression their ancestors suffered cannot be healed until the Whites have apologized enough and made sufficient financial restitution to make up for these offenses. Are the wounds they have suffered real? Yes, they are. But, as we showed in an earlier chapter, those who caused the offence are long since dead. The wounds they have suffered, therefore, can never be completely healed by anything man does. Apart from God, these wounds are like a well that cannot be filled or like a tree that is so deeply rooted that it cannot be removed. Only faith in God can pluck up this tree and cast it into the sea. Only then can healing come between the races.

It is equally important for those who were born in the shadow of racial hatred and racism. Being raised in an environment of segregation and a lack of equality, heirs to the old ways and thinking of the forefathers, an ax must be laid to the root as well as these trees plucked up and cast out of our lives, both Black and White, Red, Yellow, and Brown. Only the love of God can accomplish that in all of our lives.

Is it difficult to forgive these deep offenses? Yes, unquestionably it is. That's why the disciples asked Jesus to increase their faith. They must have been amazed when He said, *"You only need mustard seed-sized faith to do the job!"*

Processing our faith:

Often we speak of the power <u>in</u> the mustard seed. Jesus was not teaching His disciples about the power <u>in</u> the mustard seed; He was speaking of the power <u>of</u> the mustard seed. There is a difference.

The mustard seed is perhaps the smallest of all seeds. If you dropped one on a carpet, it would be very difficult to find. But if you were to plant that tiny seed, the scriptures tell us that it would grow into one of the tallest herbs in the garden! The seed does not remain as it is when it is dropped into the soil. It germinates, grows into a great tree, and produces more seed.

What happened to that tiny seed? It was changed, it was processed according to God's plan, and, as a result, it was able to produce abundant fruit. The same thing happens to our faith if we plant it in the love of God and the Word of God. If we allow it to be processed according to God's plan, it will germinate and grow; and we will be able to speak to the mountains in our lives—even the mountains of racism—and they will be cast into the sea.

But what happens when we don't process our faith according to God's plan—according to God's instructions? Consider what happens when we have a problem—say a mechanical problem—and we receive instructions from someone over the phone. When they get through, they say, *"If you go through these steps, it should run, it should work!"* If we skip some of the things we were told to do, is the advice going to work? No, it isn't. Likewise, if we are processing what God is telling us, it should be working. If it is not working, we need to ask why.

So often our first thought is, *"Well, it's because of the Devil."* We are blood-bought, born again, Holy Ghost-filled, armor-bearing children of God. Our name is written in the Lamb's book of life, and we have received **all** authority over **all** the power of the enemy. We can run through a troop, leap over a wall Why do we keep blaming everything on the Devil?

If we have faith, any obstacle, like the metaphorical mountain Jesus mentioned in Luke 17:6, should obey us. Whatever it is! It doesn't matter. It should obey us! Why? Because, in the name of Jesus, it has to move!

Certainly, the Devil is not impressed with me. If I walk up to him and say, *"Do you know who I am?"*, do you know what he will say? *"No, and I could care less?"* But if I say, **"Do you know who Jesus is?"**, do you think he will move?"

OMITTING NOTHING:

Sometimes mountains don't move like we expect, because we have overlooked the more simple things of the gospel. We need to follow God's plan, omitting nothing.

Let's look at Luke 17:7-10, which says,

> *7But which of you, having a servant plowing or feeding cattle, will say unto him by and by, when he is come from the field, Go and sit down to meat? 8And will not rather say unto him, Make ready wherewith I may sup, and gird thyself, and serve me, till I have eaten and drunken; and afterward thou shalt*

eat and drink? ⁹ Doth he thank that servant because he did the things that were commanded him? I trow not. ¹⁰So likewise ye, when ye shall have done all those things which are commanded you, say, We are unprofitable servants: we have done that which was our duty to do.

Sometimes we read this passage and become indignant about how the master is treating his servant. But I believe Jesus was teaching a simple truth here: He wants us to do all that He commands us to do, omitting nothing. You see, sometimes things seem so useless—or sometimes we get so high-minded, caught up in our own self-worth and spirituality—that we overlook the more simple things of the gospel. But it is the simple things that we must be most careful to follow. Remember, sometimes it is the smallest part that stops an entire machine! If a nineteen cent screw or a forty-four cent washer or gasket blows in a four million dollar piece of equipment, it will stop functioning! *"It is the same with our faith,"* Jesus is saying. *"Look at the simplicity and do not leave out any of the ingredients."*

We need to look at the prescription God gives in His Word and use it the way God has prescribed it. If we do, it's going to work! It has to work! Why? Because it's God's instruction. Nothing will keep it from working if we're doing it correctly. So what Jesus is saying here is, *"If you're going to prosper, you need to do what I command you to do."*

In order for faith to work, we need to process it. How do you process it? First you have to plant it. Because if you plant it, it's going to produce more!!!

A TRUE AND LIVING FAITH:

There are many lessons we can learn from the mustard seed. Jesus spoke of this plant's seeds, comparing it to the Word of God, in the parable that is recorded in Matthew 13:31-32:

Another parable he put forth unto them, he said, the kingdom of heaven is like a grain of mustard which a man took and sowed in his field, which indeed is least of all the seeds, but when it is grown, it is the greatest among herbs and becomes a tree, so that the birds of the air come and lodge in the branches thereof.

The word for *seed* here is the Greek word *sperma*, which is the same as the reproductive sperm of a male human being. The seed is for one purpose—to reproduce!

In the same way, faith should produce life in us and that life more abundantly! Faith should be a productive thing, not just in the dead letter of saying, *"I have faith"* and doing nothing with it. But as we start sowing our faith—processing our faith—as God has instructed us in this parable, it will produce life; it will produce a true and living faith. You see, a true and living faith, in us, is a faith that's going to produce a product. There's going to be fruit from the faith. But if the seed, the Word of God that is planted in us is not processed—if it is not combined with faith—it will not produce a crop.

In Hebrews 4:2, Paul spoke of the unfruitfulness that comes when we do not process our faith:

> *For* unto us was the *gospel preached as well as unto them, but the word preached did not profit them, not being mixed with faith in them that heard it.*

So you see, there's a process. We have to plant the seed, and the seed has to be planted in fertile soil.

In II Chronicles 20:20, we see an example where the Word of God came to His people, and they combined it with faith. A powerful enemy was coming **against** Jerusalem. Many other cities had already fallen to this enemy. But something even more powerful than this enemy came **to** Jerusalem: the Word of the Lord; and His word to them was one of victory! King Jehoshaphat chose to believe God. He exhorted the people to act on God's Word:

> *²⁰And they rose early in the morning, and went forth into the wilderness of Tekoa: and as they went forth, Jehoshaphat*

stood and said, Hear me, O Judah, and ye inhabitants of Jerusalem; Believe in the LORD your God, so shall ye be established; believe his prophets, so shall ye prosper.

What was Jehoshaphat saying? *"If you believe and act on what the prophets have said, God will prosper you!"* In this case, Jehoshaphat was not speaking of a material prosperity, but of prosperity in battle with an enemy that by far out-classed them. Despite the power of their enemy, God had promised them victory!

Jehoshaphat was teaching them a basic truth: The Word of God— both written and oral—is prophecy. I always teach that the Word of God is the purest form of prophecy. It is the prophetic voice of God. Whether it is written or oral, if we hear the Word of God and apply it, it will prosper us; it will produce something in our lives. But you have to add, *"and apply it"* to the prescription Jehoshapht gave the inhabitants of Jerusalem; because if we only hear the Word and do not apply it, it will not work for us. The people of Jerusalem had to go out in battle against that powerful enemy before they were going to see the great victory God had promised to bring in their lives.

EARS TO HEAR:

Do you remember what Jesus said in Revelation, chapter three? *"Those that have ears to hear…"* He wasn't talking about fleshly ears, was He? We all have ears, unless we have been in a terrible accident or were born with a birth defect. No, Jesus was not talking about ears of flesh; He was speaking about spiritual ears. Why? Because God is spirit, and He communes with spirit. God does not talk to the flesh! He communes with the spirit of man!

So Jesus says, *"Those that have spiritual ears are going to hear what the Spirit is saying to the church."* To hear what the Spirit of God is saying to our church, we have to open our spiritual ears, not our fleshly ears, our carnal hearing. Once we have heard His word, we must start processing it by faith. When God said to Abraham, *"I want you to rise, take your household and go into a land that you know not,"* what did Abraham do? He took the Word of God, processed it by faith, packed up all of his household, and struck out in faith, not knowing where he was going. He left, because God said, *"Go!"* That's processing your faith!

What would have happened if Abraham had only heard God's Word, if he hadn't combined it with faith and act upon it, if he hadn't processed it? Like unplanted seeds, it would have remained dormant—ineffective—in Abraham's life, and it would not have produced the crop God intended. As a result, God's purpose in giving it to Abraham would have remained unfulfilled. What we do with the Word of God that comes to us is so important!

A Closer Look at the Mustard Seed:

There are many lessons we can learn from the mustard seed. The hardy, little mustard seed will grow in salty water, in marshy places. It will grow where no other herbs will grow. That gives us confidence that we can grow and flourish even when we find ourselves planted in the most harsh surroundings.

The mustard seed will not mix with any other seed. If you plant some seeds, some different flowers and things, they will germinate and come up together. But if you plant any other seed with mustard seeds, the mustard seeds will not germinate. What does that mean? Our faith cannot be mixed with anything else. Our faith cannot be mixed with doubt, or it will become diluted, and it will not work. Our faith cannot be dependent upon our intellect, our emotions, or anything else the flesh can produce. It must be pure, and the purest form of faith is trust that is placed in God and nothing else. Nothing wavering!

James 1:6-8 talks of a double-minded man. The word *double-minded* means *double-spirited*. If you translate that passage, it says double-spirited. What does double-spirited mean? It means our attitude changes. One day we're up, and the next day we're down. When things are good, we're up; and when things are not good, we're down. Then we are wavering!

James tells us that he who is wavering, double-minded, double-spirited, should not believe he's going to receive anything from

God (James 1:7). Why? Because he's mixing faith and doubt together, and a mixture of faith and doubt will not work. We must have faith in God!

THE ABODE OF GOD:

Looking at verse 32 of Matthew again, we see that Jesus said that, although the mustard seed *"...is the least of all seeds, but when it's grown, the greatest among herbs. It becomes a tree so that the birds of the air come and lodge in the branches thereof."* In other words, this tiny seed grows into a tree large enough to provide security and a covering to the birds of the air. The word translated air here is *ouranos*. It is an interesting word that talks about the abode of God. What does God say to you and I when we accept Jesus as Lord and Savior? Does He not say, *"If you will believe in your heart, confess with your mouth, We will come and make our abode with you. You will be the inhabitation of the Father, Son, and Holy Ghost!"* Hallelujah!

This word *ouranos* also speaks of happiness, power, and eternity—of heaven that encompasses us. In Psalm 91, David said, *"When trouble comes, you will find me, abiding in the shadow of the Almighty."* The shadow of the Almighty becomes a covering for us when we allow God to make His abode with us. All of us! Amen?

But where does it begin? It begins with us allowing the seed of faith to take root in our lives, with processing the seed of faith God has given each of us, and allowing it to grow and produce fruit for God in our lives—fruit that will remain and bless others.

THE MOST PERSEVERING OF ALL SEEDS:

The mustard seed is the most persevering of all seeds. If that mustard seed can see one ray of light, it's going to grow toward the light. You and I need to grow toward the Light.

Do you know that a mustard seed will grow from beneath a block of stone? Even if you put a stone on top of it, that mustard seed is going to find its way out. In fact, **mustard seed has been known**

to grow through stone to get to the light! It will make its way! It perseveres. It is the most persevering of all seeds.

Sometimes we find ourselves in a hard place. If we will persevere like that tiny mustard seed, we will come out to the light! The trial of our faith will not only work patience in us, but it will also bring us into victory!

The mustard seed is so tenacious that it will grow back seven years voluntarily after the seed is planted. Seven years! Circumstances can try to plow our faith under, but if our faith and hope and trust are in God, we will be able to persevere regardless of our circumstances.

Another interesting thing about mustard is that when you look at its leaves from the top when it first comes out of the ground, it comes out like a perfect cross every time. As faith grows within us, we become more and more conformed to the image of the One who went to the cross for us.

During World War I, many Allied soldiers were victims of a new weapon that required limited manpower to kill or incapacitate entire regiments. The name of this weapon? Mustard gas. Do you know how they made mustard gas? They mixed the black mustard seeds and the white mustard seeds together. This mixture created a powerful weapon for destruction!

Do you know what God is doing in His church today? Do you remember the scripture that says, *"One puts a thousand to flight; two puts ten thousand to flight"*? God is blending Black and White into one powerful weapon! If you want to see a church that is powerful in faith, if you want to see the manifestation of the power of God, it happens only when a church comes into unity; and it has to come into racial unity first! Once we realize, that we are one family, one church, that there is one heaven to go to, one hell to stay out of, we will become a powerful weapon in God's hands—a weapon for reconstruction, not destruction. This weapon reaches its fullest potential only when there is a unity of the races.

POWER TO MOVE MOUNTAINS:

While we are speaking of powerful weapons, we need to consider the one God has made available to every believer. This weapon is not a "what"; it is a "who"—the Holy Spirit. He has been given to move the mountains in our lives that we would otherwise in no way be capable of casting down.

Now if you were going to remove a mountain, what would be the best way to do it? Dynamite! In Acts 1:8, Jesus said, *"And when the Holy Ghost is come upon you, you shall receive power."* The word for power in the Greek is *dunamis*—the dynamite, Holy Ghost, supernatural power of God.

When you're working with explosives, there is wisdom in learning how to use it properly. One of the most important things you must learn is what is necessary to keep the explosive stable until you really want it to explode. Have you ever heard of C-4, an explosive used by the military? It resembles a child's "modeling clay." When it's placed in the right place, depending upon the amount you use, it'll move almost anything permanently.

Those who have worked with C-4 know that it can dry out over a period of time and get a little flaky. When it gets flaky, it gets unstable, and it is much more difficult to know just how much to use. You may end up blowing up something you didn't want to remove. You could even end up blowing yourself up. So it is very important to keep it pliable.

Do you know what makes C-4 pliable? Mustard seed oil!

People can get a little flaky now and then too, can't they? Do you know what keeps you and I pliable? Our faith in God! No matter what arises, instead of just blowing up, flying off the handle, losing total control, our power and authority is under the divine control and direction of God! The faith in us will remove mountains in our life. It will keep us from blowing up something we didn't want to and from harming ourselves or others.

Why so much emphasis on faith, you may ask. Only an exercise in faith can change our thoughts and actions concerning one another!

What does this have to do with racism? Faith alone gives us the power to forgive the wounds our spirits and sometimes even our bodies have received at the hands of racist people. **Faith to forgive** defuses what would otherwise bring division and allows healing and restoration to take place. We must remember, to forgive is always a choice, a quality decision on our part.

GOD'S WORD TO THE CHURCH:

What is God saying to the Church? Our faith is useless unless we process it! We've got to do something about what God says. We have to be willing to obey all of the instructions of God, and, if we are willing to do that, we can *taste and see that the Lord is good*, like mustard on a hot dog or a nice big Polish sausage. God is going to bless us.

So you see, when the Word of God is rooted and grounded in us, when we process the Word of God in us, it will germinate and bring forth much fruit. John 12:24 says, *"Unless a seed falls into the ground and dies (that is, germinates), it abides alone. But if it dies it brings forth much fruit."* God wants us to bring forth much fruit in our lives!

All ye of little faith, please stand to your feet. So now you see the power of the mustard seed, Amen? There's no power in that little mustard seed, but a great power can come from it.

There is a mountain that needs to be removed in the body of Christ. It is an obstacle that bars the way to healing, unity and revival in the Church. That mountain is racism.

That little mustard seed is a picture of what God is doing in the Church. We can come to Him in the name of Jesus in this very hour, speaking authority over every mountain in every person's life—Red, Yellow, Black or White—and we can say, *"Be ye removed! In the name of Jesus! Oh, be plucked up by the roots and cast in yonder sea. In Jesus' name!"*

We need to "process" our faith. We need to take positive action to be one with each other.

It is not enough to pray for unity. Neither will unity come if we try to deny that there is a great need in individual lives regarding racism. We must act upon our faith by forgiving and receiving forgiveness, by loving and being loved. Then unity will come in the Church!

AN ANTI-IRRITANT:
There is one final characteristic of the mustard seed I want to share with you. Mustard is an anti-irritant. It's used as a balm to remove sickness without causing irritation.

Even while reading this book you may be irritated by any one of a dozen things. Certainly, the ungodly attitudes by people of a different race can be a strong irritant, and reflections from the past can cause some of our inner feelings to surface. But that is what the truth does, and then it sets us free. If you make the following prayer your prayer right now, I am confident God will honor your faith:

"Lord, I believe and I want to receive at the hands of our Lord and our God. Like the song, *Worthy is the Lamb*, Lord, I submit to your will and your way. Lord, let me take your Word—all of your Word—and process it into faith in my spirit. **Let that seed grow into a mighty tree that will produce the very presence of God in my life, bringing peace, forgiveness, and joy right now!"**

"Lord, let healing begin in our hearts; let peace fill our minds, and fill us with Your love for all of the brethren. Oh, Lord God, touch our spirits. Lord, calm the storms that are raging in bosoms of some. Step into our "boat" and say, *"Peace, be still!"* and let the wind and the waves obey You, in Jesus' name!

"Bring healing and restoration in Your Church and in all people, Lord, make us <u>one</u>! In Jesus' name. Amen.

BIBLIOGRAPHY

Kreem Abdul-Jabbar, *Leveling the Field: Athletes Score for Equality*, <u>Bet Weekend</u>, Feburary, 1998, pp. 16-17.

AFP, *UN Rights Commission Urges Sudan not to Bomb Civilian Targets.* Available at http://www.persecutedchurch.org/>. Accessed on March 22, 1999.

AFP, *UN Warns of Catastrophic Famine in Southern Sudan.* Available at Available at http://www.persecutedchurch.org/>. Accessed on March 22, 1999.

American Heritage Dictionary, Second College Edition, <u>Houghton Mifflin Company</u>, Boston, 1976.

The American Heritage Dictionary, Second College Edition, <u>Houghton Mifflin Company</u>, Boston, © 1985, pp. 60, 763.

American Psychological Association, 1996 Press Release, *APA Task Force Examines the Knowns and Unknowns of Intelligence*, <u>American Psychological Association</u> (web site): Availible at http://www.apa.org/psychnet/. Accessed Sept. 9, 2000.

American Visionaries: Frederick Douglass, <u>National Parks Services</u> . Available at http://www.cr.nps.gov/exhibits/douglass/overview.htm> Accessed on Aug. 1, 2000.

Angels in Sudan web page, *Sudan Peace Act*, featured on the "What's Happening on Captiol Hill?" section, Dec. 15, 1999. Available at http://www.anti-slavery.org/. Accessed on Mar. 2, 2000.

Anti-Slavery International, *The Persecuted Church: The Latest News*, Available at <http://www.persecutedchurch.org>. Accessed on Mar. 2, 2000.

Anti-Slavery International, *The Persecuted Church: the situation in countries around the world*, Available at <http://www.persecutedchurch.org>. Accessed on Mar. 2, 2000.

Anti-Slavery International, *Voice from the Field*, News Section, August 1999. Available at http://www.antislavery.org/nwstraf.htm>. Accessed on Sept. 2, 2000.

Sara Band, *A Necessary Cause—Women in Afghanistan*, Available from <sarabande@brandeis.edu> Accessed on 4/15/00.

Steven Barboza, *A Divided Legacy*, <u>Emerge</u>, April 1992, p. 25.

Roy Basler, Editor, *The Collected Works of Abraham Lincoln, Vol. 4 (of 9 Volumes), pp. 13-30.* Available at http://members.aol.com/jfepperson/newhaven.html. Accessed on October 29, 1999.

Roy P. Basler, Editor, et al., *The Collected Works of Abraham Lincoln: Volume 5 (of 9 Volumes), "Lincoln's speech to Congress, July 12, 1862*, New Brunswick, N.J., 1953-55, pp. 317-319. Available at http://members.aol.com/jfepperson/newhaven.html. Accessed on October 29, 1999.

Sharon Begley with Ginny Carroll in Houston and Karen Springen in Chicago, *Blood, Hair and Heredity*, <u>Newsweek</u>, July 11, 1994, pp. 24-25.

Peter M. Bergman and Mort N. Bergman, compilers, *A Chronological History of the Negro in America*, <u>New York: New American Library</u>, 1969, pg. 52.

Luther Blackwell, *The Heritage of the Black Believer*, <u>Treasure House</u>, Shippensburg, Pennsylvania, 1993.

William Branigin, *"Modern-Day Slavery"? Imported Servants Allege Abuse by Foreign Host Families in U.S.*, <u>The Washington Post</u>, 1999. Wednesday, September 29, 1999 ; Page B04

Allen Breed, *Just who—and what—is the CCC?*, <u>Prince George's Journal</u>, Sunday, February 7, 1999, section A7, page 1. http://www.persecutedchurch.org/ >. Accessed on Mar. 2, 2000.

Karen Breslau, *A Polite Kind of Race War: Inside the struggle to make a Clinton idea work*, <u>Newsweek</u>, January 26, 1998, p. 29.

Briefing Paper for the UN Working Group on the Draft Optional Protocol to the Convention on the Rights of the Child on Involvement of Children in Armed Conflicts, which met on January 10-21, 2000. Available at: <http://www.child-soldiers.org/Briefing.htm>

Dee Brown, *Bury My Heart At Wounded Knee*, <u>Bantam Books, Holt, Rinehart & Winston</u>, New York, 1972.

William Branigin, *"Modern-Day Slavery"? Imported Servants Allege Abuse by Foreign Host Families in U.S.*, <u>The Washington Post</u>, Wednesday, September 29, 1999 ; Page B04

James and Lillian Breckenridge, *What Color Is Your God? Multicultural Education in the Church*, <u>Victor Books/SP Publications, Inc.</u>, 1995.

BurmaNet News, *Amnesty Declares War on Child Armies*, BBC Report, January 12, 1999. Available at http://www.soros.org/burma/ai11299.html.

Earle E. Cairns, *Christianity Through the Centuries: A History of the Christian Church*, <u>Zondervan Publishing House</u>, Grand Rapids, Michigan, 49506, pg. 231-233.

Professor Chinweizu, *Reparations and a New Global Order: A Comparative Overview*, A paper read at the second Plenary Session of the First Pan-African Conference on Reparations, held in Abuja, Nigeria, April 27, 1993, <u>Africa Reparations Movement</u> (web site). Available at http://www.arm.arc.co.uk/ NewGlobalOrder.html. Accessed on *Sept. 9, 2000.*

Mary Louise Clifford, *The Land and People of Liberia*, <u>J. B. Lippincott Company</u>, Philadelphia,1971.

Coalition to Stop the Use of Child Soldiers, *The Use of Children as Soldiers: Questions and Answers*; December, 1999. Available at http://www.child-soldiers.org. Accessed on Sept. 9, 2000.

Chuck Colson, *Standing Up Against Slavery Today*, originally appeared in the Jubille Extra, March 1998. Available at http://www.anti-slavery.org.

James H. Cone, *God of the Oppressed*, Harper & Row Publishers, San Francisco, 1975.

Court TV, *Justice in Black and White*, August 3, 2000.

Ellis Cose, *Caught Between Two Worlds, Why Simpson couldn't overcome the barriers of race*, Newsweek, July 11, 1994, p. 28.

Geoffrey Cowley with Mary Hager in Yodohama, *The Ever-Expanding Plague: Aids--Experts point to Asia as the next epicenter*, Newsweek, August 22, 1994, p. 37.

Philip D. Curtin, *The Atlantic Slave Trade: A Census*, The University of Wisconsin Press, Madison, Wisconsin, 1969.

DATELINE NBC, *Spotlight on Slavery*, the Script of the December 12, 1996 program. http://www.anti-slavery.org. Accessed on Sept. 9, 2000.

Basil Davidson, *The African Slave Trade*, Atlantic Monthly Press, Little, Brown and Company, Boston, 1980.

Dr. Bobby J. Davis, *Help Heal the Wounds*, Miracle Faith World Outreach, Inc., Monroe, Connecticut, 1995.

Tori DeAngelis, *Psychologists Question the Findings of Bell Curve*, American Psychologist Association web site: Available at <http://www.apa.org/monitor/oct95/bell.html> Accessed on 6/9/00.

Dr. Edwin J. Derensbourg, *The Roots of Deliverance*, Abundant Life Deliverance Ministries, Lancaster, California.

Jared Diamond, *Empire of Unformity: the Great Chinese Puzzle*, Discover, March 1996, pp. 79-85.

William LaRue Dillard, *Biblical Ancestry Voyage: Revealing Facts of Significant Black Characters*, 1989.

Frederick Douglass, *What to the American Slave Is Your Fourth of July?* (given on July 4, 1852 in Rochester, New York), Afro-American Almanac. Available at http://www.toptags.com/aama/voices/speeches/forth.htm>, accessed in July 29, 2000.

Frederick Douglass, Afro-American Almanac. Available at http://www.toptags.com/aama/bio/men/freddoug.htm. Accessed on July 27, 2000.

Martin Duberman, *The Antislavery Vanguard: New Essays on the Abolitionists*, Princeton University Press, Princeton, New Jersey, 1965.

Brian Eads, *Slavery's Shameful Return to Africa*, Reader's Digest, March 1996, pp. 77-81.

Dan Eggen, Washington Post Staff Writer, *A Taste of Slavery Has Tourists Up in Arms: Williamsburg's New Skits Elicit Raw Emotions*, The Washington Post, July 7, 1999, pg. A01.

Sara Engram, *Children in bondage: It's not only in Sudan*, The Baltimore Sun, June 23, 1996, 3F. Available at http://www.anti-slavery.org. Accessed on Sept. 9, 2000.

Christian A. Fleetwood, Sergeant-Major 4th U.S. Colored Troops, *The Negro as a Soldier In the War of the Revolution*, originally given at or the Negro Congress at the Cotton States and International Exposition, Atlanta, Ga., November 11 to November 23, 1895. Afro-American Almanac web site. Available at http://www.toptags.com/aama/bio/men/freddoug.htm. Accessed on July 27, 2000.

Robert William Fogel and Stanley L. Engerman, *Time on the Cross: The Economics of American Negro Slavery*, Little, Brown and Company, Boston, 1974.

Donna Foote and Mark Miller in Los Angeles and David Schrieberg in New York, *Now Comes the Legal Odyssey*, Newsweek, June 27, 1994, p. 22.

E. Franklin Frazier, *The Negro Church in America*, Schocken Books, New York, 1974.

The Freedman and Southern Society Project, *The Chronology of Emancipation during the Civil War, "U.S., Statutes at Large, Treaties, and Proclamations of the United States of America"*, Vol. 12, Boston, 1863, pp. 1267-68. Availiable at http://www.inform.umd.edu/ARHU/Depts/History/Freedman/prelep.htm. Accessed on October 29, 1999.

Senator Bill Frist, *The Sudan Peace Act, 106th Congress, 1st Session, Bill S.1453*, Thomas Web Site. Available at http://thomas.loc.gov.

Jeff Giles with Susan Miller, Nina Archer Biddle, Susannah Patton, Allison Samuels and Patrick Rogers in New York, Pat Wingert and Farai Chideya in Washington, Karen Springen and Stanley Holmes in Chicago, Debra Rosenberg in Boston and Tim Pryor in Los Angeles, *Generalizations X*, Newsweek, June 6, 1994, pp. 62-72.

Elizabeth Gleick, *O.J. Holds the Line*, Time, December 9, 1996, p. 44.

Allen H. Godbey, *The Lost Tribes A Myth*, Duke University Press, Durham, North Carolina, 1930.

"Good Morning America: 'Fifth-graders Redeem Slaves for Cash,'" American Anti-Slavery Group Press Release, Aired Monday, August 17, 1998. Available at http://www.anti-slavery.org/. Accessed on March 22, 1999.

Christine Gorman, *A Racial Gap: Blacks undergo lifesaving lung-cancer surgery at a lower rate than whites. What can be done?*, Time, October 25, 1999, p. 136.

Joseph R. Gregory, *African Slavery—1996*, © 1996, First Things 63, May 1996, pp. 37-39.

Roger S. Greenway and Timothy M. Monsma, *Cities: Missions' New Frontier*, Baker Book House, Grand Rapids, Michigan, 1989.

Alan P. Grimes, *Equality in America: Religion, Race and the Urban Majority*, Oxford University Press, New York, 1964.

Stephen A. Grunlan and Marvin K. Mayers, *Cultural Anthropology: A Christian Perspective*, Academic Books, Zondervan Publishing House, Grand Rapids, Michigan, 1988.

John Gunther, *Inside Africa*, Harper & Brothers, New York, 1955.

Ralph Randolph Gurley, *The Life of Jehudi Ashmun: Late Colonial Agent in Liberia*, Books for Libraries Press, Freeport, New York, first published in 1835; Reprinted in 1971.

Andrew Hacker, *Two Nations: Black and White, Separate, Hostile, Unequal*, Ballantine Books, New York, 1995.

Alex Haley, *The Autobiography of Malcolm X*, Ballantine Books, New York, 1965.

Ken Ham, Carl Weiland, and Don Batten, *One Blood: the Biblical Answer to Racism*, Master Books, Arkansas, 1999.

Joshua Hammer, *Escape from Hell*, Newsweek, May 16, 1994, pp. 34-35.

Michael Harris, *Slavery, a Recurring Evil, Anti-Slavery International Annual Report, 1994-5*, Anti-Slavery International. Available at http://www.anti-slavery.org. For more information, write The Stableyard, Broomgrove Road, London SW9 9TL, United Kingdom.

Michael H. Hart, *Racial Partition of the United States,* a speech given at the 1996 American Renaissance Conference in Louisville, Kentucky. Available at <http://www.separatism.org>. Accessed on April 15, 2000.

Joyce T. Henderson, *Why African American Youth Are Attracted to Non-Christian/Non-Traditional Religions and Sects*, 1998.

Nat Hentoff, *Anybody Care About Black Slaves? Denver Kids Rescue African Slaves. Jesse Jackson Is Silent,* Village Voice, August 12, 1998. Available at http://www.anti-slavery.org/pages/reports_index.html. Accessed on Sept. 9. 2000.

Nat Hentoff, *Fifth-Grade Freedom Fighters*, The Washington Post, Saturday, August 1, 1998, pg. A15. Available at http://www.anti-slavery.org/pages/reports_index.html. Accessed on Sept. 9. 2000.

Nat Hentoff, *'I Saw My Father Cut to Pieces' : A Holocaust We Could Have Stopped*, Village Voice, February 24-March 2, 2000. Available at http://www.villagevoice.com. Accessed on Nov. 5, 1999.

Nat Hentoff, *5000 UN Soldiers Could Have Ended It: The Holocaust Without Guilt*, Village Voice, March 10-16, 2000. Available at http://www.villagevoice.com. Accessed on Nov. 5, 2000.

Nat Hentoff, *How Clean Is Amoco's Gas?*, Village Voice, June 7-13, 2000. Available at http://www.villagevoice.com. Accessed on Nov. 5, 2000.

Nat Hentoff, *Our People Were Turned to Ash: A Sudanese Woman Tells Her Story*, Village Voice, April 4, 2000. Available at http://www.villagevoice.com. Accessed on Nov. 5, 2000.

Nat Hentoff, *Rwanda overflowed with corpses: The Triumph of Evil*, Village Voice, March 3-9, 1999. Available at http://www.villagevoice.com. Accessed on Nov. 5, 2000.

Nat Hentoff, *"Running, I Can Smell the Horses': Black Slaves Not News in New York*, Village Voice, June 21-27, 2000. Available at http://www.villagevoice.com. Accessed on Nov. 5, 2000.

Nat Hentoff, *The World Is Strangely Silent: Slaughter of the Innocents*, Village Voice, April 19-25, 2000. Available at http://www.villagevoice.com. Accessed on Nov. 5, 2000.

Nat Hentoff, *Two Million Have Been Killed: 'She was 12. They Shot Her'*, Village Voice, June 28-July 4, 2000. Available at http://www.villagevoice.com. Accessed on Nov. 5, 2000.

Nat Hentoff, *We Descendants of These Slaves: Black Pastors Demand Justice*, Village Voice, July 5-11, 2000. Available at http://www.villagevoice.com. Accessed on Nov. 5, 2000.

Avaneda D. Hobbs, *From the Garden of Eden To America*, CSE Books, Forestville, Forestville, Maryland, 1997.

Randolph T. Holhut, *Challenging the Racist Science of the "The Bell Curve."* Available at: http://www.mdle.com/WrittenWord/rholhut/holhut27.htm. Accessed April 29, 2000.

Constance Morris Hope, *Liberia*, Chelsea House, 1987.

Louise L. Hornor, *Black Americans: A Statistical Sourcebook*, Information Publications, Palo Alto, California, 1998.

H. Wayne House, *Israel the Land and the People: An Evangelical Affirmation of God's Promises*, Kregel Publications, Grand Rapids, Michigan, 1998.

Desson Howe, Washington Post Staff Writer, *Putting Black Faces in Civil War Pictures* , The Washington Post, Thursday, July 16, 1998.

Earl Ofari Hutchinson, *Racial Myths Reinforce White Fears*, The Ledger, Thursday, October 26, 1995, section A, p. 15.

Michele Ingrassia and Melinda Beck, with reporting by Ginny Carroll, Nina Archer Biddle, Karen Springen, Patrick Rogers, John McCormick, Jeanne Gordon, Allison Samuel, and Mary Hager, *Patterns of Abuse,* <u>Newsweek</u>, July 4, 1994, pp. 26-33.

Island Connoissuer, *Country Studies: Abaco, Antigua, Aruba, the Bahamas, Barbados, Bermuda, Cayman Islands, Cuba, Dominican Republic, Grenada, Haiti, Jamaica, Puerto Rico.* Accessed from an Internet site, which unfortunately is no longer available.

Island Connoissuer, *Precolumbian Civilizations.* Accessed from an Internet site, which unfortunately is no longer available.

Charles Jacobs, President of the American Anti-Slavery Group, *Slavery: A Worldwide Evil,* The World & I, April 1996. <u>Anti-Slavery International</u> web site. Available at: http://www.anti-slavery.org/.Accessed on Sept. 9, 2000

Charles Jacobs, President of the American Anti-Slavery Group, *Where Are the Liberals?,* <u>Boston Globe</u>, Op Ed, July 7, 1997. <u>Anti-Slavery International</u> web site. Available at http://www.anti-slavery.org. Accessed on Sept. 9, 2000

Charles Jacobs, President of the American Anti-Slavery Group, *Halting Sudan's Slavery and Slaughter,* <u>The Boston Globe</u>, Op Ed, November 8, 1999

Jeff Jacoby, *The Slave-traders and Farrakhan,* originally appeared in <u>The Boston Globe</u>. Available at http://www.anti-slavery.org/

Charles H. Kraft, *Christianity in Culture: A Study in Dynamic Biblical Theologizing in Cross-Cultural Perspective,* <u>Orbis Books</u>, Maryknoll, New York, 1979.

Gregory Kane, *Witness to Slavery,* originally appeared in <u>The Baltimore Sun</u>. Available at http://www.anti-slavery.org/

Philip B. Kunhardt, Jr., Philip B. Kunhardt, III, and Peter Kunhardt, *Lincoln: an Illustrated Biography,* <u>Portland House</u>, New York, NY, 1992, pp. 272-273

Goran Larson, *Fact or Fraud? The Protocols of the Elders of Zion,* <u>AMI-Jerusalem Center for Biblical Studies and Research</u>, Jerusalem, 1994.

Leadership Conference on Civil Rights Report, *Justice On Trial: Racial Disparities in the American Criminal Justice System, May 2000.* Available at <http://www.civilrights.org>. Accessed on July 12, 2000.

Daniel Levine, *Race Over Reason in the Jury Box: Justice is sabotaged when jurors ignore the evidence,* <u>Reader's Digest</u>, June, 1996.

Janet Levine, *Inside Apartheid: One Woman's Struggle in South Africa,* <u>Contemporary Books</u>, Chicago,1988.

Gilbert Lewthwaite and Gregory Kane, *Witness to Slavery: Part 3,* <u>The Baltimore Sun</u>, June 18, 1996, Section 1A. Available at http://www.anti-slavery.org/ . Accessed on Sept. 9, 2000.

Library of Congress, *African American Mosaic,* Accessed on Jan. 13, 2001

Library of Congress, *The Liberator, Newspaper, Rare Book and Special Collections Division (59), May 21, 1831. Available at <http://lcweb.loc.gov/exhibits/african/lib.jpg>. Accessed on Dec. 10, 2000.*

Abraham Lincoln, *"Speeches and Writings of Abraham Lincoln: Cooper Union Address"*, February. 27, 1860. *Available at* http://www.netins.net/showcase/creative/lincoln/speeches/greeley.htm. Accessed on Nov. 2, 1999.

Abraham Lincoln and Stephen A. Douglas, *First Lincoln/Douglas Debate: Ottawa, Illinois August 21, 1858,* The Abraham Lincoln Association, http://www.alincolnassoc.com. Accessed on October 20, 1999.

C. Eric Lincoln, *The Black Church Since Frazier*, Schocken Books, New York, 1974.

Michael T. Lubragge, Chairman of the Department of Humanities Computing Project, *Manifest Destiny: The Philosophy That Created a Nation.* Available at http://odur.let.rug.nl/alfa/ For more information, write Postbus 716, 9700 AS Groningen, The Netherlands. Phone +31 50 3635974, Fax +31 50 3636855

Reinhard H. Luthin, *The Real Abraham Lincoln*, Prentice-Hall, Inc., Englewood Cliffs, New Jersey, 1960.

James C. McKinly, Jr., *Famine Looming, Sudan Curbs Relief to Rebel-held Areas*, New York Times, April 21, 1998. Available at http://www.anti-slavery.org/

William Dwight McKissic, Sr., *Beyond Roots: In Search of Blacks in the Bible*, Renaissance Productions, New Jersey, 1990.

Paul L. Maier, *Josephus: The Essential Writings*, Kregel Publications, Grand Rapids, Michigan, 1988.

Peter Marshall and David Manuel, *From Sea to Shining Sea*, Fleming H. Revell Company,Old Tappan, New Jersey, 1986.

Marshall, Peter and David Manuel, *The Light and the Glory*, Fleming H. Revell Company, Tarrytown, New York, 1977.

Ushari Ahmad Mahmud and Suleyman Ali Baldo (University of Khartoum professors*), Human Rights Violations in the Sudan The Al Dein Massacre*, 1987. Available at http://www.anti-slavery.org. Accessed on Sept. 9, 2000.

Barbara Mathias and Mary Ann French, *Forty Ways to Raise a Non-racist Child*, Harpers Perennial, New York, 1996.

Terry Mattingly, *What to Do About Religious Persecution*, The Prince George's County Journal: Religious Section, November 13, 1998, pg. A8.

August Meier, and Elliott Rudwick, *From Plantation to Ghetto*, Hill and Wang, New York, 1970.

Ricardo Mendoza, *How the West Was Won*, Available at http://members.aol.com/htmpro/index.htm

Microsoft Encarta Africana 2000, Marian Aguiar, *Rosa Louise McCauley*, Microsoft Corporation, 1999.

Microsoft Encarta Africana 2000, *Zayde Antrim, Slave Kingdoms: The Trans-Saharan Trade Route*, Microsoft Corporation, 1999.

Microsoft Encarta Africana 2000, *George Washington Carver*, Microsoft Corporation, 1999.

Microsoft Encarta Africana 2000, *Paul Cuffee*, Microsoft Corporation, 1999.

Microsoft Encarta Africana 2000, Frederick Douglass' autobiography, *Narrative of the Life of Frederick Douglass*, Microsoft Corporation, 1999.

Microsoft Encarta Africana 2000, *Martin Luther King, Jr.*, Microsoft Corporation, 1999.

Microsoft Encarta Africana 2000, *Harriet Tubman*, Microsoft Corporation, 1999.

Microsoft Encarta Africana 2000, *Booker Taliaferro Washington*, Microsoft Corporation, 1999.

N. Moore, *Pulpit Confessions: Exposing the Black Church*, Exodus Books, 1998.

Robert Morey, *The Islamic Invasion: Confronting the World's Fastest Growing Religion*, Harvest House Publishers, Eugene, Oregon, 1992.

Lance Morrow, *Manifest Destiny*, Time, February 8, 1999, p. 69.

Abdullah Yasin Muhannad, *It's Still Nation Time*, Emerge, April 1992, p. 33.

Andrew Murr and Jeanne Gordon in Los Angeles, with Vern E. Smith in Atlanta and John McCormick in Chicago, *A Shooting Stirs Tension in the Nation*, Newsweek, June 13, 1994, p. 27.

National Parks Services, *American Visionaries: Frederick Douglass*. Available at http://www.cr.nps.gov/exhibits/douglass/overview.htm> Accessed on Aug. 1, 2000.

Jim Naureckas, *Racism Resurgent: How Media Let "The Bell Curve's" Pseudo-Science Define the Agenda on Races*. Available at: <http://www.fair.org/extra/9501/bell.html>. Accessed on Sept. 9, 2000.

Mark E. Neely, Jr., *The Last Best Hope of Earth: Abraham Lincoln and the Promise of America*, Harvard University Press, Cambridge, Massachusetts, 1993.

Bruce W. Nelan, *Troops or Consequences: NATO issues a remarkable ultimatum to Milosevic and the Kosovars: Make peace, or we'll bomb you*, Time, February 8, 1999, p. 38.

The NET Bible: Study Notes, (Dallas, TX: Biblical Studies Press) 1998. Available at www.netbible.org.

No Author given, *John L. O'Sullivan's 1884 View of Manifest Destiny*, The United States Magazine and Democratic Review, http://we.go.net/docent/explore/hbent2.htm.

No Author given, *Rwanda: Punishing the guilty, maybe*, The Economist, October 12, 1996, p. 48.

No Author given, *South Africa: Black Fight*, The Economist, International Section, February 24-March 1, 1996, pp. 44-45.

No Author given, *South Africa: How wrong is it going?*, The Economist, October 12, 1996, p. 21-23.

No author given, *Time's 25 Most Influential Americans: Louis Farrakhan, Leader of the Nation of Islam,* Time, June 17, 1996, p. 67.

G. Frederick Owen, Abraham Lincoln: The Man and His Faith, *Tyndale House Publishers, Inc. Wheaton, IL, 1976.*

William Pannell, *The Coming Race Wars? A Cry for Reconcilitation,* Zondervan Publishing House, Grand Rapids, Michigan, 1993.

J. H. Parry and Philip Sherlock, *A Short History of the West Indies*, Macmillan Press, London., 1971.

Earl Parvin, *Mission USA*, Moody Press, Chicago, 1985, pp. 77-87

Perry-Castañeda Library, of the University of Texas at Austin, Frederick Douglass photograph. Their source is J.W. Thompson's book, History of the Douglass Monument, *published by the* Rochester Herald Press Rochester, *Rochester, in 1903. Available at: <http://www.lib.utexas.edu/Libs/PCL/portraits/douglass.jpg> Accessed on Oct. 16, 2000*

Wayne Perryman, *The 1993 Trial on the Curse of Ham*, Pneuma Life Publishing, Bakersfield, California, 1994.

Carlisle John Peterson, *The Destiny of the Black Race*, Lifeline Communications, Toronto, 1991.

Robert Peterson, *Only the Ball Was White*, Prentice-Hall, Inc., Englewood Cliffs, New Jersey, 1970.

Jeffrey Prescott, Will Data Make a Difference?, *The Christian Science Monitor, Thursday, May 10, 2000. Available at <http://www.civilrights.org>. Accessed on July 12, 2000.*

Debra Rosenberg in Boston, Lincoln Caplan in Washington and bureau reports, *Three for the Defense*, Newsweek, July 11, 1994, pp. 26-27.

A. M. Rosenthal, *On My Mind—Shatter the Silence*, The New York Times, October 21, 1997. Available at http://www.anti-slavery.org/

Ruldolph C. Ryser, *Publication of the Center for World Indigenous Studies*, June 1992. Available at http://odur.let.rug.nl/alfa/

Anthony Sampson, *Black and Gold*, Pantheon Books, New York, 1987.

Allison Samuels and John Leland, *Waiting to Prevail: A generation of young black actresses is making a move on Hollywood,* Newsweek, January 12, 1998, p. 59.

Carl Sandburg, *Abraham Lincoln: The War Years, Volumes 1-4*, Harcourt, Brace & World, Inc., 1939.

Linda Slobodian, *The Slave Trail: An eight part special report*, first appeared in the Calgery Sun, Available at http://www.anti-slavery.org/. Accessed on Sept. 9, 2000.

Thomas Sowell, *Ethnic America*, Basic Books, Inc., Publishers, New York, 1981.

Carlyle Fielding Stewart, *African American Church Growth: 12 Principles of Prophetic Ministry*, Abingdon Press, Nashville, 1993.

Charles C. Tansill, *Documents Illustrative of the Formation of the Union of the American States*, Government Printing Office, Washington, DC, 1927.

Jay Thorpe and Thomas G. Whittle, *A Fire on the Cross*, Freedom, 1996, Vol. 29, Issue 1, pp. 4-9.

Jonathan Tilove, *Black soldiers, unsung heroes*, The Baltimore Sun, Perspective Section, Sunday, February 14, 1999

Henry Clarence Thiessen, *Introductory Lectures in Systematic Theology*, Wm. B. Eerdmans Publishing Company, Grand Rapids, Michigan, 1968, p. 26

Bill Turque with Andrew Murr, Mark Miller, Donna Foote and Charles Fleming in Los Angeles, Nina Archer Biddle and Mark Starr in Chicago and Tessa Namuth in New York, *He Could Run, But He Couldn't Hide*, Newsweek, June 27, 1994, pp. 16-27.

Bill Turque with Mark Miller and Andrew Murr in Los Angeles, *"He's Going Nuts"*, Newsweek, July 4, 1994, pp. 23-25.

Bill Turque with Mark Miller, Andrew Murr, Jim Crogan and Tim Pryor in Los Angeles, *The Body of Evidence*, Newsweek, July 11, 1994, pp. 20-25

Merril F. Unger and William White, Jr., Editors, *Vine's Complete Expository Dictionary of Old and New Testament Words*, Thomas Nelson Publishers, New York, 1985, pg 674

W. E. Vines, *An Expository Dictionary of New Testament Words: Vol. III*, Fleming H. Revell Company, Old Tappan, New Jersey, 1996, pp.20, 21.

Barbara Vogel, S.T.O.P., American Anti-Slavery Group. Available at http://www.anti-slavery.org/ . Accessed on Dec. 23, 2000.

Geoffrey C. Ward with Ric Burns and Ken Burns, *The Civil War: An Illustrated History*, Alfred A Knopf, New York, 1998, pg. 253.

Raleigh Washington and Glen Kehrein, *Breaking Down Walls: A Model for Reconciliation In An Age of Racial Strife*, Moody Press, Chicago, 1993.

George M. Welling, Coordinator of *Computing in the Humanities*, a project of developed by the Department of Alfa-informatica at the University of Groningen in the Netherlands, *Thomas Jefferson on Slavery*. Available at <http://odur.let.rug.nl/~usa/I/pages.htm>. Accessed on Dec. 14, 2000.

Rep. Frank Wolf and Senator Arlen Specter, *The Freedom from Religious Persecution Act: H.R. 2431*. Available at <www.house.gov/wolf/free>.

UNICEF, *Children at Both Ends of the Gun*, Available at: <http://www.unicef.org>. Accessed on Mar. 13, 2000.

UNICEF, Press Release: *Children in War*, Available at: <http://www.unicef.org>. Accessed on Mar. 13, 2000.

United Nations Economic and Social Council: Commission on Human Rights, Sub-Commission on Prevention of Discrimination and Protection of Minorities, *UN Trust Fund for Contemporary Forms of Slavery/Trafficking in West Africa*, 49th Session, Geneva, August 1997. Available at <http://www.persecutedchurch.org>. Accessed on Sept. 9, 2000.

United Nations Economic and Social Council: Commission on Human Rights, Sub-Commission on Prevention of Discrimination and Protection of Minorities, *Working Group on Contemporary Forms of Slavery*, 22nd Session, Geneva, June 1997, Ref. TS/S/2/97. Available at <http://www.persecutedchurch.org>. Accessed on Sept. 9, 2000.

Bertram Wyatt-Brown, *Lewis Tappan and the Evangelical War Against Slavery*, Case Western Reserve University Press, Cleveland, 1969.

World Book Online, *The African American Journey*. Available at <http://www.worldbook.com/fun/aajourney/bh037.html>. Accessed on Sept. 9, 2000.

Biography of
Dr. G. Randolph Gurley

Dr. Gurley is an anointed preacher and teacher of God's word. He has traveled around the world for over twenty years, bringing the love of God and the truth that sets men free.

Dr. Gurley is the President of Harvest International Ministerial Fellowship. Harvest is a fellowship of Pastors and churches around the globe training indigenous leaders and planting churches. Dr. Gurley serves as Apostle and spiritual Father to over 1200 Pastors and churches worldwide.

Dr. Gurley is also Executive Vice President and Chairman of the Board of Regents of Vision International University. Vision is an international network of Bible colleges. With over 140 satellite campuses in the United States and in 100 nations, Vision is raising up leaders and training ministers to reach their own culture and nation with the Gospel.

Urban and cross-cultural ministry has always been a strong focus in the Gurleys' lives. He and his lovely wife Rev. Manon Gurley pastor The Tabernacle Church: "A City of Refuge", a racially and internationally mixed church, located in Laurel, Maryland, just outside of Washington, D.C.

Dr. Gurley teaches seminars on the subject matter of this book and many other theological subjects. He speaks at leadership conferences, graduations, and holds international evangelistic crusades in many foreign countries.

Dr. Gurley's message is one of love and unity. There is only <u>one</u> God who has only one church that consists of <u>one</u> people born again by Jesus Christ. When America grasps the truth of this statement, we will experience true revival.

To order additional copies of this book, audio tapes or other books by Dr. Gurley, or to book a seminar or speaking date write or call:

G.M.I. Publishing
P.O. Box 2690
Laurel, Maryland 20709
1-301-490-3838

Printed in the United States
59172LVS00003B/10-72